Gendering the City

Gendering the City

Women, Boundaries, and Visions of Urban Life

edited by
Kristine B. Miranne
& Alma H. Young

ROWMAN & LITTLEFIELD PUBLISHERS, INC.
Lanham • Boulder • New York • Oxford

ROWMAN & LITTLEFIELD PUBLISHERS, INC.

Published in the United States of America
by Rowman & Littlefield Publishers, Inc.
4720 Boston Way, Lanham, Maryland 20706
http://www.rowmanlittlefield.com

12 Hid's Copse Road
Cumnor Hill, Oxford OX2 9JJ, England

British Library Cataloguing in Publication Information Available

Library of Congress Cataloging-in-Publication Data

Gendering the city : women, boundaries, and visions of urban life / edited by Kristine B.
Miranne, Alma H. Young.
   p. cm.
   Includes bibliographical references and index.
   ISBN 0-8476-9450-X (cloth : alk. paper)—ISBN 0-8476-9451-8 (pbk. : alk. paper)
   1. Women and city planning.   2. Urban ecology.   3. Urban women—Social
conditions.   4. Feminist theory.   I. Miranne, Kristine B.   II. Young, Alma H.
HT166.G4614   1999
307.1′216′082—dc21   99-047148

Printed in the United States of America

Friend, Colleague, and Scholar

MARSHA RITZDORF
1946–1998

Contents

Acknowledgments   ix

Introduction   1
Kristine B. Miranne and Alma H. Young

Part I
VISIBLE OR INVISIBLE?
GENDERED URBAN BOUNDARIES

1   "Not Named or Identified": Politics and the Search for Anonymity
in the City   19
Judith A. Garber

2   "The Two Major Living Realities": Urban Services Needs of First
Nations Women in Canadian Cities   41
Evelyn Peters

Part II
INTERSECTIONS OF GENDERED BOUNDARIES:
RACE, CLASS, AND ETHNICITY

3   Identity, Difference, and the Geographies of Working Poor
Women's Survival Strategies   65
Melissa R. Gilbert

4   Boundaries Cracked: Gendering Literacy, Empowering Women,
Building Community   89
Jennifer E. Subban and Alma H. Young

5   Black Women as City Builders: Redemptive Places and the Legacy
of Nannie Helen Burroughs   105
Daphne Spain

6 Women "Embounded": Intersections of Welfare Reform and
Public Housing Policy   119
Kristine B. Miranne

Part III
CHALLENGING PLANNED BOUNDARIES

7 Theorizing Canadian Planning History: Women, Gender and
Feminist Perspectives   139
Sue Hendler with Helen Harrison

8 Resisting Boundaries? Using Safety Audits for Women   157
Caroline Andrew

9 Sex, Lies, and Urban Life: How Municipal Planning Marginalizes
African American Women and Their Families   169
Marsha Ritzdorf

10 Manipulating Constraints: Women's Housing and the
"Metropolitan Context"   183
Christine Cook, Marilyn Bruin, and Sue Crull

Epilogue: Cracks, Light, Energy   209
Beth Moore Milroy

Index   219

About the Editors and Contributors   227

Acknowledgments

The initial idea for this volume came from our own experiences of being participants on a set of panels organized by Judith Garber and Robyne Turner for the Urban Affairs Association (UAA) conference in 1994. These integrated panels, the first of their kind at this conference, focused on issues of gendered research and the city. Their efforts led the way for ongoing provocative and spirited discussions of gender relations as they are played out within the urban arena. At the 1997 UAA meeting, we in turn organized a series of three panels under the rubric of "Gender and the City." Most of the authors included in this volume presented their work at that conference. Although not all participants at the panel sessions contributed to this book, we do want to especially thank Meredith Ramsay and Robyne Turner for comments and critique. In addition, we appreciate the enthusiastic response among urban scholars who attended the conference, indicating that there is a definite (and growing) interest in the interconnected themes of this volume: spatial and social boundaries, the multiplicities of women's lives, and the urban setting.

As we began putting this book together, several other individuals provided advice, comments, and support. We would like to thank Sallie Marston and David Perry for their assistance during the initial proposal phase of the volume. We would also like to thank Liz Bondi as well as several anonymous reviewers for their thought-provoking comments and questions. We are grateful to Sabrina Williams, Angela Guy-Lee, and Bonnie Wright for their patience and diligence in the final stages of manuscript production. Finally, Brenda Hadenfeldt of Rowman and Littlefield was instrumental in leading us through this entire process.

On a personal note, we would like to thank our families for their support and understanding of this "labor of love." Thank you, Rodney, Rachel, and Johanna. Thank you, Dennis and Alden.

Introduction

Kristine B. Miranne and Alma H. Young

The field of urban studies has long reflected a gender bias in both the construction of theory and the avoidance of research that directly addresses women's lived experiences. Within the last two decades, however, there has been an emerging body of research on feminist issues relating to gender and the urban environment. The starting premise is the recognition in the current literature that: first, women's and men's experiences in the city are different and that these differences center largely on relations of inequality; second, that women's active use of space and time often results in changes to the spatial and social structure of the city; and third, that structural changes can alter gender relations within the city. We expand this discussion by looking more critically at how women use and change the space and time they inhabit within the urban environment.

We do this through the use of the concept of boundary. The essays in this volume reveal the interconnectedness between socially constructed gender relations and the visible and invisible boundaries that affect how women use urban space. This concept of boundaries enriches the imagery of cities and the actions that women take within them. Boundaries are complex structures that establish differences and commonalities between individuals and groups. Boundaries may be maintained, crossed, resisted, reconfigured. Because they exhibit much flexibility, boundaries may be permeable and inclusive. Socially constructed, boundaries remain volatile and dynamic. Thus, the concept provides interpretations of the ways in which urban spaces are generated by social relations, and, in turn, of how social relations result in distinct spatial forms within the city. The specific social relations we are most concerned with are those expressed in gender—the relations between men and women, between women and women, between women and the state—over time and within specific contexts. Relations among women and between women and the state are emphasized in this volume. We speak of "gendering" to symbolize that it is a dynamic process, one that West and Zim-

1

merman (1987) have called "doing gender." It is also a structure, a set of "institutionalized social relationships that, by creating and manipulating the categories of gender, organize and signify power at levels above the individual, from cultural meanings to government policies" (Ferree, Lorber, and Hess 1999, xix; also see Lorber 1994).

The integration of gender (along with other multiplicities of women's lives) into urban space has been evolving over the past twenty years as an area of study. The explicit call for theories of gender to be included within the multidisciplinary field of urban studies, however, has a more recent vintage. In this volume we further this agenda by looking in greater depth (and thus with a narrower focus) at the lives of women in the city. The conceptual framework of boundary allows us to ask more detailed and intriguing questions about how (and why) women act to create lives for themselves within the urban environment.

As editors, we challenged our contributors by asking them to respond to three separate, yet interrelated, foci. These foci became the major themes that guide this volume. First, the authors were asked to address boundaries conceptually and methodologically. Under what conditions are boundaries visible? When are they invisible? What does it mean for women to be "bounded"? Are women bounded by others, or do they work to maintain the boundaries established by others? For what purposes might women create boundaries of their own? Might women create boundaries to keep themselves from others? Do boundaries create alternative space(s), and for whom is this space created? Because of the separation of different roles and functions within the city, and because women often find themselves within separate and less powerful space, women resist, (re)configure, and (re)construct the boundaries they encounter. What might be the basis for such action? How are socially constructed boundaries made visible? What occurs at the intersection(s) among (multiple) boundaries?

These are powerful questions and remind us that "woman" is not an essential category; instead, we begin to see the similarities and diversities of women's lives as constructed by and through their gendered, racial, ethnic, and sexual identities. This is the intent of the second focus. By investigating individual and collective experiences, the chapters in this volume reveal how women create their own histories and construct relations with each other, with men, and with the urban processes played out in space. Looking at the construction of the city through the lens of the multiplicities of women's lives acknowledges that the category "woman" cannot be stripped of the other forms of oppression that impinge upon women in their daily lives. Thus we get a richer sense of how women negotiate their way in the city, in particular, the ways in which the intersection of gender and race (or ethnicity or sexual identity) affects women and either limits or encourages actions. We ask in what ways can this intersection be seen as a boundary, and what are the possibilities for action from this vantage point?

The third focus of this volume centers on challenging conventional notions of how urban space is used by looking at how women work the edges of boundaries to create new spaces for themselves. The authors were encouraged to describe how women imagine space and how they actualize it in practice. The result, as defined by women themselves, is a series of alternative visions of social and spatial boundaries within the urban environment. The extent to which visions are incorporated or stymied by governmental and other regulatory bodies as they establish boundaries (physical and otherwise) is also explored. Although some of these visions may be invisible to government, they remain operating principles for many women. It will become apparent as the reader continues that none of these three organizational themes is truly separate. Rather, all three interact with each other in provocative and intriguing ways.

FEMINIST RESEARCH METHODS

All of the research presented in this volume employs feminist research methods, an emerging and somewhat controversial means of inquiry in urban studies. Although some researchers have questioned whether it is possible to identify certain methods as uniquely feminist, it has been demonstrated that there is a feminist approach to research grounded in both an older positivist-empirical tradition as well as a new, postempirical one.[1] Feminist methods are also part of an intellectual movement that represents a shift away from traditional social science methodology (Nielsen 1990; Westkott 1990). The theories that frame these methods can be rendered feminist in a number of ways. Gender comprises a central focus, and gender relations are seen as neither natural nor immutable. Gendered status is viewed as a product of sociocultural and historical processes (Chafetz 1988). Thus, for feminists, the categories of man and woman are not presumed to be givens (Andrew and Milroy 1988).

In feminist research, it is necessary to engage in a historical, theoretical, and political process that results in women being considered subjects as well as objects of study (Hartsock 1990). We want to develop an account in which women's perspectives are not subjugated or disruptive knowledges but rather as primary and constitutive of their everyday world. Thus, feminist research must be grounded in an epistemological base that indicates knowledge is possible. As a social construction, knowledge is partly autobiographical and, therefore, gender biased. Knowledge is gained by talking and by listening—"an everyday and deeply political form of praxis" (Forester 1989, 113); knowing can be tacit or intuitive (Sandercock and Forsyth 1992). From these concepts of knowing come a social science not only about women but also for women.

Feminist research also needs a theory of power that recognizes that everyday activity contains an understanding of the world (Hartsock 1990; Smith 1987). For women, their standpoint within the everyday world brings into view "the fundamental grounding of modes of knowing developed in a ruling apparatus. The ruling apparatus is that familiar complex of management, government administration, professions, and intelligentsia, as well as the textually mediated discourses that coordinate and interpenetrate it" (Smith 1987, 108). In this manner, the disjuncture between women's experiences and the modes of knowing make the ruling apparatus visible.[2] Social science inquiry should be more than a litany of facts about women within a patriarchal society; it should instead evaluate the consciousness of women (Westkott 1990). In doing so, we draw new boundaries in scholarship, pedagogy, and practice.

Feminists of all disciplines also argue for a "connected knowing" (Belenky et al. 1986). This concept is multifaceted and can be defined, first, as a relationship between researcher and the object of research (as opposed to a separation between the two); and, second, as a discussion of the politics of theory and method and of the origins and implications of theoretical hierarchies (Sandercock and Forsyth 1992). In this sense, the concept of understanding or knowing "is widely taken to include knowing from without, by way of observation, and also knowing from within, experientially, empathetically, and intuitively" (Andrew and Milroy 1988, 176).

Inherent in this process is the linkage between understanding and change in the phenomenon of space. "Changing" refers to the altering of concepts, methods, theories, and languages we use to investigate the everyday world. It also reflects a redefinition of the criteria that are the bases of our knowledge. The determination to connect understanding and change, however, is more than a research methodology—it is also a political act. Following Fincher and Jacobs' lead, we are looking at the interconnectedness of power and identity as not just difference but as a *located* politics of difference (1998, 2). In so doing, scientific enterprise and politics are brought face-to-face, not unlike other developed theories and methods that take human agents and their actions into account. We suggest that by starting with a feminist standpoint, researchers can challenge old boundaries and draw new ones.

LEGACIES OF UNDERSTANDING GENDER AND THE CITY

The body of research presented within this volume builds in very specific ways on works from the 1980s and 1990s in the area of women and the urban environment. That work started with earlier, essentially descriptive, studies that focused on the differences between women's and men's experiences and perceptions of the city, emphasizing in particular the spatial constraints experienced by women and the gender roles played within. Then came investigations centered on gender relations that stressed relations of inequality in which men (and their institutions) systematically use physical, political, and economic power to subordinate women. The seminal work by Acker (1988) on the institutional aspects of patriarchy showed us that to understand local politics fully, attention must be paid to gender. A concern with gender highlights issues of power and social organization, and provides for greater depth in understanding the world(s) women inhabit within the city.

Much of the evolving work on the "analysis of women's activities and experience and the nature of their oppression in urban areas" (Little, Peake, and Richardson 1988, 1) was developed by feminist geographers, who were troubled by the prominence of a male bias in their own field (also see Jones, Nast, and Roberts 1997). Little, Peake, and Richardson further declared that their contribution to the literature on women in urban environments was to

> illustrate that an understanding of the nature of women's lives and activity patterns—that is, their active use of space and time—affect, and are affected by, spatial structure and environmental change. . . [we] come to understand that as gender relations change so does the way in which men and women create, reproduce, and change the environments in which they live. In turn, the environment and its transformation reflects, reproduces and alters gender relations. (1988, 12)

Along with other feminist geographers, they help us to see the reciprocal relationship between women and urban environments. As women adjust their use of space and time, they create new environments and reconfigure existing ones. Thus, we see that bounded places and spatialized identities are not static. Investigating the processes and power relations that produce bounded areas enables us to better comprehend how urban women are contained and enact their identities within these spaces. Furthermore, it helps us understand how women's alternative visions of urban space help them to stretch and, sometimes, break the bounds that contain them.

Feminists in other disciplines, such as the sociologist Daphne Spain (1992) and political scientists Judith Garber and Robyne Turner (1995), have also added to our understanding of the relationship between women and the city. In turn, Caroline Andrew and Beth Moore Milroy (1988) have provided feminist analyses of how and why urban areas are structured as they are. They look specifically at the junction between physical urban structure and the socioeconomic practices that shape it and spring from it. Thus, they study gender relations through an examination of urban structures and processes, giving special attention to the historical contingency of both and the fact that both are constructed in line with dominant interests. These authors suggest that "the special contribution of [their] work is to highlight the tension between production and reproduction which have traditionally been linked activities for women only, and to challenge theories that value one to the disadvantage of the other" (Andrew and Milroy 1988, 178). They also stress the theme of the relationship between understanding situations and changing them. How can we build understanding that simultaneously escapes sexism and recognizes the need to change current affairs? Women experience cities differently from men specifically because of the gender asymmetries that are embedded in distinct institutions and local institutional relationships.

We would argue that the value of feminist theory is vested in a political stance that points out how conventional models of what constitutes "normal" and typical gender-based behavior marginalizes many people in our society. It shows how institutions (like planning) are deeply intertwined with a gender system that establishes expectations for individuals and society, with a resulting impact on the economy, politics, and the family. In order for women not to be marginalized, their urban experiences need to be taken into account when local policies are made; thus an institutional perspective from which to look at women and the city (Garber and Turner 1995) is instructive.

With this in mind, our contributors have challenged the institutional ways in which cities have been designed, developed, and maintained, and offer alternative visions of how, as active agents, women can address issues of empowerment, oppression, and exclusion/inclusion. The authors also recognize the contexts within which the descriptions of women's worlds are proposed. They address the broad cultural, economic, and political forces that situate gendered relations within the historical development of U.S. and Canadian cities. Their empirical studies reveal the power of patterns that assert themselves in space. U.S. cities provide rich examples of how certain patterns—that is, the dominance of issues of race and ethnicity—impact spatial arrangements and social relations. Because of the widespread acceptance of racial/ethnic segregation, the American public has come to tolerate deep social inequities (see Goldsmith 1997). As a counterpoint, the ethnic diversity found in Canada has contributed to the construction of more heterogeneously spatial and social communities within Canadian cities. The Canadian case studies herein explore to what extent social inequalities and the resultant use of spatial boundaries influence gender relations within Canada.

Until quite recently, European cities have avoided the racial-caste character of U.S. cities. But now Europe's cities are threatened by a new social geography that diminishes their vibrancy. William Goldsmith (1997) argues that this threat is due to (hidden) American influences, and that it is important to focus on the way that Americans structure and use their cities. In this vein, we concentrate on cities in North America, with the understanding that there are implications for divining how women interact within urban areas throughout the world. The discussion goes beyond the description of policies for restructuring city form, however, as the authors explain how historic context, current circumstance, and the production of alternative visions of the city allow for explanations as to how women can seek the power to shape their urban environment.

In response to our major themes, the volume is divided into three sections: Visible or Invisible? Gendered Urban Boundaries; Intersections of Gendered Boundaries: Race, Class, and Ethnicity; and Challenging Planned Boundaries. We have placed chapters within these three sections because their major contribution to the debate falls within a specific theme. At the same time, all of the chapters cut across all three main themes. In large measure, this is due to the collaborative discussions among the contributors and the editors.

VISIBLE OR INVISIBLE? GENDERED URBAN BOUNDARIES

The construct of boundary is a powerful tool for understanding women's lives in the city; we see boundaries as multiple and intersecting, provisional and shifting. It is critical that we also view boundaries as an enabling force—a process women use to create enclaves of similarity and support. We often think of a boundary as a physical place/space that is negative (as in keeping people out). However, we are reminded by authors in this section that boundaries can also be positive (for maintaining relations within). They can form a social space that delineates who belongs and who does not. Boundary can also have a psychological sense, suggesting what is safe and what is not. However, urban women do not live within such neat categories. Women's lives are a constant transitioning across boundaries: accompanying men to "their" places, going into spaces that have been closed to them (such as city streets at night), or creating new or alternative spaces that transcend boundaries, both visible and invisible. Some women transgress boundaries (for example, prostitutes plying their trade, or others who may be allowed to enter the male domain if they have male attributes); others work to maintain boundaries, accepting the gendered division of labor. Boundary can also be thought of as an intersection, that point at which one is poised to enter a new territory; as such, the concept opens up the possibilities that may await women and the city. The different authors all grapple with the idea of boundary, and seek to understand how (and why) the women they study have found ways to explore and exploit boundaries, and with what results.

Indeed, how women respond to these boundaries and interconnections is a key to how they live their lives. Do they accept these boundaries? Or, do they envision other alternatives, and make the boundary a site of resistance as they (re)-configure and (re)construct it? Urban women often do resist spaces imposed upon them, for reasons ranging from survival to political consciousness. As Caroline Andrew reminds us in chapter 8, "women's experience in the city is one of movement in the margins, between and through categories, connecting rather than distinguishing and relishing contradictions rather than rejecting them." During this process, what happens to the spatial and social forms of the city? Borders in space and place are inseparable from social boundaries—boundaries that we define to be the formation of identity and the production of difference. This is apparent as the contributors discuss the individual and collective experiences of women in the city. Although the reality of urban space must be investigated, we must also come to understand how women see themselves within that space.

Women's interpretation of their space can lead to a wider connectedness with city life rather than being disadvantaged by the segmentation of space. Evelyn Peters brings this to light in chapter 2 in her investigation of the spatiality that organizes First Nations women's narratives about their needs for services in urban areas throughout Canada. Beyond a description of the range and nature of the services, Peters explores underlying geographies of these native women as they construct their own maps of meaning. In so doing, these women break down some of the boundaries they find in the city.

Judith Garber in chapter 1 adds an intriguing twist to the argument about boundaries as she probes the complex question of how anonymity in the city contributes to the urban condition. The everyday struggles she outlines are conducted around specific identity categories by which some individuals have come to be placed in the sociospatial architecture of the city (see Fincher and Jacobs 1998; Massey 1994). Garber queries how identity, collective empowerment (of women, gays, and lesbians), and the honoring of diversity/plurality are related. Inherent in her analysis is the concept of power relations embedded in the anonymity of the public sphere of strangers—a contradiction of urban anonymity that allows some to stay out of harm's way but condemns others to unrecognizability in urban life. Thus we see how boundaries can be created within cities to protect and embolden those within.

By viewing urban space in multiple ways, investigations are opened that allow for alternative visions of what the city could be. Such views reveal the simultaneous coexistence of social interrelations and interactions on all spatial scales—here, particularly, within the city. Accepting that urban space is constructed in many ways suggests the complex matrix of historical, social, sexual, racial, and class positions that women occupy. Our working definition of "boundary" encourages the reader to reevaluate aspects of urban life from the viewpoints of women and other marginalized groups who, although often silent, are an integral part of the urban landscape.

INTERSECTIONS OF GENDERED BOUNDARIES: RACE, ETHNICITY, AND CLASS

We posit that a gendered and differentiated perspective of women is the preferable grounding for inquiry—preferable because, as the excluded group, women's perspective is often more inclusive and critically coherent than the dominant group (Di Stefano 1990). A central theme within feminist thought has been the assertion that all women are oppressed, the implication being that women share a common experience. This is not true. Although sexism may be a system of domination, it has never been the sole determinant of oppression, since race, ethnicity, class, and sexual preference are also critical in determining the extent to which sexism oppresses individual women in their daily life experiences. The matrix of domination that women "experience (and resist) exists on three levels, namely the level of personal biography, the group level of the cultural context created by race, class, gender [ethnicity and sexuality], and the systematic level of social institutions" (Collins 1991, 364).

This attention to the interlocking nature of gender, race, ethnicity, class, and sexuality shifts the focus of investigation from one aimed at explicating these elements to one whose goal is to determine what the connections are among these systems. This is a critical distinction; previously, the tendency has been to determine one primary form of oppression and then address the remaining types of oppression as variables within the system that is defined as most important. Resisting one primary form of oppression, African American feminists have focused on the triple jeopardy of racism, sexism, and classism as a conceptualization of African American women's status (King 1988). From this starting point, these feminists are now exploring the dynamics of multiple identities and the interaction between these factors, seeking to develop new theoretical interpretations of the interaction itself (Collins 1991).

Although it is impossible to separate structure and thought from the historical and material conditions determining the lives of its producers (Berger and Luckman 1967), it is critical that the history of multiple identities not obscure the ways in which women actively seek to construct their social worlds. Individual experience, embedded within a set of social relations, produces both the possibilities and limitations of that experience. To explain and understand any human social behavior, we need to know the meaning attached to it by the participants themselves (Nielsen 1990; Smith 1987). What is at issue is not just women's everyday experience, but also the relations that underlie it and the connections between the two. This is why feminist concepts of empowerment, women's consciousness, and the intersection of boundaries need to be brought to the forefront. These concepts help us understand how women—who, because of their visibility are defined by a special status within society—negotiate their way around boundaries and often find themselves "choosing the margin" (hooks 1990). Although it is difficult to develop feminist ideologies that bring in all the complexities of women and their lives, it is precisely for this reason that we should undertake the effort (Barrett and McIntosh 1985; King 1988).

The complexities of the research investigation require feminists to pay particular attention to women's narratives as played out within their social worlds. Daphne Spain in chapter 5 details how, in the beginning of this century, African American women were able to contribute to constructing "redemptive spaces" in which women, men, and children found protection from the harsh conditions of the industrializing city. Her focus on the words and actions of specific individuals who led these efforts reveals how women of this time built institutions through interconnections with other women and voluntary organizations. Though bounded by social realities on many levels, their vision of what the city could be allowed these women to reconfigure their space and, in turn, to expand their social relations.

It is critical that we move women's knowledge from its inception within women's experiences to a recognition of the ways that women's places in social organization obscure the diversity of their lived experience. The juncture between the experience and the manner in which that experience is expressed is the focus of much of the empirical work reported in this volume. By focusing on the survival strategies of working poor women, Melissa Gilbert demonstrates in chapter 3 how their location within various systems of power relations can shape the social and spatial boundaries of their lives. In addition, she reveals how African American women and white women record different histories and different relationships, adding to the complexity of Gilbert's argument while still enabling us to see some of the commonalities across their experiences.

Jennifer Subban and Alma Young in chapter 4 discuss the process through which a group of African American women come to a critical consciousness of their experiences and, in so doing, are able to situate themselves within the political and economic structures. The vehicle for this consciousness is literacy training, which seeks to foster within the women a capacity for community building. The women's literacy status is conceived of as a boundary, one that has a dual function: it isolates the women from the larger society while providing solace among those who are left behind—the solace that comes from recognizing others with whom you share commonalities. But the literacy training also reminds them that isolation from mainstream society is problematic and points them in the direction of extending their boundaries.

Kristine Miranne in chapter 6 investigates how federal devolution is concurrently transforming welfare policy and public-housing policy. Poor women and their families are the ones who most feel the impact of these changes, as they often access welfare and housing assistance at the same time. Women thus find themselves "embounded" when they are isolated from state resources. Therefore, the challenge for women is to transcend the intersections among the multiple boundaries of social policies as they work from the margins to create new opportunities for themselves and their families.

As various experiences are described, and the significance of these experiences as a ground for the critique of dominant institutions and ideologies of society is realized, these authors begin to reveal the methodological challenges to constructing an account of the world that is sensitive to the realities and multiplicities of women's lives. In this way, they help us to understand further the sense in which both women and the city are socially constructed. We see how the city changes spatially and socially through the responses of women, in both proactive and reactive ways, to the oppressions they find in the city. In turn, the social and spatial processes found in the city change not only the way that women are perceived by others but also how they come to perceive of themselves. It is this dynamic of social construction that is captured in this volume.

CHALLENGING PLANNED BOUNDARIES

In her seminal work, *The Death and Life of Great American Cities* (1961), Jane Jacobs writes:

Objects in cities—whether they are buildings, streets, parks, districts, landmarks, or anything else—can have radically differing effects, depending upon the circumstances and contexts in which they exist. Thus, for instance, almost nothing useful can be understood or can be done about improving city dwellings if these are considered in the abstract as "housing." City dwellings—either existing or potential—are *specific* and particularized buildings are always involved in *differing, specific processes.* (440) [emphasis in original]

It is apparent that the general reluctance of planning to recognize the gender implications of women's needs is a function of the actual process of policy making moreso than its content (Little 1994, 9). The contributors to this volume see planning as a process, one that includes more than a litany of how women should be part of the planning endeavor. Rather, they propose a reconceptualized, open-ended set of alternatives and options that opposes the implementation of a fixed vision, which characterizes much of today's urban planning.

Within the last two decades, we have seen an urban feminist movement directed toward a better understanding of women's disadvantaged position within the city whose form reflects a male orientation (Mackenzie 1989; Wilson 1991; also see Greed 1994; Staeheli and Clarke 1995). Clara Greed further points out that the male-dominated world of urban planning debates whether "it should confine itself to purely physical issues or take on social policy"—as if the two could, or should, be separated (1994, 22). As more and more women assume nontraditional roles and activities, they have to operate within an urban, built environment that has literally been man made. Yet "the built environment is often seen as a benign background to the human drama rather than a force which shapes our lives in profound ways" (MacGregor 1995, 26).

As increasing numbers of women assume these so-called nontraditional responsibilities, it becomes clear that the built environment is not able to meet women's changing needs. Deconstructing that environment reveals aspects of urban life that would look considerably different if the needs of all women and other marginalized groups were taken into account. By arguing for a change in the agenda of cities, the authors challenge traditional patterns and the institutions that create and sustain them. They examine the extent to which we can envision new spaces within the city by providing a better understanding of how diverse social groups interact, how urban space can enhance such interaction, and what roles formal and informal laws, by-laws, policies, and other measures should play. They critique the concept of public and private that spatially segregates home and the workplace. Charged with changing the assumptions that have (mis)guided the planning profession for so long, their theoretical and empirical work support MacGregor's statement that the "public" must become an integrated "publics" where diverse needs, aspirations, and experiences are included (1995, 42).

The experience of land users must not only be reflected in the planning process but also be legitimated as a source of knowledge to be used as a guide for planning and community development (Sandercock and Forsyth 1992). Knowledge that comes from women's activity, however, is frequently misrepresented or absent altogether from the discourse of the public world. Smith (1987) refers to this gap in social knowledge as a "line of fault." For example, we must remember that African American feminist thought, though possibly recorded by others, is produced by African American women. There is an underlying assumption that not only will women share a commonality of experience but also that it will be unique to their identity. Because of the multiplicities of their lives, women have many different identities. Living within these identities may produce certain commonalities of outlook, but the inherent diversity results in different expressions of these commonalities. It has become apparent as we continue to investigate women's experiences that we do not think of "identities as solidified around one or two social traits such as ethnicity, or gender, or stage in the life cycle, or sexuality; identities are conceived as a process, as performed, and as unstable" (Pratt 1998, 26).

This leads to a new "geography of opportunity"—women, through politics of identity and politics of place, can formulate strategies to create new spaces and possibilities within cities. In order to understand how women can contribute to the social, economic, and political agendas set within the urban environment, we need a better understanding of women's place within the history of planning. Sue Hendler in chapter 7 discusses the boundaries that have been established in Canada between the formal planning profession, populated largely by men, and community planning, led to a large extent by women. She asks what the implications might have been for physical and social planning if the divisions between formal planning and community planning had not been so sharp. Hendler deconstructs Canadian planning history to show how women fare under three different interpretations. Hendler also calls for the production of planning texts that empower by recognizing the need to accommodate the complexity of space, place, and agency.

Although women's experiences in cities may reflect movement between and through spaces, they are still constrained by boundaries that are defined by time, space, and segmentation of social relations. In her work on safety audits in Canada, Caroline Andrew in chapter 8 states that a gendered perspective of urban space must take into account the symbolic representation of that space. In particular, how can women gain ownership of space that, until now, they have not been able to access freely (such as city streets at night)? Andrew argues further that planning initiatives, such as safety audits, must lead to concrete results, be woman centered, and be related to the social construction of spaces.

The politics of location, where the geographies of women reflect identity politics and relational differences, can be seen in the gender and racial bias of municipal zoning regulations. Officials never planned environments that were gender specific, even when traditional gender roles were in place, because "a notion of women's experience as a basis for making plans did not exist" (Liggett 1992, 24). Current zoning policies in many North American cities support nuclear (traditional) families and actually penalize women because of changes in family and household structure. In chapter 9, Marsha Ritzdorf draws on examples from municipal land use planning and zoning to argue that the concept of a "deviant African-American family" frames a policy discourse that discriminates against black women and their families. Here we see an example of boundaries being drawn that are exclusive, designed to keep certain groups out. Housing, planning, and zoning policies have limited the rights and access to resources of those who live within urban spaces bounded by the social construction of their families and communities. This social construction is reflected by a set of planning and legal regulations that conspires to keep African American women and their families in the margins. The action that we see is clearly institutional and reactive, and its impact minimizes the ability of African Americans to actualize their urban vision.

Christine Cook, Marilyn Bruin, and Sue Crull examine in chapter 10 how women conceptualize their housing and neighborhood choices. Within cities, many poor women are relegated to housing that appears to be inadequate and that is located in impoverished neighborhoods. Do women initially choose or decide to remain in such housing because of income, racial identity, or lack of education? Or are they committed to the social networks that contribute to the construction of their space? The authors suggest that women do manipulate the constraints placed before them by reconfiguring and resisting these boundaries. Women often do this silently, however, as these authors find that housing problems experienced by poor single mothers and their families are often overlooked by political leaders in the efforts to revitalize and reconstruct cities. The current focus on the economic opportunities available to residents of the metropolis must be broadened to include a better understanding of women's housing and neighborhood conditions.

All of the chapters in this volume offer a contextual vision of the city by looking at the "multiple grids of difference and complex and varied links between place and identity formation" (Pratt 1998, 27). The authors outline how linking sustainability (as revealed through the women's lives) and feminist visions of the urban environment will enable us to achieve a stronger sense of urban place (Spain 1995). How can women critique the social, economic, and political agendas set within urban space? How does the concept of boundaries help reveal the agendas that have been established? How can women become empowered through their expertise at devising strategies to live within cities? Because women are not typically at the intersections where policy decisions are made, we call for mechanisms that reinforce women's knowledge, for analyses of the social and spatial aspects of the city related to women's lives, and for processes that indicate to women that they can resist, (re)configure, and (re)construct the boundaries they encounter.

EPILOGUE

This volume makes a significant contribution to the study of women and the city in four significant ways. First, the book helps us to understand further the sense in which both women and the city are socially constructed. Through both the proactive and reactive responses of women to the oppressions they find in the city, the city changes spatially and socially. In turn, the social and spatial processes found in the city change not only the way that women are perceived by others but also how they come to perceive of themselves. Second, it adds to studies, still embryonic, that look at the construction of the city through the lens of the multiplicities of women's lives—in terms of gender, race, ethnicity, sexuality, and nationality. By acknowledging the differences as well as the similarities of women, we get a richer sense of how women negotiate their way in the city. Third, the volume reminds us how women find ways to challenge the boundaries that constrain them while creating new boundaries to encompass who they are and the lives that they want to lead in the city. Fourth, this volume offers alternative visions of what the relations of women to their environment can be in cities. That, in turn, gives us different conceptions of gender relations and spatial forms within the city.

As editors, we chose not to end the book with a conclusion; rather, we asked Beth Moore Milroy to comment on the past development of urban, woman-centered research, on the current pressing issues as revealed by the contributors to this book, and on future avenues. She reminds us that the feminist agenda must continue to include practice as well as theory. Thus, she urges us to look for new paths, to rethink conceptualizations and practices, as we probe more deeply the body/city interplay. She is particularly concerned with finding new ways of looking at multiplicity, so that we move away from thinking of it as separate pieces. Instead, she suggests that we use concepts like métissage, seriality, and mimesis, which enable us to see the range of possibilities in women's lived experiences. We come to conceptualize how diverse people can use city spaces without their "differences" being explicitly questioned. These conceptualizations, though raising complex issues, give us a different set of lenses through which to view women's lives in the urban arena.

NOTES

1. Nielsen (1990) defines "postempirical" as a turning point in the contemporary philosophy of science, epistemology, sociology of knowledge, and related fields. This turning point is characterized by work directed toward the development of an alternative to scientific methods for the study of the cultural and social world.

2. Smith's definition of the ruling apparatus, however, refers to more than the sphere of men from which women have been excluded. As a concept, the ruling apparatus exposes the intersection of those institutions organizing society by basis of their gender sub-

text and division of labor. As the dominant mode of ruling, the structure of the apparatus transcribes the local and particular actualities of lives into generalized and abstracted forms (Smith 1987).

REFERENCES

Acker, J. 1988. "Class, Gender, and the Relations of Distribution." *Journal of Women and Culture and Society* 13: 473–497.

Andrew, Caroline, and Beth Moore Milroy, eds. 1988. *Life Spaces: Gender, Households and Employment.* Vancouver: University of British Columbia Press.

Barrett, Michele, and Mary McIntosh. 1985. "Ethnocentrism and Socialist Feminist Theory." *Feminist Review* 20: 23–48.

Belenky, Mary Field, Blythe McVicker Clinchy, Nancy Rule Goldberger, and Jill Mattuck Tarule, eds. 1986. *Women's Way of Knowing: The Development of Self, Voice, and Mind.* New York: Basic Books.

Berger, Peter L., and Thomas Luckman. 1967. *The Social Construction of Reality.* New York: Anchor Books.

Chafetz, Janet Saltzman. 1988. *Feminist Sociology: An Overview of Contemporary Theories.* Itasca, Ill.: Peacock.

Collins, Patricia Hill. 1991. "Learning from the Outsider Within: The Sociological Significance of Black Feminist Thought." In *Beyond Methodology: Feminist Scholarship as Lived Research,* edited by Mary Margaret Fonow and Judith A. Cook. Bloomington: Indiana University Press.

Di Stefano, Christine. 1990. "Dilemmas of Difference: Feminism, Modernity, and Postmodernism." In *Feminism/Postmodernism,* edited by Linda Nicholson. New York: Routledge.

Ferree, Myra Marx, Judith Lorber, and Beth B. Hess, eds. 1999. *Revisioning Gender.* Thousand Oaks, Calif.: Sage Publications.

Fincher, Ruth, and Jane M. Jacobs. 1998. *Cities of Difference.* New York: Guilford Press.

Forester, John F. 1989. *Planning in the Face of Power.* Berkeley: University of California Press.

Garber, Judith, and Robyne S. Turner, eds. 1995. *Gender in Urban Research.* Thousand Oaks, Calif.: Sage Publications.

Goldsmith, W. W. 1997. "The Metropolis and Globalization: The Dialectics of Racial Discrimination, Deregulation, and Urban Form." *American Behavioral Scientist* 31: 299–310.

Greed, Clara H. 1994. *Women and Planning: Creating Gendered Realities.* London: Routledge.

Hartsock, Nancy. 1990. "Foucalt on Power: A Theory for Women." In *Feminism/Postmodernism,* edited by Linda Nicholson. New York: Routledge.

hooks, bell. 1990. "Choosing the Margin as a Space of Radical Openness." In *Yearning: Race, Gender and Cultural Politics.* Boston: South End Press.

Jacobs, Jane. 1961. *The Death and Life of Great American Cities.* New York: Random House.

Jones III, John Paul, Heidi Nast, and Susan R. Roberts, eds. 1997. *Thresholds in Feminist*

Geography: Difference, Methodology, and Representation. Lanham, Md.: Rowman and Littlefield.

King, Deborah. 1988. "Multiple Jeopardy, Multiple Consciousness: The Context of Black Feminist Ideology." *Signs* 14: 42–72.

Liggett, Helen. 1992. "Knowing Women/Planning Theory." *Planning Theory* 7: 22–30.

Little, Jo. 1994. *Gender, Planning, and the Policy Process.* Oxford: Pergamon Press.

Little, Jo, Linda L. Peake, and Pat Richardson, eds. 1988. *Women in Cities: Gender and the Built Environment.* New York: Macmillan Education.

Lorber, Judith. 1994. *Paradoxes of Gender.* New Haven, Conn.: Yale University Press.

MacGregor, Sherilyn. 1995. "Deconstructing the Man Made City: Feminist Critiques of Planning Thought and Action." In *Change of Plans: Towards a Non-Sexist Sustainable City,* edited by Margaret Eichler. New York: Garamond Press.

Mackenzie, Suzanne. 1989. *Visible Histories: Women and Environments in a Post-War British City.* Montreal: McGill-Queens University Press.

Massey, Doreen. 1994. *Space, Place, and Gender.* Minneapolis: University of Minnesota Press.

Nielsen, Joyce M. 1990. *Feminist Research Methods: Exemplary Readings in the Social Sciences.* Boulder: Westview Press.

Pratt, Geraldine. 1998. "Grids of Difference: Place and Identity Formation." In *Cities of Difference,* edited by Ruth Fincher and Jane M. Jacobs. New York: Guilford Press.

Sandercock, Leonie, and Ann Forsyth. 1992. "A Gender Agenda: New Directions for Planning Theory." *Journal of the American Planning Association* 58: 49–58.

Smith, Dorothy. 1987. *The Everyday World as Problematic: A Feminist Sociology.* Boston: Northeastern University Press.

Spain, Daphne. 1992. *Gendered Spaces.* Chapel Hill: University of North Carolina Press.

———. 1995. "Sustainability, Feminist Visions, and the Utopian Vision." *Journal of Planning Literature* 9: 363–369.

Staeheli, Lynn, and Susan Clarke. 1995. "Gender, Place, and Citizenship." In *Gender in Urban Research,* edited by Judith Garber and Robyne Turner. Thousand Oaks, Calif.: Sage Publications.

West, Candace, and Don Zimmerman. 1987. "Doing Gender." *Gender and Society* 1: 125–151.

Westkott, Marcia. 1990. "Feminist Criticism of the Social Sciences." In *Feminist Research Methods,* edited by Joyce McCarl Nielsen. Boulder: Westview Press.

Wilson, Elizabeth. 1991. *The Sphinx in the City: Urban Life, the Control of Disorder and Women.* London: Viagro.

PART I

VISIBLE OR INVISIBLE?
GENDERED URBAN BOUNDARIES

Chapter 1

"Not Named or Identified": Politics and the Search for Anonymity in the City

Judith A. Garber

anonymous: not named or identified; lacking individuality, distinction, or recognizability

—*Merriam-Webster's Collegiate Dictionary*, 10th ed.

The sociologist Lyn Lofland has written: "City living is possible only because a city is not, in fact, a totally anonymous sort of place. . . . That is, one can live as a stranger in the midst of strangers only because important elements of 'strangeness' have been removed" (1973, 29). Although Lofland's statement makes great intuitive sense, in fact there are almost no descriptors for urban society that are used more predictably than "anonymous." Urban sociologists and historians have traditionally viewed cities as confluences of strangers, treating anonymity as a defining attribute of urbanity (Bender 1993; Jackson 1961; J. Jacobs 1961; Lofland 1994, 1998; Sennett 1970, 1994; Wirth 1938; also see Swanson 1993; Wilson 1993). For certain political theorists, cities epitomize the democratic public sphere because of their openness to what and who is unknown (Berman 1986; Walzer 1986; Young 1990). Recently, urban anonymity has enjoyed a renaissance among lesbian, gay, and feminist scholars, who have focused on its heightened relevance to people whose group affiliations render them "strange" in nonurban settings (Faderman 1991; Grube 1997; Haeberle 1993; Kennedy and Davis 1993; Valentine 1993; Weisman 1992).

Across these varied literatures, and over time, anonymity is treated as inherent in urbanity and inherently linked to the most vital characteristic of urban places: publicity. That is, cities are defined, at least in the ideal, by their robust public spheres and public spaces, of which anyone can partake. Urban publicity is unmarked by internal boundaries that would segregate and exclude, and it is unintrusive in that people are not required to reveal any more about themselves than they choose. Because publicity is only part of what it means to be urban, anonymity does not pervade every nook and cranny of cities (see A. Jacobs 1997), but anonymity is *available* for those who want to take advantage of it. Because of its accessibility to all sorts of groups, anonymity is used to signify the kinds of ideal geographical, social, and civic spaces in which identity differences are accepted instead of being subsumed into the mainstream or repelled.

This chapter examines the empirical claim that anonymity has been a primary goal for women, gays, lesbians, and members of other marginalized groups who seek out the city, as well as the normative claim to which it is strongly connected—that anonymity enhances the character of the city as a public place. I argue that this empirical claim is incomplete and confused and that this normative claim is vacuous. Whereas anonymity holds concrete, unassailable appeal in terms of the security of groups that live under scrutiny and threat, cities are at least as compelling to nonmembers of the monolithic community because they offer the opportunity for social, cultural, and political identity. Anonymity has a complex and deeply paradoxical relationship to the search for identity in the city. Considered outside of this context, however, anonymity has limited political content. Ultimately, my design is to show that anonymity cannot contribute much to a vision of an urban public sphere in which members of groups marginalized by their identities can gain political standing.

WHO SEEKS ANONYMITY?

In current scholarship, anonymity is most apt to be associated with gay men, lesbians, and, less often, all women. Anonymity serves as a fundamental explanation for why members of these groups settle in urban areas rather than villages, towns, and small cities. But the anonymity of the city is relevant to anybody who looks, acts, sounds, or generally seems different from the *actual* or *perceived* norm in nonurban places. Obviously, norms are highly idiosyncratic to particular places and times, but in North America and Europe this category of people seeking anonymity could conceivably include culturally specific groups such as habited Catholic nuns, nonspeakers of the majority language, Hell's Angels, Rastafarians, or sari-wearing East Indian women; those whose distinctiveness stems from their bodily characteristics, such as people with evident disabilities; and numerous others who might stand out for a mixture of reasons, most notably prostitutes, mixed-identity families, the homeless, the ostentatiously tattooed or pierced, "artistic types," or children.

Stated as a general proposition, particular kinds of people consciously seek anonymity, and they favor cities, where anonymity is more likely to be found. The image of cities as sites of anonymity is assumed to be emblazoned in the minds of people who gravitate there. As Iris Marion Young puts it, "deviant or minority groups find in the city . . . a cover of anonymity" (1990, 238). Young's expansive statement is primarily a comment on the nature of cities, and it exists within a larger, normative, political theory, but it also endorses the common empirical wisdom about anonymity-seeking. Such claims about the relationship between group characteristics and anonymity in the city are frequently backed by interviews, historical materials, and received knowledge. Gill Valentine has found that, in an unnamed, medium-sized English city, "urban areas are seen as more anonymous, and hence lesbians believe it is easier to manage and control others' images of their sexual identity in such an environment" (1993, 398). As Elizabeth Kennedy and Madeline Davis discovered in Buffalo, "in the first half of the twentieth century" the city "was large enough to allow the anonymity necessary for lesbians to separate their social lives from work and family" (1993, 10). In post–World War II Toronto, according to John Grube, for many gay men, "homosexuality . . . was placed in one zone of social discourse, the public anonymity of the street and park" (1997, 131). These are only a few examples of the empirically grounded claims made about anonymity (see, for example, Munt 1995, 118; Rayside 1991, 145; Senelick 1991, 338–342), but they reveal that, in different countries at various points in time, cities have been associated with groups that are subject to scrutiny and control, because the unbounded, unintrusive character of urban publicity cultivates the anonymity these groups seek.

WHY SEEK ANONYMITY?

So far, I have not bothered to define anonymity. This is because, on a basic conceptual level, it is not terribly controversial. The conventional understanding of anonymity is very nearly like the dictionary definition—that is, the state of being unnamed, unidentified, unrecognized. I believe—although this is not part of the formal definition—that anonymity is also commonly supposed to have some affinity with the qualities of invisibility and hiddenness. (Whether any of these are positive or negative conditions is a separate issue.) Of course, anonymity exists primarily in the eye of the beholder—that is, people do not in fact lack their own, personal identities simply because they are "not named or identified" from the outside. One's *group* identities, in contrast, tend to be much more heavily dependent on being revealed to or identifiable by others.

In practice, the concept of anonymity turns out to be more murky and problematic than might be expected. Work that lauds anonymity as a benefit of urban living for particular groups, and especially for lesbians and gay men, tends to use the term in conjunction with concepts whose proximity to it is dubious. Life in the big city, to which anonymity is linked conceptually and in practice, is vaguely portrayed as a corrective to the most fundamental problems—invisibility and isolation—encountered by groups who, because of societal sanctions, often attract unwanted and negative attention (Haeberle 1993, 2; Kennedy and Davis 1993, 29, 66; also see D'Emilio 1983, 100; Valentine 1993, 402). This urban, anonymous life is supposed to engender safety (in numbers) (Valentine 1993, 398), belonging (to a "critical mass") (Haeberle 1993, 2), expression (of one's identity), and solidarity or community (with people who are similar) (Kennedy and Davis 1993, 10, 29, 66).

Often, writers move effortlessly between anonymity and identity as if they were part of a seamless whole. Lillian Faderman observes, for instance, that World War II–era military service deposited lesbians in the United States in "large metropolitan areas where they could meet others like themselves" (1992, 127). At the same time, "many women also came . . . to work in factories during the war and they, like ex-military women, stayed because they found the anonymity of the big city to be more compatible with what became their life choices" (126). David Rayside refers to cities as places "where a degree of anonymity is possible, and where people of a like mind are easier to find" (1991, 145). Young says that, for people who differ from the social norm, the search for anonymity in the city is accompanied by the discovery of "a critical mass unavailable in the smaller town" (1990, 238).

The flaw in this formulation is apparent, for much of the language that is used to evoke the benefits of the anonymous urban life suggests anonymity's exact opposites, visibility and identification. It is evident how anonymity, impersonality, and freedom might be closely related to each other (although they are not synonymous); in contrast, the connection between anonymity and belonging or visibility is not at all immediately obvious. For Young, at least, identity group affiliation and anonymity are both necessary to achieve the ideal of "social differentiation without exclusion" (1990, 238–239), an observation that suggests there is a *relationship* between being anonymous and being identified with or within a group. The important, difficult questions of how anonymity contributes to this urban condition, where the two goals are in tension or contradiction, and how the relationship between them can best be explicated are, however, left untouched by the use of anonymity as a rough substitute for identity.[1]

Whatever the benefits of being able to express one's identity or to discover a critical mass of people like oneself—and however much these capacities are rooted in urbanity—they are plainly not equivalent to being anonymous. I am skeptical that a direct connection between anonymity and identity can be made for the purposes of an empirical account of why members of marginalized groups come to cities or, ultimately, a normative account of how cities support a meaningful public sphere in which diversity is actively included in both social and political life. At best, it is possible, having acknowledged a relationship between anonymity and identity, to locate points of paradox, indefiniteness, and movement in the search for anonymity, and to include these in an explanation of why people have historically looked to the city for acceptance of their specific identities.

THE COMPLEXITY OF LOCATIONAL CHOICES

Claims about anonymity rest on the observation that, historically, cities have been magnets for the kinds of people who stand out and thus risk subtle suffocation or outright punishment in nonurban settings. This observation reveals one, pedestrian fact about human nature: People have a deep interest in living where they are less apt to be harassed simply because of their association with a disfavored group or culture. It does not shed light on the other significant factors shaping people's choices, such as the tradeoff between short-term and long-term goals. In looking more closely at the search for anonymity in urban settings, it appears that safety through anonymity has primarily been an immediate, limited goal, existing alongside the more persistent, broader goal of safety through nonanonymity.

Anonymity and Life after Anonymity

There is conflict within the set of goals that drive people's locational choices. The presence of this conflict is evidenced by the fact that anonymity and identity, although not equivalent, have both served to some degree as goals sought by members of scrutinized groups. A critical question in assessing the significance of anonymity-seeking is to what extent anonymity is appealing in and of itself, and to what extent it is merely a survival strategy that members of some identity groups employ until more successful or appealing strategies come along.

A mountain of evidence about historical and present conditions documents the scrutiny that homeless people, leftists, homosexuals, feminists, prostitutes, and members of "minority" racial and cultural groups receive both as individuals and as groups. There is simply no question that many people have gathered in cities because of a desire to be free of the (negative) attention inescapable in smaller places where such divergences from the norm are condemned. For an individual who can mask or regulate the perception of identity, living in cities allows the separation of one's job and family from one's sexual, social, and political lives. People can protect a core dimension of their identity from the prying eyes of families, neighbors, landlords, and coworkers, who may well hold real power over them (see, for example, Kennedy and Davis 1993, 55; Valentine 1993).

Understood in this context, anonymity appears as a largely "defensive" strategy (Haeberle 1993, 7), historically used by gays and lesbians who felt they *had* to hide their group identification. Interestingly, this urban strategy may actually be a carryover from experiences in rural or other "nonmetropolitan areas where gays and lesbians are forced to rely much more on invisibility and anonymity" (Kramer 1995, 201) to hide prohibited behavior and associations. Even though the social mix, size, and impersonality of big cities are consistently regarded as providing the more reliable setting for keeping under cover, the deep logic of anonymity-seeking in urban areas is not about becoming genuinely liberated or included any more than it is in small towns.

In anonymous big cities, moreover, the instrumental strategy of defensive anonymity is not an end in and of itself. It does not appear to supersede the durable goal of no longer having to be defensive, at least for gays and lesbians, although neither has it disappeared. John D'Emilio stresses the constant tension between hiding and wanting to create and participate in a collective identity (1983, 40). Gay men in particular have engaged in community-formation strategies that are both self-conscious and highly attentive to the urban context. Parallel efforts to parlay the comfort level provided by urban anonymity into actual displays of identity can be seen in various cultural and ethnic groups, including, in many cities throughout the world, observant Muslims and aboriginal peoples. For these groups, too, there has been a dynamic between relying on defensive anonymity and overtly displaying identity, albeit on the groups' own terms.

In cities, how space is occupied and employed is an indicator of the extent to which the quest for anonymity has been replaced by the desire for legitimation and acceptance of group identity. Space contributes to identity formation—local space can be queer, feminist, or populist, although it usually is not. Former San Francisco Supervisor Harry Britt recognized that relationship when he made the provocative assertion: "When gays are spatially scattered, they are not gay, because they are invisible" (Castells 1983, 138; also see Kramer 1995). Admittedly, Britt's observation has significantly less force in the age of cybercommunications; nevertheless, the ability to form neighborhoods that approximate coherent local communities, which is something that only cities can easily provide to multiple groups at once, remains crucial to identity formation. Following the model of so many immigrant groups, gay men in many cities have consciously fused residential, retail, commercial, and public space into coherent, place-based communities. Gays in San Francisco "created a gay community by living in certain neighborhoods, by operating businesses, by meeting in bars." Through this mechanism, the area around Castro Street developed into "a gay territory" that "is not only a residential space but also a space for . . . business . . . for leisure and pleasure, for feasts and politics" (Castells 1983, 151).

Identity stemming from the creation of a city-within-a-city is only one of the forms that the relationship between urban space and identity can take. As Lawrence Knopp argues in his study of gay identity in several cities: "The forging of identities through the economic and political colonization of territorial spaces . . . is much facilitated . . . where there is a critical mass of middle-class white men" (1998, 159), and where antigay oppression does not prevent spatial concentration. These conditions exist, he found, in New Orleans, Minneapolis, and, to a lesser extent, London and Sydney. In other contexts, such as in Edinburgh, "the contesting of everyday urban spaces for various social, political, and even sexual purposes (including, frequently, transgressive ones) is much more central to gay male identity formation" (159). Knopp's point—that territorial "colonization" is not the *sole* pattern of identity formation, and that the specific *kind* of identity it produces is not necessarily well-rounded or radicalizing—is quite compelling. It is not inconsistent, though, with the idea that over the long term, identity is more decisive than anonymity in shaping the urbanization of marginalized groups.

Identity and Political Presence

The political development of identifiable communities is not incidental or subordinate to their social, economic, or cultural dimensions. As Castells stresses, political organization is both a method and a result of identity formation, or what I call life after anonymity. The intensive organizing and activism that is necessary for a group to progress from invisibility, isolation, and powerlessness to political presence cannot occur in a context of anonymity. Indeed, any self-conscious political action can only be reasonably read as a collective effort to *overcome* invisibility. From the individual perspective, casting off the cloak of anonymity requires the assumption of some risk, and therefore it, too, is difficult to interpret as anything other than a weighing of competing (personal and political) goals. However, an urban public sphere conceived as a true confluence of strangers would seem to obstruct the movement of groups toward political identity or presence. There is scant basis among strangers—even respectful strangers—for the kinds of alliances that are prerequisite to major social changes, or even the barest level of group-interest articulation and empowerment. This is definitely not to say that all political gains come through action that occurs squarely in the public sphere or is directed towards the state.[2] Efforts to reconceptualize politics and publicity notwithstanding, the move over time to a more fully public, political presence for groups marked as "different" explains why "Don't ask, don't tell"[3]—which is predicated upon enforced anonymity—is an intolerable step backward from "We're here, we're queer"—which constitutes a refusal to remain anonymous.

The dynamic of politicization is not identical for all groups in the city. For women, who are sometimes said to benefit from anonymity, the relationship between anonymity, identity, and political presence cannot be the same as it is for communities defined primarily by characteristics such as ethnicity, color, or sexual orientation. Aside from lesbian local communities (not all of which are urban), women do tend to be spatially scattered; women do not live in homogenous place-based communities. It is therefore difficult to chart women's political presence as a simple function of the development of a critical mass in a particular spot in a city.

Nonetheless, the notion that identity is equivalent to life beyond anonymity, and that identity replaces anonymity as a goal of urban living, is pertinent to women's political activism. In diverse urban places, including poor neighborhoods that are *de facto* communities of women and children and other neighborhoods where women do not predominate, women's political empowerment is directly related to their ability to self-identify and to identify themselves to others as (certain kinds of) women (such as, mothers, public housing residents, homeowners, immigrants, Latinas, whites, victims of violence), though usually not as feminists. The creation of a group identity and political consciousness among women in geographical communities is often applied to issues affecting the particular places where they live and their lives in those places (Breitbart and Pader 1995; Feldman, Stall, and Wright 1998; Pardo 1998; Pulido 1997; Rabrenovic 1995).

Living alongside other women does not invariably cultivate gender-based political identity, but the connection between neighbors, neighborhood issues, and political action is relatively natural. At the citywide scale, women's political activism depends heavily on a transition from invisibility to identity. Women may be unnamed or unidentified for a variety of reasons: if they belong to the large class of undocumented immigrants who provide informal labor in urban areas; if they are in any number of cultural or domestic settings that enforce a strict, gendered division between the public and private spheres; if the state delegitimizes or depoliticizes their identities; or if they are not known to women on the other side of race, ethnicity, sexual orientation, or class boundaries. Studies of women's politicization in cities, whether carried out in formal or informal political spheres (Andrew 1995), confirm that invisibility of one sort or another must be actively acknowledged, worked with, and mitigated (Bookman and Morgen 1988; Hondagneu-Sotelo 1998; Kendrick 1998).

The Complexity of Cities

The claim that anonymity draws people to cities and shelters them depends not only on the nature of people's choices but also, of course, on the nature of cities themselves. As discussed at the beginning of this chapter, cities are said to be inherently more hospitable to women, lesbians, gays, other minority groups, and strangers, because anonymity is a basic quality of urbanity. According to the typical narrative about how cities draw in newcomers, in urban areas there exists a level of tolerance for diversity and nonconformity that is simply unattainable in towns, villages, the countryside, and suburbs.

The disagreement between the view that anonymity is something to be celebrated and the view that it is something to be overcome only highlights the pervasive agreement that cities are anonymous. On one side, many urban scholars present anonymity by means of a basically hopeful account of the possibilities of life within the context of urban "disorder" (Sennett 1970). Anonymity is good because, along with other things, it contributes to individual freedom, diversity, and a rich public sphere. But the vision of cities as anonymous also helps to undergird anti-urban sentiment. From this position, anonymity is a marker for what is bad about cities, including individual freedom, deviance, social mixing, and danger (Lofland 1998, chap. 6). What is notable is that, despite the fundamental differences embedded in these two views of urbanity, both assume the city's basic quality as a confluence of strangers.

This characterization of cities as anonymous may be legendary,[4] but in fact cities are highly complex places, which suggests that there is no direct or predictable correlation between urban publicity and anonymity. Cities are anonymous on certain dimensions, in certain places, at selected times—but not always or everywhere. Just as the reasons for immigration to the city are complex, so is the city, and it follows that observations about the logic behind locational choices are necessarily as much about cities as about people. Bonnie Menes Kahn confirms this complexity by making what appear to be flatly contradictory assertions about why people come to cities. She states, in keeping with the conventional wisdom, that people "have chosen city life to escape the curse of tradition and the clutches of small-town acquaintances. They have sought the relief of anonymity. Social escape makes men free" (1987, 15). At the same time, however, Kahn makes the less conventional, but equally convincing claim that cities "consist of social strangers whose object is the relief of anonymity—or new attachments" (13).

Perhaps unintentionally, Kahn is supporting the contention that cities provide both relief in anonymity and relief from it. This very argument, that belongingness and identity are as intrinsic to urbanity as autonomy and anonymity, is fundamental to the work of Jane Jacobs (1961) and other urbanists who have thought deeply about the nature of cities, community, and the public sphere. Therefore, when Lyn Lofland, who has written extensively and perceptively on stranger-relationships in the city, says, "To experience the city is, among many other things, to experience anonymity" (1973, ix), these "other things" are meant to be taken seriously. It is true that "everybody" may recognize the urban public realm as "the site of total anonymity, impersonality, isolation, [and] alienation" (Cahill and Lofland 1994, xi; see also Lofland 1994, 26). Because the geographic and social boundaries of the public sphere are often faint, however, what count as public behavior and public relationships are difficult to pin down, in the same way that specific qualities of the urban public sphere itself are difficult to agree upon (Berman 1986; Walzer 1986).

In contrast to the complexity of urban space, many mentions of anonymity-seeking rely on an unworkably strict division between the public and private pockets of the city. According to this duality, anonymity is unnecessary within the boundaries of the private, because standing out is possible and at times even desirable. In the public sphere, however, the ability to be anonymous is tantamount to blending into the city's diversity. This could allow open expression of identity but may furnish nothing more than the chance to get lost in the crowd. Although, as discussed earlier, it is commonly recognized that both anonymity and identity have prevailed in urban life for people who are judged "different," this recognition has not typically rested on serious consideration of physical or metaphorical bridges between the public arena of anonymity and the private arena of identity.

These bridges do, however, exist. First, there are subtle gradations in cities of which locates—parks, shopping malls, cafes, libraries, condominiums, streets—are public and private on legal, physical, or social grounds (McKenzie 1994; Sorkin 1992). Second, within any public and private places, anonymity and identity are just two points on a broad spectrum. Whether cities are anonymous therefore rests on individual factors such as the extent to which people want to be identifiable and on structural factors such as the "open-mindedness" or "closed-mindedness" of specific urban spaces (Walzer 1986). Finally, wildly divergent identities, including no identity, can be "practiced" within a single piece of urban territory. Whether a physical space encourages anonymity or identity is contingent on how that space changes over time, in addition to whether metaphoric "spaces" (social, political, cultural, sexual) overlay it.[5] Thus, anonymity is dependent on people displaying or hiding various roles as they move from home to work, bar, park, school, street, synagogue, or city hall within one seemingly coherent part of the city.

TOLERANCE AND THE RIGHT TO BE LEFT ALONE

How identity, collective empowerment, and the honoring of plurality are related to each other is, ultimately, at least as much a normative issue as an empirical one. Indeed, for Iris Young, anonymity is included squarely within the criteria for her "normative ideal of city life" (1990, 236–241). In this sense, Young echoes and participates in the established tradition of urban sociology and democratic theory, in which anonymity, the public sphere, and a healthy city life are defined with reference to one another. And although cities are generally not a direct, normative concern in the feminist, lesbian, and gay work that mentions anonymity-seeking, by extension the city plays a key role in providing the feminist or queer "good life."

In considering what anonymity might contribute to a political theory of the city, it is crucial to ask what, if anything, is political about being anonymous, and whether there are any political qualities that are distinctive to anonymity. In answer to these questions, it is not evident that anonymity has any unique political content. Although it has certain similarities to tolerance (of "difference") and to the right to be left alone, which are important elements of any political theory that celebrates plurality, both of these aspects are distinguishable from anonymity. Furthermore, unlike tolerance or the right to be left alone, anonymity is not comprehensible as a political relationship, and it is unconvincing as a political characteristic of urbanity.

Tolerance

What passes for anonymity frequently bears a striking resemblance to the core political value of tolerance. Clearly, cities are regarded as places where people are more tolerant of differences from the norm or from themselves; moreover, they are willing to tolerate differences in practice as well as in theory. Here, tolerance is a basic, liberal, political value that is limited to putting up with, or declining to persecute, what is *unlike* and even *disliked*. In this sense, tolerance has similar effects to anonymity, because it commands that people's particularities be treated essentially as if they were unrecognizable or invisible. In contrast to anonymity, though, tolerance permits substantive discussion about group values and characteristics, about relationships between people, and about how these are to be regarded politically.

Anonymity also evokes tolerance in another, fuller sense. Cities are tolerant in that urban norms may actually incorporate diverse and divergent behaviors and identities. Seeking anonymity may be confused with seeking out places where progressive values about race, sex, or culture are actually institutionalized. Certainly, violation of accepted gender roles looms large in the literature about anonymity-seeking. Thus, it makes sense to recognize that urban gender norms are more forgiving, or tolerant, than those in most smaller places. With respect to this issue, Lynn Appleton (1995) and others have argued that all localities are patriarchal, but different types of localities have identifiable "gender regimes," which incorporate local economic, social, cultural, geographic, and political patterns. These factors combine to produce radically different gender forms: The "public patriarchy" of cities exists in distinction to the "private patriarchy" of suburbs. Public patriarchy is marked by the integration of (middle-class) women into the labor force and thus into the public realm, although obviously not with advantages equivalent to men's. The importance of economic changes in disrupting traditional domestic and geographic arrangements has been discussed in a wide range of historical research. The move to cities by unmarried women and homosexuals is seen as a consequence, beginning in the nineteenth century, of industrialization and urbanization, which produced wage labor outside of the family unit (D'Emilio 1983, 10–11; D'Emilio 1992, 12–13; Stansell 1986). Later, other economic changes due to wars (Faderman 1992, 119–130) and, in the United States, the migration of African Americans to northern cities (Lemann 1991), created recognizable urban neighborhoods in which working (married and unmarried) straight women, lesbians, or gay men could exist in relative comfort.

The relaxation of urban gender norms also has strongly social underpinnings. Although cities are often presumed to be male, precisely because they are connected with the public sphere (Wolff 1990), in actuality cities can be considered more female socially than other local forms (Wilson 1991). Though less so now than in the past, the mere presence in North American cities of so many female-headed households (and so many females generally) in close proximity to each other has supported social networks that deviate from heterosexual, nuclear family mores, if only because multiple forms of child care and various "familial" arrangements are possible (see, for example, Stansell 1986). In "the gender realm" itself, "there is open internal dissension" (Appleton 1995, 48). This, too, is facilitated by the easier communication of nonmainstream ideas about gender within the denser social networks of cities, and by the tolerance of "more open discussion of sexuality" (D'Emilio 1983, 22) in selected urban cultural and social milieus. The more gay men, unmarried women, and childless couples move to the city, the more the practice of atypical gender norms intensifies and perpetuates this public version of patriarchy.

The greater demand for (and reliance on) collective welfare policies in cities reflects the politicization of these other dimensions of the gender regime. Because of the high need for social benefits like welfare, public housing, and day-care, and because urban gender expectations have been more likely to accept state intervention into family structures, political support for such policies has been higher in cities. State intervention into the sexual and familial dimensions of the lives of unmarried female urban recipients of social assistance has sometimes attempted to impose mainstream gender norms, but it also has at other times, as with public housing and welfare requirements, actually demanded that they be subverted (Spain 1995).

The spatial arrangements of the city also reflect its level of tolerance. Exclusionary and homogenizing land-use controls are certainly not unknown in big cities, but towns and suburbs have considerably more egregious records of enforcing social conformity through land-use regulations. Larger cities are more likely to be zoned to allow high-density, non-single-family, residential development, and they are less likely to restrict the number of unrelated people who may live together. Such spatial factors have a direct and often overt relationship to a locality's tolerance of alternative gender and sexual regimes.

The Right to Be Let Alone

In thinking about the political content of anonymity, the following comment about the public realm of the city is quite pertinent: "A commonly understood rule proscribing staring at others in acknowledgment of their right to be let alone makes it possible to convey effectively by staring that someone *is* a target of special curiosity or design" (Cahill 1994, 11; emphasis in original). This observation is striking because it bears an uncanny resemblance to the endorsement for anonymity that is contained, but rarely articulated, in the feminist, gay, and lesbian literature I have been discussing. People who wish neither to be stared at nor to suffer the consequences that frequently follow staring seek out big cities— "here people let one another alone" (Sennett 1994, 358).

Being let alone, or the closely related right to privacy, is a deeply political consideration. It should go without saying that characteristics like color, sexual orientation, sex, age, citizenship status, nationality, physical and mental ability, and wealth presently mean that some people do not benefit from a full complement of privacy rights; therefore, any political theory must speak to how such rights should be defined, extended to everybody, and safeguarded (see, for example, Babst 1997). The right to be let alone constitutes the central tenet of liberalism. It may also, however, be taken in the context of postmodernism or any other framework that values plurality and particularity. Privacy may also serve as an element of any argument against the presumption that the need for individual rights has been superseded or that rights are actually detrimental to justice or equality. In any case, a normative political vision of the diverse city must recognize individuals' privacy rights as being essential to a democratic public sphere.

It is extremely important, however, to emphasize that the history of group progression from anonymity to identity suggests that if people can control *how* they are paid attention to—say, if they are among similar and sympathetic people—then this is normally preferable to being left totally alone. Even breaches of anonymity that occur in public, by strangers who do not share your identity, may be accepted or welcomed, depending on the circumstances and the individuals involved (Gardner 1994). And this is why cities are important, because the chances are higher that you do not have to be let totally alone (A. Jacobs 1997).

The keys to privacy rights are unavoidably individual integrity and autonomy. There must, in any case, be an individual in this formulation. This is where the endorsement of anonymity-seeking diverges from the insistence on the right to be let alone, and it is another reason why it is difficult to take anonymity seriously as an element of normative theories of the city, of public life, or of difference. Since anonymity presumes the absence of individuals and identity, relying on anonymity means there is no way to protect individuals who identify with disfavored groups, a concern that lies at the heart of the notions of privacy and rights.

THE LIMITS OF ANONYMITY AS A NORMATIVE IDEAL

Any political theory of the city must place privacy-enjoying, tolerated individuals in a framework in which the full range of group identities are honored *and* in which political action animated by those identities can take place. Positing anonymity as a pillar of urban publicity will only carry this discussion so far, however. First, anonymity is flawed as an ideal for the city because, like the urban public sphere itself, it is not equally accessible to all groups. Second, anonymity often manifests itself as a proliferation of separate, identity-based enclaves within the city, rather than as genuine publicity that renders the city open to all people.

The Inequality of Anonymity

As urban anonymity is usually imagined, its primary attraction is that it provides a safe haven for conspicuous human characteristics, whether physical, social, or cultural. In practice, anonymity is not equally available to everyone who might want it. On one level, visible and otherwise obvious identities may impede the quest for anonymity. As D'Emilio has pointed out, "Unlike many groups— women and African Americans, for instance—in which one's identity is clear for the world to see, most gay men and lesbians have the option to remain invisible"

(1992, 151). D'Emilio's observation does not go far enough, though, for it is important to remember that visibility is also relative to the norm. Thus, Kennedy and Davis document the fact that the anonymity of lesbians in Buffalo, mentioned earlier, only applied to white lesbians until the city's black population reached a certain size (1993, 65). It is not only deeply ironic that being anonymous depends on not standing out too much, but also that the claim that anonymity protects the marginal is undermined by the realization that the marginal always will stand out the most.

On another level, anonymity is, like any social relation, nonneutral and imbued with power. Therefore, in many places, anonymity is notably racialized. For example, in comparison with private and semipublic spaces, "On [American] public streets blacks have the greatest exposure to strangers and the least protection against overt discriminatory behavior, including violence" (Feagin 1991, 102). Because they are regarded by many whites as part of the threat posed by "the street," at least in North American cities, black, Aboriginal, Latino, and Asian young males are notably subject to levels of surveillance, control, and harm that negate their capacity to be strangers. In other words, anonymity does not work to preserve the prerogatives of those people who enter urban public space having been pre-identified as posing a threat.

Anonymity is pervasively gendered—women on the street are objects of comment and approach, in part because they are assumed to have (and do have) less "ownership" of public space. Janet Wolff (1990) argues that, in literature and in life, women have historically been precluded from engaging in "the fleeting, anonymous encounter and the purposeless strolling" that marks the public sphere of the modern city (but see Swanson 1993; Wilson 1993). In contemporary cities, attention ranging from solicitous to benign to threatening regularly breaches women's anonymity. Particularly with respect to violence on the street, women, who are "unable to regulate their interactions with male strangers in public places, are robbed of an important privilege of urban life: their anonymity" (Weisman 1992, 69; also see Greed 1994).

The ability to be anonymous is shaped at the conjunction of sex and sexuality. Lesbians and bisexual women are less able than homosexual men to invoke anonymity in ostensibly "gay" public situations (Kennedy and Davis 1993, 30; Valentine 1993, 409). The least conformist presentations of gender are the most disavowed in the straight and homosexual mainstreams (Phelan 1996). Because they *are* so nonconformist, butches and drag queens are more vulnerable to unwanted notice or other interventions on city streets (also see Gardner 1994; Munt 1995).

Finally, for many of the same reasons that anonymity is not completely available to some people, it can actually be perilous to others. Closely related to the power relations embedded in the anonymity of the public sphere of strangers is the terrible contradiction of urban anonymity that allows some people to stay out of harm's way yet that condemns others—prostitutes, the mentally ill, runaway youth, and anyone who lives on the street—to unrecognizability in life and, literally, unidentifiability in death. For some of these people, the city's anonymity may possibly begin as a means of escape, as it does for other groups, but in the end, for the extremely marginalized and vulnerable the city is evidently *too* anonymous.

Anonymity as Pluralism

One problem with anonymity is that it has no room for politics if it is understood strictly as being unnamed, unidentified, or unrecognized. As I have shown, though, anonymity is usually not understood in this way; in fact, anonymity-seeking is frequently confused with, or at least not sufficiently distinguished from, identity-seeking. This mushy version of anonymity—which, again, is what really seems to be operating in the current work on anonymity-seeking—presents another problem from the perspective of a normative political vision of the city, in that it has a tenuous link with the ideal of urban publicity. Here, anonymity is not an attribute of the city as a whole, but of some bounded part of the city. A budding hip-hop artist can escape the scrutiny and control of her rural Alabama hometown to a precise cultural niche located in Los Angeles where she may fit in and flourish; a cheating spouse in any big city can reduce the chances of being recognized by retreating to an hourly rate hotel with other people engaging in nonmarital trysts; communities whose shared identity lies in class, color, language, or ethnicity concentrate in what are often quite clearly defined spaces in the city.

Exercising anonymity understood in this way may simply be a matter of segmenting the city into parts where you are relieved that you can be anonymous and parts where you do not have to be, and of negotiating the boundaries and contradictions between the two. Whatever one's reasons for becoming anonymous, from this perspective anonymity consists of revealing yourself or your group identity only within a relatively controlled corner of the big city. This anonymity speaks to the benefits of the existence of a proliferation of homogenous, separate, place-based communities, not to the robust publicity of city life. In contrast, robust, urban, public spheres and public spaces countenance the overt demonstration of most identities, in most city streets, most of the time. In terms of a political theory of the city, anonymity conceived of as plural communities is not very enlightening, because there is nothing fully public or essentially urban about it.

Unfortunately, there are very few places to look for examples of a political theory in which specificity is actually integrated into the urban public sphere rather than replaced by a kind of pluralist version of anonymity. Although Iris Young is rightly recognized for going beyond liberal tolerance to advocate a substantive acceptance of differences, her picture of the city, including its anonymity, also looks strikingly like a plurality of identity-based communities. In

Young's urban public sphere, people do not abhor difference and maybe even find it interesting or "erotic" (1990, 239–240); furthermore, she outlines structural mechanisms for representing difference in local public policy. Nevertheless, we are left without a sense of what it means, in political terms, for Young's "deviant or minority groups" to seek anonymity at the same time that they seek identity and community in cities.

We might look for guidance toward Richard Sennett's insights into the urban *acceptance* of others' difference and suffering, where suffering both precedes and stems from difference. Sennett observes that "the body accepting pain is ready to become a civic body, sensible to the pain of another person, pains present together on the street, at last endurable—even though, in a diverse world, each person cannot explain what he or she is feeling, who he or she is, to the other." He admonishes, further, that the "civic trajectory" is "to live together as exiles" (1994, 376). Unfortunately, Sennett does not elaborate on what this acceptance of pain means politically, but he rests an intensely political concept—the civic—on neither looking away from nor having to conceal what is painful (or by extension, unpleasant, scary, or strange). In making this strong connection between recognition and citizenship in the city, Sennett allows us to imagine an urban public sphere that lives up to the ideal of being both unmarked by internal boundaries and unintrusive. Crucially, while Sennett clearly does not deny the importance of strangers to the city, or demand that people reveal more of themselves than they choose, his urban public sphere also promises to move beyond anonymity or invisibility as a goal of urban life.

CONCLUSION

Anonymity is undeniably helpful in accounting for the attractiveness of cities to people escaping scrutiny, threat, and control. However, the desire to be anonymous is heavily counterbalanced by the desire for and the development of group identity, including political presence; indeed, the feminist, lesbian, and gay literature that discusses anonymity often fails to distinguish it explicitly from identity. In normative terms, anonymity is easily confused with the core political values of tolerance and privacy. Political agency is, moreover, seemingly at odds with anonymity, because access to anonymity is unequally distributed among city dwellers. Anonymity does not advance postmodern, feminist, or queer visions of an ideal urban publicity that genuinely embraces "difference;" instead, anonymity turns a blind eye to difference or ensconces it in a plurality of bounded communities within the city. Examining closely how anonymity operates within each of the various public spheres—political, cultural, social, sexual—that cities encompass, and defining carefully the complex relationship between anonymity and identity might elicit a more politically enlightening version of anonymity. Nevertheless, a concept so closely associated with invisibility as anonymity cannot explain the increased visibility over time of gay men, lesbians, and women in cities, and being "not named or identified" is a limiting, not a liberating, political project.

NOTES

I would like to thank Bob Beauregard for his careful and very helpful reading of an earlier version of this chapter, Ana Annalise Acorn, Talja Blokland-Potters, Kathy Ferguson, Cheryl Hall, and Shane Phelan for their comments. I am also grateful to the Department of Political Science at the University of Hawaii for providing me a wonderful working environment while I wrote the initial draft of this chapter.

1. A conceptual link between anonymity and identity might be found in the idea of tipping points, past which anonymity turns into identity. In the United States, tipping points are part of the familiar landscape of racial and ethnic succession in urban and suburban areas, but they apply to other demographic and cultural changes, too. For example, gay bars hidden in mixed neighborhoods may over time become bars in gay neighborhoods, without any shift in the geographical boundaries of the neighborhood. At first, the bars (and their patrons) are anonymous within the larger context of the city by some combination of choice and necessity. Later, both bars and patrons are part of a culturally identifiable space (Cahill 1994, 9; Lofland 1973, 130)—after all, neighborhoods cannot really be anonymous. The same dynamic applies to residential locations, whereby a diverse "neighborhood . . . perceived to be tolerant" transforms itself into a visible lesbian "residential ghetto" (Valentine 1993, 398) precisely because it begins to be identifiable as such. In these examples, anonymity and visibility are clarified, and their urban context illuminated, by emphasizing the mechanism of relationships between them.

2. For example, it has been shown that urban "bar culture," which has both private and public elements, and which exists in quasi-public space, initiated a movement toward lesbian and gay identity formation and in this way served as a "crucible for politics" (see Kennedy and Davis 1993, 29). More theoretically, a significant amount of feminist, queer, and postmodern work has attempted to dramatically expand the definition of the political use of urban space, whether public or private (Bell and Valentine 1995; Ingram, Bouthillette, and Retter 1997; Massey 1994; Watson and Gibson 1993).

3. Since 1993, this phrase has constituted the core of official policy regarding homosexual men and women serving in the U.S. military.

4. At least, the attraction of the anonymous city is one legend. Another, made in Hollywood, Broadway, and the American psyche, goes like this: Young women and men flock to "the big city" (New York or Los Angeles) to seek fame and possibly fortune, both of which entail casting off the cloak of anonymity. Here, though, the legends often intersect, at least in fictional accounts. Finding that the city is indeed a cold, cruel and anonymous place, these optimistic young people from Iowa farms and Ohio towns manage to rise above the city or, in the case of women, find a man to rescue them from urbanity.

5. Lawrence Knopp makes a related point when he argues: "Anonymity, voyeurism, tactility, motion, etc. are all human experiences that can be, and arguably have been, sexualized and desexualized in a variety of places and fashions (and for a variety of reasons), throughout history. Thus they bear no *necessary* relationship to the city. The issue is . . .

how and why urban space has been sexualized in the particular ways that it has" (1995, 160 n. 7; italics in original).

REFERENCES

Andrew, Caroline. 1995. "Getting Women's Issues on the Municipal Agenda: Violence against Women." In *Gender in Urban Research*, edited by Judith A. Garber and Robyne S. Turner. Thousand Oaks, Calif.: Sage Publications.

Appleton, Lynn. 1995. "The Gender Regimes of American Cities." In *Gender in Urban Research*, edited by Judith A. Garber and Robyne S. Turner. Thousand Oaks, Calif.: Sage Publications.

Babst, Gordon A. 1997. "Community, Rights Talk, and the Communitarian Dissent in Bowers v. Hardwick." In *Playing with Fire: Queer Politics, Queer Theories*, edited by Shane Phelan. New York: Routledge.

Bell, David, and Gill Valentine, eds. 1995. *Mapping Desire: Geographies of Sexualities*. London: Routledge.

Bender, Thomas. 1993. "The Erosion of Public Culture: Cities, Discourses, and Professional Disciplines." In *Intellect and Public Life: Essays on the Social History of Academic Intellectuals in the United States*. Baltimore: Johns Hopkins University Press.

Berman, Marshall. 1986. "Take It to the Streets: Conflict and Community in the Public Sphere." *Dissent* 33: 476–485.

Bookman, Ann, and Sandra Morgen, eds. 1988. *Women and the Politics of Empowerment*. Philadelphia: Temple University Press.

Breitbart, Myra Margulies, and Ellen-J. Pader. 1995. "Establishing Ground: Representing Gender and Race in a Mixed Housing Development." *Gender, Place, and Culture* 2: 5–20.

Cahill, Spencer E. 1994. "Following Goffman, Following Durkheim in the Public Realm." In *Research in Community Sociology: The Community of the Streets*, Supp. 1, edited by Spencer E. Cahill and Lyn H. Lofland. Greenwich, Conn.: JAI Press.

Cahill, Spencer E., and Lyn H. Lofland. 1994. "Introduction." In *Research in Community Sociology: The Community of the Streets*, Supp. 1, edited by Spencer E. Cahill and Lyn H. Lofland. Greenwich, Conn.: JAI Press.

Castells, Manuel. 1983. *The City and the Grassroots: A Cross-Cultural Theory of Urban Social Movements*. Berkeley: University of California Press.

D'Emilio, John. 1983. *Sexual Politics, Sexual Communities: The Making of a Homosexual Minority in the United States, 1940–1970*. Chicago: University of Chicago Press.

———. 1992. *Making Trouble: Essays on Gay History, Politics and the University*. New York: Routledge.

Faderman, Lillian. 1991. *Odd Girls and Twilight Lovers: A History of Lesbian Life in Twentieth-Century America*. New York: Columbia University Press.

Feagin, Joe R. 1991. "The Continuing Significance of Race: Antiblack Discrimination in Public Places." *American Sociological Review* 56: 101–116.

Feldman, Roberta M., Susan Stall, and Patricia A. Wright. 1998. " 'The Community Needs to Be Built by Us': Women Organizing in Chicago Public Housing." In *Community*

Activism and Feminist Politics: Organizing across Race, Class, and Gender, edited by Nancy A. Naples. New York: Routledge.

Gardner, Carol Brooks. 1994. "A Family among Strangers: Kinship Claims among Gay Men in Public Places." In *Research in Community Sociology: The Community of the Streets*, Supp. 1, edited by Spencer E. Cahill and Lyn H. Lofland. Greenwich, Conn.: JAI Press.

Greed, Clara A. 1994. *Women and Planning: Creating Gendered Realities*. London: Routledge.

Grube, John. 1997. " 'No More Shit': The Struggle for Democratic Gay Space in Toronto." In *Queers in Space: Communities/Public Places/Sites of Resistance*, edited by Gordon Brent Ingram, Anne-Marie Bouthillette, and Yolanda Retter. Seattle: Bay Press.

Haeberle, Steven H. 1993. "Cliques, Crowds, and Clubs: A Comparative Look at Gays and Lesbians as Interest Groups in Urban Politics." Paper presented at the Annual Meeting of the American Political Science Association, Washington, D.C., August 31–September 3.

Hondagneu-Sotelo, Pierrette. 1998. "Latina Immigrant Women and Paid Domestic Work: Upgrading the Occupation." In *Community Activism and Feminist Politics: Organizing across Race, Class, and Gender*, edited by Nancy A. Naples. New York: Routledge.

Ingram, Gordon Brent, Anne-Marie Bouthillette, and Yolanda Retter, eds. 1997. *Queers in Space: Communities/Public Places/Sites of Resistance*. Seattle: Bay Press.

Jackson, J. B. 1961. "The Many Guises of Suburbia." *Landscape* 11: 22–24.

Jacobs, Andrew. 1997. "Lonesome Town: Or Is It Just a Myth?" *New York Times*, June 8, Section 13, 1.

Jacobs, Jane. 1961. *The Death and Life of Great American Cities*. New York: Vintage Books.

Kahn, Bonnie Menes. 1987. *Cosmopolitan Culture: The Gilt-Edged Dream of a Tolerant City*. New York: Atheneum.

Kendrick, Karen. 1998. "Producing the Battered Woman: Shelter Politics and the Power of the Feminist Voice." In *Community Activism and Feminist Politics: Organizing across Race, Class, and Gender*, edited by Nancy A. Naples. New York: Routledge.

Kennedy, Elizabeth Lapovsky, and Madeline D. Davis. 1993. *Boots of Leather, Slippers of Gold*. New York: Routledge.

Knopp, Lawrence. 1995. "Sexuality and Urban Space: A Framework for Analysis." In *Mapping Desire: Geographies of Sexualities*, edited by David Bell and Gill Valentine. London: Routledge.

———. 1998. "Sexuality and Urban Space: Gay Male Identity Politics in the United States, the United Kingdom, and Australia." In *Cities of Difference*, edited by Ruth Fincher and Jane M. Jacobs. New York: Guilford Press.

Kramer, Jerry Lee. 1995. "Bachelor Farmers and Spinsters: Gay and Lesbian Identities and Communities in Rural North Dakota." In *Mapping Desire: Geographies of Sexualities*, edited by David Bell and Gill Valentine. London: Routledge.

Lemann, Nicholas. 1991. *The Promised Land: The Great Black Migration and How It Changed America*. New York: Vintage Books.

Lofland, Lyn H. 1973. *A World of Strangers: Order and Action in Urban Public Space*. New York: Basic Books.

———. 1994. "Observations and Observers in Conflict: Field Research in the Public

Realm." In *Research in Community Sociology: The Community of the Streets*, Supp. 1, edited by Spencer E. Cahill and Lyn H. Lofland. Greenwich, Conn.: JAI Press.

———. 1998. *The Public Realm: Exploring the City's Quintessential Social Territory.* New York: Aldine de Gruyter.

Massey, Doreen. 1994. *Space, Place, and Gender.* Minneapolis: University of Minnesota Press.

McKenzie, Evan. 1994. *Privatopia.* New Haven: Yale University Press.

Munt, Sally. 1995. "The Lesbian Flâneur." In *Mapping Desire: Geographies of Sexualities*, edited by David Bell and Gill Valentine. London: Routledge.

Pardo, Mary. 1998. "Creating Community: Mexican American Women in Eastside Los Angeles." In *Community Activism and Feminist Politics: Organizing across Race, Class, and Gender*, edited by Nancy A. Naples. New York: Routledge.

Phelan, Shane. 1996. "Queer Citizenship and Public Discourse." Paper presented at the Annual Meeting of the American Political Science Association, San Francisco, September 2–September 6.

Pulido, Laura. 1997. "Community, Place, and Identity." In *Thresholds in Feminist Geography: Difference, Methodology, Representation,* edited by John Paul Jones III, Heidi J. Nast, and Susan M. Roberts. Lanham, Md.: Rowman and Littlefield.

Rabrenovic, Gordana. 1995. "Women and Collective Action in Urban Neighborhoods." In *Gender in Urban Research*, edited by Judith A. Garber and Robyne S. Turner. Thousand Oaks, Calif.: Sage Publications.

Rayside, David. 1991. *A Small Town in Modern Times: Alexandria, Ontario.* Kingston: Queen's University Press.

Senelick, Laurence. 1991. "Private Parts in Public Places." In *Inventing Times Square: Commerce and Culture at the Crossroads of the World*, edited by William R. Taylor. New York: Russell Sage Foundation.

Sennett, Richard. 1970. *The Uses of Disorder: Personal Identity and City Life.* New York: Alfred A. Knopf.

———. 1994. *Flesh and Stone: The Body and the City in Western Civilization.* New York: Norton.

Sorkin, Michael, ed. 1992. *Variations on a Theme Park: The New American City and the End of Public Space.* New York: Hill and Wang.

Spain, Daphne. 1995. "Public Housing and the Beguinage." In *Gender in Urban Research*, edited by Judith A. Garber and Robyne S. Turner. Thousand Oaks, Calif.: Sage Publications.

Stansell, Christine. 1986. *City of Women: Sex and Class in New York, 1789–1860.* New York: Alfred A. Knopf.

Swanson, Gillian. 1993. " 'Drunk with the Glitter': Consuming Spaces and Sexual Geographies." In *Postmodern Cities and Spaces*, edited by Sophie Watson and Katherine Gibson. London: Routledge.

Valentine, Gill. 1993. "(Hetero)sexing Space: Lesbian Perceptions and Experiences of Everyday Spaces." *Environment and Planning D: Society and Space* 11: 395–413.

Walzer, Michael. 1986. "Pleasures and Costs of Urbanity." *Dissent* 33: 470–475.

Watson, Sophie, and Katherine Gibson, eds. 1993. *Postmodern Cities and Spaces.* London: Routledge.

Weisman, Leslie Kanes. 1992. *Discrimination by Design: A Feminist Critique of the Man-Made Environment.* Chicago: University of Illinois Press.

Wilson, Elizabeth. 1991. *The Sphinx in the City.* London: Virago.

———. 1993. "The Invisible Flâneur." In *Postmodern Cities and Spaces*, edited by Sophie Watson and Katherine Gibson. London: Routledge.

Wirth, Louis. 1938. "Urbanism as a Way of Life." *American Journal of Sociology* 44: 1–24.

Wolff, Janet. 1990. "The Invisible Flâneuse: Women and the Literature of Modernity." In *Feminine Sentences.* Cambridge: Polity Press.

Young, Iris Marion. 1990. *Justice and the Politics of Difference.* Princeton: Princeton University Press.

Chapter 2

"The Two Major Living Realities": Urban Services Needs of First Nations Women in Canadian Cities

Evelyn Peters

Since the late 1940s, there has been increasing migration of First Nations people[1] from the largely rural reserves to which they were confined through a variety of colonial practices, to urban centers in Canada. First Nations women[2] have been overrepresented in this migration process. The little work extant that addresses the lives of First Nations women in Canadian cities documents the ways in which cultural origins and colonial histories shape the strategies they use to cope in the urban environment (Culleton 1983; Maracle 1992; Peters 1984; Shorten 1991).

Feminist geographers have only begun to produce work that addresses spatialities of daily life for women like those of the First Nations in European and North American cities. In 1990, Rickie Sanders noted that "geographic gender studies have fallen victim to the myth of 'universal womanhood' and have not been sensitive to the experiences and contributions of women from various races and classes" (1990, 228; see also Boys 1990, 249). Increasingly, feminist geographers have acknowledged the need for, as Allison Blunt and Gillian Rose note, "the elaboration of other geographies that resonate with the forms of oppression faced by women who are not middle class and white" (1994, 4; see also McDowell 1993, 310; Rose 1993). To date, there is a small but growing body of work in feminist geography that explores how to theorize the relationship between gender and other facets of power and identity (Kobayashi and Peake 1994; Larner 1995; Ruddick 1996), and that examines the effect of race and ethnicity on aspects of women's lives in European and North American cities (see Gilbert 1997).

A prerequisite for creating a more inclusive geography is a critical assessment of the significance we attach to a variety of analytical categories. Early feminist work in geography quickly came to realize that a meaningful analysis of women's

41

lives required reorienting and redefining existing concepts and theories (Macken-zie 1989). More recently, feminist geographers have built on these insights to emphasize that incorporating diversity and difference requires more than just adding third world women, women of color, or indigenous women to the theoreti-cal frameworks which have served as standards for our discipline (Boys 1990; Gilbert 1998; Radcliffe 1994; Rose 1993; Sanders 1990, 230). Instead, an inclu-sive feminist geography means critically assessing the degree to which the frame-works we use are appropriate for understanding the lives of people who have often been excluded from their formulation. In other words, as Peake notes, ad-dressing difference "affects not only the ways we interpret our empirical find-ings; implicatively, it also requires that we address the terms on which we con-duct our research" (1993, 419).

It is also important to explore the specificity of the relationships between the city and women of various cultural, national, and racialized origins. As Brah (1992,) points out, different groups have been defined differently under varying circumstances and on the basis of different signifiers of difference. Moreover, people's varied responses to processes of definition have the result that the sig-nificance of spaces and places is negotiated and contested. In addition to recog-nizing the importance of the intersection of race, ethnicity, and gender in wom-en's lives in the city, it is important to explain the connection for a particular group. To date, there is very little work which explores the geographies of the daily lives of First Nations women in urban areas.

This chapter focuses on the spatiality that organizes First Nations women's descriptions of their needs for services in urban areas in Canada. The intent is not to provide a comprehensive description of the range and nature of services needed, but instead to explore the spaces, boundaries, and territories implicated in First Nations women's expressions of their needs and critiques of what is cur-rently available. Exploring these underlying geographies can obviate some of the taken-for-granted geographical frameworks that often underlie discussions of women and urban environments, and it may work to displace taken-for-granted assumptions that the maps of meaning we feminist researchers employ are equally meaningful for all women in urban areas.

In this analysis I do not wish to suggest that the First Nations women's needs do not overlap with the needs of other women in the city—that their requirements are primarily exotic and different. Like other women in cities, First Nations women need safety in private and public space, access to employment and urban services, and affordable suitable housing. I also do not wish to use the term "First Nations" as an essentialized category—natural, static, and unrelated to particular geographies and histories. However, like the Maori women described in Wendy Larner's (1995) article,[3] many First Nations women have employed their differ-ence from non-Aboriginal women in the struggle against the effects of colonial-ism (Brant and Brant 1995; Maracle 1992; Osennontion and Skonaganleh:ra 1989). Moreover, their history as Aboriginal peoples creates political and cultural geographies that do not always match those of the groups and organizations that organize service provision in urban centers. This chapter explores some aspects of this mismatch in order to emphasize the diverse spatialities of women in cities. It begins with a short description of the data on which the analysis is based, then describes the colonial maps of gender and cultural identity that form an important basis for First Nations women's engagement with the city. Finally, it presents First Nations women's arguments regarding the need for culturally appropriate services and analyzes the maps of meaning underlying these arguments.

SOURCES AND METHOD

The major sources of information on First Nations women's needs in urban areas in this chapter are interventions by First Nations women to the 1992–1993 Public Hearings of the Canadian Royal Commission on Aboriginal Peoples. The Canadian Royal Commission on Aboriginal Peoples was established April 23, 1991, to "examine the economic, social and cultural situation of the Aboriginal peoples of the country" (Royal Commission 1992, 1). In 1992 and 1993 the Commission held extensive Public Hearings in all parts of Canada, with a total of 2,067 intervenors in 96 different communities. Of these, 309 interventions focused on urban issues (Royal Commission 1994, 100); and of these, 43 First Nations women addressed issues related to the needs of First Nations women living in the city. I examined only presentations by First Nations peoples because their historic experiences with the Indian Act and its regulation of identity and residence are different than those of Métis and Inuit peoples.

The Commission dedicated considerable resources to the process of encouraging Aboriginal people from different cultures, perspectives, and ways of life to participate. Hearings were held in many Aboriginal communities, both central and isolated, across Canada. Nevertheless, it is impossible to claim any kind of "representativeness" for the submissions analyzed here, nor was it my intention to provide an analysis that describes the general perspective of First Nations women. Instead, I wish to interrogate the seeming "naturalness" of boundaries and regions used to organize urban services through this analysis.

COLONIAL GEOGRAPHIES OF INDIAN STATUS AND GENDER

British colonial policy adopted in the 1830s had three major goals: to protect, to civilize, and to assimilate First Nations people (Tobias 1983). These policies quickly took on a distinctive geography that segregated First Nations people on small reserves under the rhetoric of "protection" and that defined urban areas as hostile to First Nations' cultures and communities. By the turn of the century, almost all First Nations people lived on reserves. Migration from reserves to urban areas began to increase in the 1950s, however, and at present almost half of all First Nations people live in cities.

Colonial policies affected women's roles in their communities in complex ways. One major impact was on women's roles in political decision making. Among many First Nations peoples, women held important and essential political decision-making roles. Beginning in 1869, however, legislation allowed only First Nations men to vote or to run for office in band councils, the governing body of the group. Though women and men resisted the imposition of this political system, and though women were allowed to participate in the band political system through legislation passed in 1951, the legacy appears to be that women continue to be excluded in various ways from political life in many First Nations communities today (Royal Commission 1996, 21–83).

Colonial policies also had implications with respect to legal status. Since the earliest days of Canadian "Indian policy," Indian status has been a prerequisite for Aboriginal rights and eligibility for government services. Although early policy did not differentiate between men and women for the determination of Indian status, by 1857 women's status became dependent on that of their husband or father. Between 1857 and 1985, Indian women marrying non-Indian men lost their Indian status.[4] Women "marrying out" represent almost all of the First Nations people who lost their Indian status since 1857 (Jamieson 1978). In 1985, the Indian Act was amended to eliminate the possibility of loss of status through out-marriage[5] and to allow individuals who had lost their status to apply for reinstatement.

Legal status is not a determinant of cultural identity, but it is an important marker for many First Nations peoples. Legal status is a prerequisite for eligibility for federally funded programs and services for Indian people. Until 1985, residency and status were also connected—only status Indian people had rights to live in reserve communities. After 1985, status and band membership were split, and band councils were given responsibility for the latter. Band membership is now the prerequisite for residency on the reserve.

A First Nations person's residency off the reserve community of origin is significant for two major reasons. First, beginning in the early 1960s, the federal government insisted that its constitutional responsibility for status Indians applies only to Indians living on reserves and that status Indians living off the reserve become the responsibility of the provinces for the purpose of most social services. Though the rhetoric of this position appears to have softened somewhat recently (Department of Indian Affairs 1997), the reality is that there are very few federally funded programs and services available to status Indians living off reserves. With few exceptions, municipal and provincial governments have not introduced programs and services specifically for status Indians, preferring instead to address their needs through mechanisms targeted to poverty populations. Second, despite the ongoing commitment of urban organizations like the Friendship Centres to meet the needs of First Nations people in cities, reserves remain the primary locus of cultural affiliation and community for many First Nations people.[6] As Sandra Lovelace argued to the Human Rights Committee of the United Nations in 1977, the loss of rights of residency on reserves meant "the loss of the cultural benefits of living in an Indian community, the emotional ties to home, family, friends and neighbors, and the loss of identity" (cited in Davies 1985, 771).

Since the early 1950s when residency data began to be collected systematically by the Indian Affairs Branch (now the Department of Indian Affairs), registered Indian women have been more likely than registered Indian men to live off reserves and in urban areas (Gerber 1977; Royal Commission 1996). Table 2.1 shows that the majority of adult, registered, Indian women live in urban areas, whereas the majority of adult, registered, Indian men live on reserves. The reasons for these differences are not well understood and they may have to do with differences in employment opportunities for men and women, responsibilities for children's education and other services, access to social assistance, and other factors. However, First Nations women's submissions to the recent Royal Commission on Aboriginal Peoples also implicated the erosion of women's roles in First Nations communities by the colonial imposition of a patriarchal system of governance and identity (Adams 1992; Courchene 1993; Ellison 1992; J. Fontaine 1992; Standingready 1993), coupled with high levels of violence that impact most severely on women and children (Croxon 1993; Gamble 1992; Meconse 1992; Sillett 1995; Wilson 1992).

Table 2.1 Registered North American Indian Men and Women, Fifteen and Older, On Reserve and Off Reserve in Urban Areas, 1991

	On reserve		Urban off reserve	
	Male	*Female*	*Male*	*Female*
All Registered Indians				
Number	51,363	47,946	37,088	54,219
Percent	58.1%	46.9%	41.9%	53.1%
Reinstated Registered Indians[a]				
Number	7,099	7,209	13,372	21,214
Percent	34.7%	25.4%	65.3%	74.6%

Source: Author's tabulations, Aboriginal Peoples Survey Data Base, *Statistics Canada*, 1991.

Notes: These calculations omit individuals living off the reserve in rural areas. These individuals represent a small minority of First Nations people. The Aboriginal Peoples Survey does not contain information concerning approximately 58,000 individuals living on unenumerated Indian reserves. Aboriginal Peoples Survey data were employed rather than Department of Indian Affairs Indian Register data because Register data do not identify urban residency.

[a]Individuals who regained their Indian status pursuant to the 1985 amendments to the Indian Act. This includes individuals who had lost their status and their descendants.

Since 1985, it may also be that women who "married out" are more likely to continue to be excluded from band membership and therefore reserve residency. Data from the 1991 Aboriginal Peoples Survey show that women were over-represented in the Bill C-31 population—the group reinstated after the 1985 amendments to the Indian Act—and that even though both men and women in this group are more likely to live off rather than on reserves, the proportion of women living off reserves is higher than that of men.[7]

Table 2.2 compares some of the characteristics of adult, registered, Indian women living on and off reserves, and all adult women in urban areas. The Indian population is generally younger than the non-Indian population, but there are fewer women 50 and older in the urban Indian population than in the reserve Indian population. Participation rates are considerably higher for urban Indian than for reserve Indian women, and the participation rates for urban Indian women are almost as high as they are for all women living in urban areas. Unemployment rates are almost identical for Indian women living on reserves and in urban areas but are more than twice as high as rates for all women in urban areas.

**Table 2.2	Comparison of North American Indian Women, Fifteen and Older, to All Women in Urban Areas, 1991**

	Registered North American Indian Women		All women in urban areas
	On reserve	Off reserve in urban areas	
Age: 15–24	31.5%	29.0%	—
25–49	48.5%	57.7%	—
50+	20.0%	13.2%	—
Participation rate[a]	35.8%	52.9%	60.2%
Unemployment rate	27.4%	25.7%	9.9%
Education < gr. 9	35.4%	15.1%	12.6%
Total income in 1990 < $2,000	28.3%	22.7%	8.9%[c]
Total income in 1990 > $40,000	0.8%	13.1%	7.2%
Head of lone-parent family[b]	14.0%	25.9%	12.0%
Access to an elder	46.3%	26.5%	—
Number	47,946	54,219	8,537,375

Sources: Author's calculation, *Aboriginal People's Survey,* 1991; *Statistics Canada Catalogues* 93-339 and 93-340.

Notes: Nonresponses and not applicable responses are not included in calculations. Aboriginal Peoples Survey data were employed instead of Canadian census data because the former refers to people who identify themselves as Aboriginal, whereas census data are based on Aboriginal ancestry.

[a]Participation rates are the people in the labor force (working or looking for work) as a percentage of the population for that group.

[b]This percentage is based on number of families rather than on the population 15 and older.

[c]For all women, this is the percentage earning less than $2,999.

The incidence of very low income is very high for both reserve and urban Indian women, compared to all women in urban areas. At the same time, some Indian women in urban areas seem to have found employment with a good income, such as in some civil service positions. Although the proportion of women who head up lone-parent families is almost the same for reserve and all urban women, the proportion of urban Indian women who are lone parents is almost twice as high. Finally, Table 2.2 shows that Indian women in urban areas have less access to elders, an important cultural resource, than Indian women living on reserves.

Unemployment rates and low income are reflected in housing conditions for urban Indian women. Indian women are substantially more likely than non-Indian women and Indian men to live in housing that is inadequate, unsuitable, and too expensive for their income levels (Spector 1995, 70–71). Housing needs are particularly serious for lone-parent households, most of which are mother-led. In comparison to approximately 12 percent of all Canadian households with core housing needs (that is, their housing is inadequate, unsuitable, or unaffordable), 64 percent of status Indian, lone-parent households have core housing needs (CMHC 1997, 3). Limited access to suitable housing may be particularly problematic for First Nations women in urban areas. Some research suggests that women's roles in organizing households and offering shelter play an important part in the day-to-day coping strategies of urban First Nations people.[8]

Clearly, statistics cannot fully describe the urban experience for Indian women. Available data, however, do indicate that although the city represents opportunities for employment and education for some women, it represents poverty and substandard housing for other women. At the same time, it is important to remember that there are considerable variations in the situations of First Nations women in different urban areas, and that needs for services may therefore vary considerably. Moreover, a focus on the discourse around service needs may result in an impression that no services currently exist for Aboriginal people in urban areas. Yet Aboriginal people, particularly in large urban centers, have worked to provide organizations and programs to meet the needs of urban Aboriginal people. Aboriginal women appear to have been the catalyst for the emergence of many of these initiatives (Royal Commission 1996, 578). By way of example, Table 2.3 describes service and political organizations in Winnipeg in 1994. Winnipeg is an urban center with a well-developed set of urban Aboriginal institutions.[9] Some of these organizations have a very long history and others have been established in recent years. Collectively, these organizations provide a fairly broad range of services to Aboriginal peoples.

NEEDS OF FIRST NATIONS WOMEN IN CITIES: ISSUES OF CULTURE AND GEOGRAPHY

In their submissions to the Commission, First Nations women called for a recognition of their presence and their needs in urban areas. Clearly, urban First Na-

Table 2.3   Aboriginal Institutions in Winnipeg, 1994

Organization	Primary focus	Year Established
A-Bah-Nu-Gee Child Care	child and family services	1984
Aboriginal Centre Inc.	social services, community and economic development	1990
Aboriginal Council of Winnipeg	political	1990
Aboriginal Literacy Foundation	education	1990
Aiyawin Corporation	housing	1983
Anishinabe Oway-Ishi	employment	1989
Anishinabe RESPECT	employment	1981
Bear Clan Patrol Inc.	safety	1992
Children of the Earth High School	education	1991
Indian Family Centre Inc.	religious/social services	1973
Indian Métis Friendship Centre	cultural/social services	1959
Ikwe Widdjiitiwin	shelter for native women	1989
Iwkewak Justice Society	justice	1986
Kinew Housing	housing	1970
Ma Mawi Chi Itata Centre	child and family services	1984
Manitoba Association for Native Languages	language education	1984
MMF—Winnipeg Region	political	NA
Native Clan	inmates	1970
Native Employment Services	employment	1972
Native United Church	religious	NA
Native Women's Transition Centre	housing	NA
Neechi Foods Community Store	economic development	NA
Nee-Gawn-Ah-Kai Day Care Centre	child care	1986
Original Women's Network	women's resource center	NA
Payuk Inter-Tribal Housing Co-op	housing	1985
Three Fires Society	cultural	1982
Winnipeg Council of First Nations	political	1991
Winnipeg Native Families Economic Development Corporation	social services, community and economic development	NA

Sources: Clatworthy, Hull, and Loughren (1995); Peters (1998). (See also Black 1993; Dubec 1992; King 1992; Maguire 1992; Sears 1993; Thusky 1993; Webster 1992; Young 1992.)
NA: not available.

tions women are a heterogeneous group whose diversity reflects age, class, sexual orientation, Nation, social status, and ability. Yet the submissions to the Commission demonstrated some common themes with respect to their needs and the issues they identified as crucial. Below are summaries of some First Nations women's arguments about the need to address their cultural origins in the provision of services, followed by an exploration of some of the geographies that are implicated in this attempt.

The Importance of Services Appropriate to First Nations Cultures

The following materials are organized according to the framework presented in a 1994 conference presented by the Organisation for Economic Co-operation and Development on women's housing and service needs in the urban environment. The conference was held in Paris in October of 1994 and had representatives from 27 countries; the proceedings were subsequently published (OECD 1995).

Urban Services Responsive to the Needs of Women and Children

The 1995 OECD publication argued that, because of women's role in child rearing and their overrepresentation as heads of lone-parent families, adequate and appropriate design of social infrastructure and provision of community services was of particular importance for them. The poverty of many First Nations women living in the city and their predominance as lone parents suggest that urban services play a crucial role in their well-being in the city. First Nations women's submissions to the Royal Commission underlined their needs for a variety of services in the city (Royal Commission 1996, 575–579). Jackie Adams (1992, n.p.) clearly addressed these issues in her presentation in Port Alberni, British Columbia.

> We want native women's transition homes and a safe house locally, a native women's drug and alcohol treatment center, a native women's resource center to provide counselling services and all abuse prevention measures. Native women need liaison workers between the native community and the Ministry of Social Service and Housing because many native women fear and dislike dealing with the white, middle class social workers. Native women need a center to help mothers deal with the impact of the residential school system to learn how to deal with the feelings of loss and anger, to learn how to empower ourselves and to redevelop our traditional native parenting skills. Native women need day care resources to enable them to further their education, develop life skills and seek employment. Urban native women want recreational funding for their children, in order to develop self-esteem and healthy lifestyles.[10]

A recurring theme in First Nations women's submissions was the need for services that not only address their situation as women in the city but also take account of their needs as First Nations women. Some of these needs derive from perceptions of racism and inequitable treatment for Aboriginal women in non-Aboriginal organizations. In Winnipeg, a representative of Ikwe Widdjiitiwin, a shelter for Native women, argued that Aboriginal women face stereotyping throughout the service system: "Our women face racism and systemic stereotyping at every turn. For aboriginal women, this racism and stereotyping is rampant right through the system, from the police to the courts, child welfare agencies to Income Security. Although the law is supposed to treat everyone equally, we all know this is not an aboriginal reality" (Hall 1992, n.p.).

In Saskatoon, Kula Ellison (1992, n.p.) poignantly described the fears of First Nations women in making a decision to go to a shelter for battered women: "I would like also to give another example. When our women go to Interval House in Saskatoon, non-native workers try to take our children away. But when a non-native woman goes in they don't even bother to try to take her children away. They are there to comfort her and give her counseling." Darlene Hall pointed out to the Commissioners that many First Nations women face multiple challenges when they arrive in the city, and that mainstream organizations may not be able to deal adequately with these combinations: "A large number of our women are victims of childhood sexual abuse, have drug or alcohol problems or are involved with the child welfare system. Often these problems have been on-going. Thus, when they are forced to leave their family and communities, they must deal with all of this, the abuse plus trying to live in an environment that is totally alien to what they are used to" (1992, n.p.).

Catherine Brooks, Executive Director of Anduhyaun, a shelter for Aboriginal women in Toronto, pointed out that women who attempt to seek help often find they are the only Aboriginal women in the group: "One of the things that happened is when Aboriginal women who are seeking to deal with emotional problems and issues in their life would go to these mainstream agencies they were not able to receive a service which was appropriate to them. For one thing, they were often the only Aboriginal women there in the group. You can imagine what that would be like" (1992, n.p.). In contrast, services provided by Aboriginal organizations were able to meet the cultural and spiritual needs of Aboriginal women, and to contribute to healing, regaining of identity, and increased confidence, both because women could find roles and identities for themselves as Aboriginal women, and because the process of providing services leads to empowerment. Jackie Esquimox-Hamelin (1993, n.p.) described the experience of the Gazhaadaawgamik Native School in Toronto:

> It was and is the vision of the parents and community members to have a child care centre in this urban setting that helped their children retain their native languages and cultural identity. . . . In order to realize our goal of full immersion it was necessary to create a team of language specialists who, we are proud to say, are First Nation grandmothers. They deliver a language and cultural program for the children, the staff and the families that encompasses the emotional, mental, spiritual, and physical development of all individuals. . . . As the children identify with these teachings a greater degree of a positive self esteem and identity are obtained.

Other women also described the positive results from the provision of urban services that incorporated Aboriginal people, perspectives, and history (see Adams

1992; Brooks 1992; Ellison 1992; Hackett 1993; King 1992; Sears 1993; Sillaby-Smith 1993; Van Heest 1993).

Affordable, Safe, Home and Community Environments

The OECD document pointed out women's needs for affordable housing, particularly since they are most likely to be heads of lone-parent families. The report also noted that "women are very sensitive to the quality of the neighbourhood environment, both for themselves and because of their children. Safety both in the neighbourhood and within their own homes is a critical issue which should be addressed" (1995, 12).

First Nations women's submissions to the Commission addressed both of these issues. They pointed out, however, that the experiences of First Nations women are related to their cultural origins as well as to their gender. For example, Marilyn Fontaine (1992, n.p.), President of the Aboriginal Women's Unity Coalition, highlighted some of Aboriginal women's experiences on Winnipeg streets:

> Some examples that we have experienced in Winnipeg in regard to this sexual exploitation and the violence against children and women are: The Carl Edward Krantz case, which was the most visible, young aboriginal girls raped by non-aboriginal men on the streets of Winnipeg, the murder of aboriginal women, in fact there are still two outstanding murders of young women that have not yet been resolved, and that is Susy Hollins and Carolyn Duck; the harassment of aboriginal women and children in the Lord Selkirk area by non-aboriginal men looking for . . . sex; the sexual exploitation of children and women by non-aboriginal johns.

In addition to their particular safety needs on the streets and in their homes, First Nations women also face unique challenges in finding housing. Housing is particularly difficult to find when one is a woman, Aboriginal, and a single parent. In Brantford, Lisa Maracle (1993, n.p.) told the Commissioners: "I have been denied housing because of my skin colour. I have been denied housing because I am a single Mom. Being a Native and being a single Mom really is discouraging because you can't get anywhere; you have that double-whammy put on you" (see also Adams 1992; Brooks 1992; Giroux 1993).

Limited access to suitable housing is particularly problematic for Aboriginal women in urban areas. It means that, in addition to the challenges of healing, cultural survival, poverty, and single parenthood, women often have to deal with all of the problems associated with substandard housing. Women's roles in organizing households and offering shelter are important in the day-to-day coping strategies of urban Aboriginal people. Having a place to stay keeps community members off the streets, and allows reserve residents access to urban services. Being able to offer a place to stay may be a prerequisite for maintaining ties with communities of origin, since kin and friends can come and stay for a few days.

The ability to provide emergency shelter for friends and family is essential in the context of evictions, condemned housing, and family violence.

Political Participation

The OECD report emphasized the need "for women to participate in urban policy and planning processes and for these processes to be made more gender sensitive" (1995, 59–60). First Nations women also spoke of the importance of women's participation in decision making. However, although the women recognized the need to participate in a variety of governmental and administrative organizations to effect decision making sensitive to their needs, their main emphasis was on self-government and the importance of women's participation according to culturally defined roles. This was eloquently stated by Margaret King in Saskatoon (1992, n.p.):

> The relevance to the Aboriginal women is to be able to contribute to society as mothers, grandmothers, and great-grandmothers. We are aware of the political, social, mental, and spiritual issues which our people are facing and confronting each day, whether we live on the reserve or off the reserve.
>
> The area of self-government in the first years is going to necessarily involve a lot of programs and dollars that will be spent on family issues. Family issues are women's issues and women's issues are society's issues. So I think that women have to have a place within the government structures of any Indian government that is set up, whether it be at the Band level or the provincial level or the national level. . . .
>
> I think in our traditional systems of government there were always women's councils and these women were asked to advise the people. . . . And that role and responsibility is such a great one that we have to provide within our governing systems a role for those women to participate; not on an equal basis but a basis which respects their essential role in the development of our communities. . . . I view the role of Indian women in our communities as so essential in the development of children to be strong human beings, to be balanced human beings, and that traditional role of women has been weakened and undermined in our communities by the influence of other societies. I think we have to respect our own culture and tradition in the development of our future leaders, because it is the women who will be the influence. (See also Contin 1993; Fontaine 1993; Olstrop 1993)

First Nations women pointed to the disruption of women's roles in governance through the imposition of the colonial band council system, and called for the restoration of political structures which recognized women's contributions (Adams 1992; Courchene 1993; Fontaine 1992; Manyfingers 1993; Nepinak 1993; Standingready 1993; Wilson 1992).

GEOGRAPHIES OF CULTURE AND NATIONHOOD

A close examination of First Nations women's submissions to the Commission elucidates that providing services appropriate to the needs of First Nations women and children requires rethinking taken-for-granted geographies that separate urban and rural, on and off reserve, cities and First Nations territories. In other words, addressing the needs of First Nations women involves addressing colonial geographies that have employed spatial separation to differentiate between "us" and "them"—between First Nations people and settlers. Geographies of settlement, political jurisdiction, and administrative responsibility are intrinsic to designing positive, appropriate, and effective initiatives.

The Implications of Reserve Geographies

A recurring theme in First Nations women's submissions concerned the lack of support for First Nations cultures and identities in urban areas. At the 1993 Round Table on Urban Issues organized by the Royal Commission on Aboriginal Peoples, participants noted the difficulty for "the survival of Aboriginal identity in an environment that is usually indifferent and often hostile to Aboriginal culture" (Royal Commission 1993, 2). In Toronto, Sharon McIvor (1992, n.p.), Western representative of the Native Women's Association of Canada, described the impact of First Nations women's loss of status when they marry non-Native men: "The statutory banishment of Aboriginal women from their communities when they married non-Aboriginals means that they have had to raise their children in settings where they were discriminated against and could not learn traditional Aboriginal culture." Colonial settlement patterns that separate First Nations communities from urban centers mean that women who migrate to urban areas are often without the support of elders and healers. Ms. Jolene Wasteste (1993, n.p.), youth group representative of the Regina Friendship Centre, noted: "We believe that our heritage, culture and religion are what makes us human beings. It is very difficult in the city to learn about these things because many of the knowledgeable people who know about it and can help us with it don't live here. We must have help and resources so that we can reach out to these people and build a connection between us and them" (see also Christmas 1992). Knowledge of spiritual practices, healing medicines, and many women's teachings are minimally accessible in urban areas. For many Aboriginal women living in cities, it is particularly important to have access to mentors, such as the Grandmothers or Clan Mothers, but access to such Elders is limited. Accordingly, receiving traditional guidance and grounding— places where strength is found—is difficult in urban centers.

Similarly, First Nations women are often cut off from their extended family and the community they left behind on the reserve. The Aboriginal Women's Council of British Columbia noted that:

We do know that, in many instances, life for aboriginal women off-reserve can be even more problematic especially if they are lacking the prospects for employment. These women have less support systems and services available to them and they are often very much alone, without the physical or emotional support of family members (which in some cases they enjoyed on the reserve). Unemployed and left to their own devices, they often feel alienated and alone, helpless, powerless, and "without a voice." (1992, 43)

In Thunder Bay, Bernice Dubec (1992, n.p.), Chair of the Thunder Bay Native Interagency Council, indicated that "the urban factors which negatively affect the Aboriginal family are numerous and complex. The problems confronting Aboriginal families are compounded by the absence of their extended families and community support systems."

These issues are directly related to colonial practices that defined First Nations cultures as incompatible with urban life, and that confined First Nations people to reserves separate from urban centers. Research for the Royal Commission found that, despite the work of many organizations in urban areas, strong and supportive cultural communities were absent in most (Royal Commission 1996). Providing First Nations women living in cities with access to their culture and community, then, requires addressing these geographies.

Geographies of Rights

Urban First Nations and Treaty women (women whose ancestors signed treaties) argue that programs and funding for women living on reserves should be made available to women in cities, as a function of their Aboriginal and Treaty rights. Vicki English (1993, n.p.), in Calgary, stated the issue clearly:

> When Native women choose to leave the reserve for an education and a better way of life for them and their children, they receive less monies in programs and funding in comparison to . . . other Native women who choose to remain on the reserve. These women can no longer be penalized for attempting to move away from the margins and to the centre of society. Monies for off-reserve housing, education and medicare, among other necessities, must be secured due to the fact that we do not lose our treaty rights outside the boundaries of the reserves. We, as a treaty Indian population, cannot fall once more under the auspices of the government's assimilation policies. We recommend that this Commission adhere to the mobility of our rights as treaty Indian women.[11]

In the past, movement off the reserve was seen to represent an attempt to assimilate into non-Aboriginal society. This assumption provided an important rationale for the withdrawal of almost all federal government services to First Nations people once they left reserves. First Nations women have rejected this assumption and challenged the geographies of responsibility for services defined by federal and provincial governments. Geographies of funding have an important symbolic component. Provincial and municipal services to First Nations people in urban areas are usually directed toward the alleviation of poverty, but First Nations women see these services as part of what they have earned through Treaty negotiations with the Crown, now represented by the federal government. These Treaty rights should not be limited by place of residence. In Vancouver,

B.C., a representative of the United Native Nations made this point about not being able to access her Treaty rights because she lived off her reserve: "My name is Sherry Small; I come from a village called L'Cal'Za which is located on the Nass River. I am Nisga'a. The Federal government refers to my ancestral home as a reserve and they refer to me as a registered Status Indian living off reserve. Therefore, I am unable to exercise my birthright as a Nisga'a due to my residency" (Small 1993, n.p.).

Political Participation

First Nations women's representations concerning political participation also have a geography that challenges contemporary boundaries drawn by federal, provincial, and municipal governments. First Nations women have fought the exclusion from political structures on reserves that urban residency brings. They have argued that First Nations women living in cities should be able to participate in reserve politics because reserve lands and communities represent links with their cultures and traditions. In Saskatoon, Margaret King (1992, n.p.), a representative from the Saskatoon Urban Treaty Indians, indicated:

> We have been meeting as a group since February here in Saskatoon. Part of the reason we got together is that as off-reserve people we have no access to our political institutions. Forty to 50 per cent of our people live off the reserve and the political structures that are in place now do not represent 50 to 60 per cent of the people here in Saskatchewan, and that government is not recognizing the rights of people who live off the reserve to be represented through those organizations. We have tried in our structure to have a liaison or linkage with our reserve communities because those communities represent the culture and traditions of our people and the lands that were given in treaties. And we respect that those lands have to be protected through our reserve-based organizations. However, we do not accept that because we live off the reserve that we cannot participate in those governing structures at our reserve communities.[12]

In Montreal, Dolores Andrés (1993, n.p.), of the provincial organization for Aboriginal women, told the Commissioners that current legislative definitions prevented communities of origin from providing services and meeting their responsibilities to community members in urban areas: "[B]ecause of the interpretations of the Indian Act made by the governmental institutions, the rights of the urban aboriginal women are not recognized and sometimes the communities are unable to help them owing to these legislative interpretations."

Clearly, introducing reserve-based political representation and service delivery for First Nations people living in cities could introduce virtually unmanageable complexity for some urban areas where First Nations populations come from many different communities, and this is not the place to attempt to provide solutions. What is important here, however, is to recognize that the differentiation between urban and reserve areas created by federal and provincial legislation and practice does not match the cultural reality or the maps of identity of many First Nations women in cities.[13]

CONCLUSION

In summary then, First Nations women's submissions to the Royal Commission insisted on the need for culturally appropriate services, the continuing need for access to reserve communities and cultures for urban residents, the importance of Aboriginal rights in the urban milieu, and the desire for participation in First Nations governing structures that cross the boundaries between city and reserve. In this way, First Nations women create imaginary geographies of government responsibilities for funding and delivering services that unite rather than fragment communities, recognize traditional territories of First Nations people, and allow access to the land and cultural communities of origin. They challenge colonial and contemporary boundaries between on reserve and off reserve, reserve and city. Through their submissions and their practices, they resist spaces of Indian cultures and rights imposed on them by various levels of government through the spatial organization of funding and service provision. They also resist pressures to be like "all other urban residents" by insisting on the relevance of First Nations cultures and nations in the city.

These are not the familiar geographies that feminist geographers have used to make sense of women's lives in the city. First Nations women's maps of identity and nation indicate the need to pay attention to the fact that the spatial frameworks that women use to give significance to their lives vary among women of different cultural and racial origins. At the same time, these spaces also demonstrate the importance of paying attention to the situation of *particular* groups of women in any exercise of remapping. Gilbert (1998), for example, has recently suggested that feminist geographers should reexamine the significance of the "spatial entrapment" model, arguing that local support networks represent a source of strength for African American women. Although this issue is not well researched for First Nations women, it is likely that many of their support networks are structured differently—relying less on neighborhood ties and more on contacts with communities of origin outside cities (see, for example, Peters 1984). The challenge for feminist geographers, then, is to recognize the multiple ways in which all women organize their daily lives in urban areas.

NOTES

The title of this chapter comes from Jennifer Wood's (1993, n.p) submission to the Royal Commission.

We would like to begin by informing you that we, the First Nations People, have come together to create a new organization which incorporates the *two major living realities*. Firstly, the reality of being First Nations, Cree Ojibway, Dakota, Dene, etcetera. Secondly, the reality of living the urban environment, the City of Winnipeg.

Our newly created organization is based on our Nationhood which recognizes our nationality from birth and our heritage with no loss of identity and nationality as a consequence of residence or location.

As a Council [the rights of off-reserve Indians] is an issue of great concern to us. Our membership and its elected Council of citizens of Nations whose ancestors entered into Treaties in good faith with the Federal Government. The use of the Sacred Pipe in the Treaty Ceremonies represented the Supremacy of God, Faith and Honesty. In exchange for sharing the resources and our land itself with the European Settlers, we received certain benefits and rights for "as long as the sun shines, rivers flow and the grass grows."

These rights were directly related to the Aboriginal title in our Traditional Lands. Our ancestors never or would not agree to arbitrary policies of successive government in limiting the exercise of Treaty Rights and benefits solely on reserves. (Emphasis added)

1. I use the term "First Nations" to refer to people who identify themselves as such, including people who are and are not registered pursuant to the Indian Act. By "Aboriginal peoples" I mean the descendants of the indigenous peoples in Canada, including First Nations peoples, Métis, and Inuit. Métis are not registered under the Indian Act, and are peoples who emerged from unions between First Nations and non–First Nations peoples. Inuit are northern peoples. I use the term "Indian" when I refer to Euro-Canadian constructions of First Nations peoples, especially when I am referring to government collected documents. Registered Indians are First Nations people registered under the Indian Act.

2. In designating the category "First Nations women," I do not mean to suggest that they constitute a homogeneous group. Many First Nations women call themselves by their Nation of origin—Cree, Gwitchin, Tsimshian, etc.—and emphasize the cultural differences among them. However, First Nations women have experienced in common the discriminatory elements of the Indian Act and the social construction of spaces where Aboriginal people have been assigned in the colonial imagination and in fact. On this issue then, they constitute an "imagined community" (Mohanty 1990, 4, following Anderson 1983) with a common context of struggle.

3. In her paper, Wendy Larner explores the issue feminists face in supporting Maori women's differentiation between themselves and non-Maori women as a strategy for critiquing colonialism, but at the same time rejecting the essential nature of these differences.

4. Conversely, non-Indian women marrying Indian men gained status as Indian.

5. First Nations individuals could also lose status through other means, which varied at different times—for example, by moving to the United States, joining the army or the clergy, or obtaining a postsecondary education. All of these possibilities were also eliminated in the amendments.

6. The first Friendship Centre was created in Winnipeg in the late 1950s in order to meet the needs of migrating Aboriginal people. There are now Friendship Centres in many urban areas in Canada, and they continue to fulfill very important service and cultural roles.

7. The Aboriginal Peoples Survey (APS) was a postcensal survey conducted in 1991. Surveyors contacted individuals who indicated on the 1991 Canadian Census that they had Aboriginal origins. The APS asked individuals if they identified with an Aboriginal group. People who answered in the affirmative were interviewed concerning a wide range of issues.

8. See, for example, Guillemin (1975) and Peters (1984).

9. This list does not represent all Aboriginal organizations in the city, but it does include those that are managed by Aboriginal people and that are autonomous of other organizations, urban based, and urban focused. There are several features of the Winnipeg situation that appear to be unique. Unlike most urban areas with large Aboriginal populations, Winnipeg has two organizations, the Aboriginal Centre Inc. and the Winnipeg Native Family Economic Development Corporation (WNFED), which have focused on community development and attempted to provide interagency links and networks.

10. See also Black 1993, Dubec 1992; King 1992; Maguire 1992; Sears 1993; Thusky 1993; Webster 1992; Young 1992.

11. See also Adams 1992; Andrés 1993; Cloutier 1992; Crook 1992; Ellison 1992; Fontaine 1992; Funk 1993; Guilbeault 1993; Hanson 1993; King 1992; Maguire 1992; White-Patmore 1992; Wood, 1993.

12. See also Coyle 1993; Fontaine; Ronnenberg, 1993.

13. It is important to recognize that some First Nations women in cities are alienated from their communities of origin, often because of violence, and that they may look to urban-based organizations to represent them and provide services.

REFERENCES

Presentations to the Public Hearings, Royal Commission on Aboriginal Peoples

These references can be found in: Royal Commission on Aboriginal Peoples, *The Electronic Series: Public Hearings*, CD-ROM (Ottawa: Minister of Supply and Services, 1993).

Aboriginal Women's Council (B.C.). 1992. *Traditional Self-Government, Economic Development and Aboriginal Women*. Submission to the Royal Commission on Aboriginal Peoples Intervenor Participation Program, February.

Adams, J. 1992. Urban Native Women's Issues, Public Hearings, Royal Commission on Aboriginal Peoples, Port Alberni, B.C., May 20.

Andrés, D. 1993. Association des femmes autochthones du Québec, Public Hearings, Royal Commission on Aboriginal Peoples, Montreal, Quebec, May 27.

Black, Brenda. 1993. Georgian Bay Native Women's Association, Public Hearings, Royal Commission on Aboriginal Peoples, Orillia, Ontario, May 14.

Brooks, C. 1992. Executive Director, Anduhyaun Inc., Public Hearings, Royal Commission on Aboriginal Peoples, Toronto, Ontario, June 26.

Christmas, G. 1992. Native Justice Court Workers, Public Hearings, Royal Commission on Aboriginal Peoples, Halifax, Nova Scotia, November 4.

Cloutier, E. 1992. Val D-Or Friendship Centre, Public Hearings, Royal Commission on Aboriginal Peoples, Val D-Or, Quebec, December 1.

Contin, J. 1993. Georgian Bay Native Friendship Centre, Public Hearings, Royal Commission on Aboriginal Peoples, Orillia, Ontario, May 13.

Courchene, J. 1993. Indigenous Womens Collective. Public Hearings, Royal Commission on Aboriginal Peoples, Winnipeg, Manitoba, June 3.

Crook, A. 1992. Public Hearings, Royal Commission on Aboriginal Peoples, Fort Simpson, Northwest Territories, May 26.

Croxon, C. 1993. Public Hearings, Royal Commission on Aboriginal Peoples, North Bay, Ontario, May 10.

Coyle, K. 1993. Public Hearings, Royal Commission on Aboriginal Peoples, Toronto, Ontario, June 4.

Dubec, B. 1992. Chair, Thunder Bay Native Interagency Council, Public Hearings, Royal Commission on Aboriginal Peoples, Thunder Bay, Ontario, October 27.

Ellison, K. 1992. Aboriginal Women's Council of Saskatchewan, Saskatoon Aboriginal Women's Local, Public Hearings, Royal Commission on Aboriginal Peoples, Saskatoon, Saskatchewan, October 28.

English, V. 1993. Calgary Native Women's Shelter, Public Hearings, Royal Commission on Aboriginal Peoples, Calgary, Alberta, May 26.

Esquimox-Hamelin, J. 1993. Gazhaadaawgamik Native School, Public Hearings, Royal Commission on Aboriginal Peoples, Toronto, Ontario, June 2.

Fontaine, J. 1993. President, Board of Directors, Aboriginal Legal Services of Toronto, Public Hearings, Royal Commission on Aboriginal Peoples, Toronto, Ontario, June 2.

Fontaine, M. 1992. President, Aboriginal Women's Unity Coalition, Public Hearings, Royal Commission on Aboriginal Peoples, Winnipeg, Manitoba, April 23.

Funk, S. 1993. Vice-President, Aboriginal Council of Winnipeg, Public Hearings, Royal Commission on Aboriginal Peoples, Winnipeg, Manitoba, June 2.

Gamble, S. 1992. Public Hearings, Royal Commission on Aboriginal Peoples, Brandon, Manitoba, December 10.

Giroux, A. 1993. Calgary Aboriginal Urban Affairs Committee, Public Hearings, Royal Commission on Aboriginal Peoples, Calgary, Alberta, May 26.

Guilbeault, M. 1993. Vice-Chair, Winnipeg First Nations Tribal Council, Public Hearings, Royal Commission on Aboriginal Peoples, Winnipeg, Manitoba, June 3.

Hackett, F. 1993. Indian Homemakers of B.C., Public Hearings, Royal Commission on Aboriginal Peoples, Vancouver, B.C., June 2.

Hall, D. 1992. Ikwe Widdjiitiwin, Public Hearings, Royal Commission on Aboriginal Peoples, Winnipeg, Manitoba, April 23.

Hanson, A. 1993. Student, Scott Collegiate, Public Hearings, Royal Commission on Aboriginal Peoples, Regina, Saskatchewan, May 10.

King, M. 1992. Saskatoon Urban Treaty Indians, Public Hearings, Royal Commission on Aboriginal Peoples, Saskatoon, Saskatchewan, October 28.

Maguire, D. 1992. Drug and Alcohol Counselor, Friendship Centre, Public Hearings, Royal Commission on Aboriginal Peoples, Halifax, Nova Scotia, November 4.

Manyfingers, G. 1993. Presentation by the Calgary Native Women's Shelter, Public Hearings, Royal Commission on Aboriginal Peoples, Calgary, Alberta, May 26.

Maracle, L. 1993. Public Hearings, Royal Commission on Aboriginal Peoples, Brantford, Ontario, May 14.

McIvor, S. 1992. Western Representative, Native Women's Association of Canada, Public Hearings, Royal Commission on Aboriginal Peoples, Toronto, Ontario, June 26.

Meconse, G. 1992. Vice-President, Native Mediation Inc. Public Hearings, Royal Commission on Aboriginal Peoples, Winnipeg, Manitoba, April 22.

Nepinak, B. 1993. Presentation by Aboriginal Women in the Canadian Labour Force, Public Hearings, Royal Commission on Aboriginal Peoples, Winnipeg, Manitoba, November 17.

Olstrop, J. 1993. Crisis Counselor, Calgary Native Women's Shelter, Public Hearings, Royal Commission on Aboriginal Peoples, Calgary, Alberta, May 26.

Ronnenberg, D. 1993. Saskatoon Urban Treaty Indians. Public Hearings, Royal Commission on Aboriginal Peoples, Saskatoon, Saskatchewan, October 28.

Sears, D. 1993. Atenlos Women's Group, Public Hearings, Royal Commission on Aboriginal Peoples, London, Ontario, May 12.

Sillaby-Smith, D. 1993. Public Hearings, Royal Commission on Aboriginal Peoples, Orillia, Ontario, May 14.

Sillett, M. 1995. Commissioner, Public Hearings, Royal Commission on Aboriginal Peoples, Montreal, Quebec, May 25.

Small, S. 1993. United Native Nations, Public Hearings, Royal Commission on Aboriginal Peoples, Vancouver, B.C., June 2.

Standingready, L. 1993. Public Hearings, Royal Commission on Aboriginal Peoples, Regina, Saskatchewan, May 11.

Thusky, V. 1993. President, Les femmes Autochtomes en milieu urbain, Public Hearings, Royal Commission on Aboriginal Peoples, Montreal, Quebec, May 27.

Van Heest, N. 1993. Public Hearings, Royal Commission on Aboriginal Peoples, Vancouver, B.C., June 2.

Wasteste, J. 1993. Youth Group, Regina Friendship Centre, Public Hearings, Royal Commission on Aboriginal Peoples, Regina, Saskatchewan, May 10.

Webster, E. 1992. Vice-President, Indigenous Women's Collective Winnipeg, Public Hearings, Royal Commission on Aboriginal Peoples, Manitoba, April 22.

White-Patmore, I. 1992. National Urban Aboriginal League, Public Hearings, Royal Commission on Aboriginal Peoples, Edmonton, Alberta, June 11.

Wilson, V. 1992. Aboriginal Women's Council of Saskatchewan, Saskatoon Aboriginal Women's Local, Public Hearings, Royal Commission on Aboriginal Peoples, Saskatoon, Saskatchewan, October 28.

Wood, J. 1993. Board Member, Winnipeg First Nations Tribal Council, Public Hearings, Royal Commission on Aboriginal Peoples, Winnipeg, Manitoba, June 3.

Young, D. 1992. Founding President, Indigenous Women's Collective, Public Hearings, Royal Commission on Aboriginal Peoples, Winnipeg, Manitoba, April 22.

Other References

Anderson, B. 1983. *Imagined Communities: Reflections on the Origin and Spread of Nationalism.* New York: Verso.

Blunt, Allison, and Gillian Rose, eds. 1994. *Writing Women and Space: Colonial and Postcolonial Geographies.* London: Guildford Press.

Boys, Jos. 1990. "Women and the Designed Environment: Dealing with Difference." *Built Environment* 16, 4: 249–256

Brah, A. 1992. "Difference, Diversity and Differentiation." In *'Race', Culture and Difference,* edited by J. Donald and A. Rattansi. London: Sage Publications.

Brant, Castellano M., and Jan Hill. 1995. "First Nations Women: Reclaiming Our Responsibilities." In *Diversity of Women: Ontario, 1945–1980,* edited by Joy Parr. Toronto: University of Toronto Press, 232–251.

Canada Mortgage and Housing Corporation (CMHC). 1997. "Housing Need among Off-reserve Aboriginal Lone Parents in Canada." *Research and Development Highlights: Socio-economic Series*, 34.

Clatworthy, Stewart, Jeremy Hull, and Neil Loughren. 1995. "Urban Aboriginal Organizations: Edmonton, Toronto and Winnipeg." In *Aboriginal Self-Government in Urban Areas*, edited by Evelyn Peters. Kingston: Queen's University, Institute of Intergovernmental Relations.

Culleton, Beatrice. 1983. *In Search of April Raintree*. Winnipeg: Pemmican Publications Inc.

Davies, Maureen. 1985. "Aboriginal Rights in International Law: Human Rights." In *Aboriginal Peoples and the Law: Indian, Metis and Inuit Rights in Canada*, edited by Bradford W. Morse. Ottawa: Carleton University Press.

Department of Indian Affairs. 1997. *Gathering Strength: Canada's Aboriginal Action Plan*. Ottawa: Minister of Public Works and Government Services Canada, 1997.

Gerber, Linda. 1977. *Trends in Out-Migration from Indian Communities Across Canada*. Ottawa: Department of the Secretary of State.

Gilbert, Melissa R. 1997. "Feminism and Difference in Urban Geography." *Urban Geography* 18, 2: 166–179.

———. 1998. " 'Race,' Space, and Power: The Survival Strategies of Working Poor Women." *Annals of the Association of American Geographers* 88, 4: 595–621.

Guillemin, Jeanne. 1975. *Urban Renegades: The Cultural Strategy of American Indians*. New York: Columbia University Press.

Jamieson, Katherine. 1978. *Indian Women and the Law in Canada: Citizens Minus*. Ottawa: Advisory Council on the Status of Women.

Kobayashi, Audrey, and Linda Peake. 1994. "Unnatural Discourse. 'Race' and Gender in Geography." *Gender, Place and Culture* 1, 1: 225–243.

Larner, Wendy. 1995. "Theorising 'Difference' in Aoteara/New Zealand." *Gender, Place and Culture* 2, 2: 177–190.

Mackenzie, Suzanne. 1989. "Women in the city." In *New Models in Geography*. Vol. 2: *The Political Economy Perspective*, edited by R. Peet and N. Thrift. London: Unwin Hyman.

Maracle, Lee. 1992. *Sundogs: A Novel*. Penticton, B.C.: Theytus Books.

McDowell, Linda. 1993. "Space, Place and Gender Relations: Part II. Identity, Difference, Feminist Geometrics and Geographies." *Progress in Human Geography* 17, 3: 305–318.

Mohanty, C. 1991. "Cartographie of Struggle: Third World Women and the Politics of Feminism." In *Third World Women and the Politics of Feminism*, edited by C. Mohanty, A. Russo, and L. Torres. Bloomington, Ill.: Indiana Univ. Press, 1–47.

Organisation for Economic Co-operation and Development (OECD). 1995. *Women in the City: Housing, Services and the Urban Environment*. Paris: OECD.

Osennontion (Marilyn Kane) and Skonaganleh:ra (Sylvia Maracle). 1989. "Our World: According to Osennontion and Skonaganleh:ra." *Canadian Woman Studies/Les Cahiers de la Femme* 10, 23: 7–19.

Peake, Linda. 1993. " 'Race' and Sexuality: Challenging the Patriarchal Structuring of Urban Social Space." *Environment and Planning D: Society and Space* 11: 415–432.

Peters, Evelyn J. 1984. *Native Households in Winnipeg: Strategies of Co-Residence and*

Financial Support. Research and Working Paper No. 4. Winnipeg: Institute of Urban Studies, University of Winnipeg.

———. 1998. "Subversive Spaces: First Nations Women and the City." *Society and Space* 16: 665–685.

Radcliffe, S. 1994. "(Representing) Post-Colonial Women: Authority, Difference, and Feminisms." *Area* 26: 25–26.

Rose, Gillian. 1993. *Feminism and Geography.* Minneapolis: University of Minnesota Press.

Royal Commission on Aboriginal Peoples. 1992. *Opening Statements on the Occasion of the Launch of the Public Hearings of the Royal Commission on Aboriginal Peoples.* Winnipeg, Manitoba.

———. 1993. *Aboriginal Peoples in Urban Centres: Report on the National Round Table on Aboriginal Urban Issues.* Ottawa: Minister of Supply and Services.

———. 1994. *Customized Data from the 1991 Aboriginal Peoples Survey.* Ottawa: Research Directorate.

———. 1996. *Perspectives and Realities.* Vol. 4. Ottawa: Minister of Supply and Services.

Ruddick, Sue. 1996. "Constructing Difference in Public Spaces: Race, Class, and Gender as Interlocking Systems." *Urban Geography* 17: 132–151.

Sanders, Rickie. 1990. "Integrating Race and Ethnicity into Geographic Gender Studies." *The Professional Geographer* 42, 2: 228–230.

Shorten, Lynda. 1991. *Without Reserve: Stories from Urban Natives.* Edmonton: NeWest Press.

Spector, Aron. 1995. *The Housing Conditions of Aboriginal People in Canada, 1991.* Ottawa: Canada Mortgage and Housing Corporation.

Tobias, John. 1983. "Protection, Civilization, Assimilation: An Outline History of Canada's Indian Policy." In *As Long as the Sun Shines and the Water Flows: A Reader in Canadian Native Studies,* edited by Ian Getty and Antoine Lussier. Vancouver: University of British Columbia Press.

PART II

INTERSECTIONS OF GENDERED BOUNDARIES: RACE, CLASS, AND ETHNICITY

Chapter 3

Identity, Difference, and the Geographies of Working Poor Women's Survival Strategies

Melissa R. Gilbert

Thirty years of attempts to reform Aid to Families with Dependent Children (AFDC), more commonly referred to as welfare, culminated in the Personal Responsibility and Work Opportunity Act of 1996, which eliminated the federal guarantee of cash assistance to poor parents and children and replaced it with a system that contains stringent work requirements and time-limited assistance. Underlying the repeal of welfare is a powerful academic and popular analysis of poverty that reduces poverty to, or explains it by, "race," gender, unemployment, and the urban environment.[1] In this essentialist analysis, poverty is believed to be caused by the supposedly maladaptive culture of the "urban underclass," commonly understood as African Americans living in inner-city neighborhoods. Some feminists have tried to counter this retrogressive analysis of poverty by pointing out that it is mostly women and their children who are impoverished. This analysis, however, has not provided an effective critique nor a basis for organizing precisely because it privileges gender over other forms of power and inequality.

My purpose in this chapter is to argue that an effective feminist and antiracist critique of, and basis for organizing against, the prevailing explanation of poverty and the resulting policy reforms requires a nonessentialist analysis of how identity and difference are constructed, maintained, and contested through space and place. I draw on my research on the survival strategies of working poor women in Worcester, Massachusetts, to demonstrate how such an analysis helps to make sense of women's everyday experiences of poverty. By focusing on the strategies of working poor women, I can counter the dominant narratives about poverty (that is, passive, ghetto, unemployed, African American "welfare queens") in which the underclass thesis is embedded and that a feminist analysis that privileges gender cannot effectively critique.

IDENTITY, DIFFERENCE, SPACE, AND PLACE

Critical race theorists and feminist theorists have rejected essentialist explanations of difference and identity. "Race" and gender are not determining biological categories; rather, they are socially constructed, historically and geographically specific concepts that have real effects on people's lives (see, for example, Jackson and Penrose 1993; Kobayashi and Peake 1994; Omi and Winant 1994). Using a nonessentialist epistemology, we can most usefully understand "race" and gender as processes whereby people become racialized and gendered.[2] Difference has been further reconceptualized in terms of multiple axes of interconnected and mutually transformative power relations (such as "race," gender, sexuality, class, age, and so on) (see, Brewer 1993; Collins 1990; Kobayashi and Peake 1994; for a review in feminist urban geography, see Gilbert 1997a). For example, racialized identities are gendered (and classed and so forth). Therefore, subjectivity is constructed through multiple, shifting, and often contradictory identities. This conceptualization of subjectivity retains the possibility of a feminist politics based on affinities and coalitions while acknowledging the very real differences among women.

Simultaneously, critical geographers have rejected essentialist conceptualizations of space and place (see Massey 1993, 1994; Soja 1989). As opposed to conceptualizing space as existing independently of objects (space as a container) and, therefore, having independent causal powers, nonessentialist conceptualizations of space see space as existing through the interrelationships of objects (social relations). Like difference, space is socially constructed although it has real effects on people's everyday lives. Social relations are constituted spatially, and geographers use the term "spatiality" to indicate that space and social relations are mutually constituted processes. Massey (1993) argues that a more progressive sense of place sees places as processes of social relations rather than as bounded enclosures, and as having multiple meanings and identities.

As many geographers have noted, spatial metaphors such as positionality, location, displacement, and boundaries have been widely used in the feminist literature (as well as in postmodernist and postcolonial literatures) to indicate the contingent nature of differences and identities (Pratt and Hanson 1994; Rose 1993; Smith and Katz 1993). Feminist geographers (as well as other geographers) have been demonstrating that the significance of space is not just metaphorical. Rather, identity and difference are constructed, fixed, and contested through space and place (Aiken et al., 1998; Fincher and Jacobs 1998; Jones et al. 1997; Keith and Pile 1993; for a review in feminist urban geography, see Gilbert 1997a). Therefore, trying to construct a feminist politics based on coalitions and affinities requires analyzing how boundaries (both spatial and social) are created, maintained and resisted.

Although the constraining aspects of the boundedness of women's lives have tended to be highlighted in feminist analyses, it is also important for the construction of a feminist politics based on coalitions to understand how boundaries are utilized as well as resisted. For example, a potential outcome of boundedness is rootedness—the extent to which someone is bound to a place through personal relationships, habits of behavior, emotional ties, and the like. The spatial boundedness of women's lives may be enabling as well as constraining as women use rootedness in the construction of individual or collective survival strategies.

THE POVERTY DEBATES: THE "URBAN UNDERCLASS"

In the mid-1960s, the civil rights movement and urban riots shifted discussions of poverty from those about rural, often white, populations to a concern with African American urban poverty (Abramovitz 1996; Katz 1989; Piven and Cloward 1997; Quadagno 1994). Most of the attention on poverty is now directed at the so-called urban underclass—a concept that is highly racialized and gendered. The urban underclass is argued to be a subset of the poor who exhibit "pathological" values and behaviors including welfare dependency, female-headed households, teenage pregnancy, unemployment, and drug use.[3]

The urban underclass also focuses on place and a conceptualization of space as either abstract space or space as a container. This leads to behavioral explanations of poverty rather than analyses of relations of power and inequality. Poor people are literally fixed in space as "underclass" people who live in "underclass" neighborhoods. Hughes (1989, 1990) has argued that the focus on "underclass" census tracts leads to the ecological fallacy in which people are defined literally by where they live. It is mistakenly assumed that people who live in the same bounded place (census tract) have similar attributes and behaviors. This focus inevitably leads to an environmentally deterministic view of neighborhoods as having the same effect on the behavior of all people who live in that neighborhood.

In addition to shaping our understanding of the causes of poverty, conceptualizing space as a container contributes to how we construct and represent difference and results in further essentializing the category of African American. Racist accounts of poverty are partially made possible by the process of racialization of African Americans through our bounding of the ghetto.[4] In popular discourse, the inner city is constructed as a place of immorality, crime, and poverty that is inhabited primarily by racialized minorities. By treating the inner city as a bounded enclosure or contained space, we neglect the connections between the inner city and the rest of society such as the processes that form residential segregation and poverty.

Thus, by fusing essentialist conceptualizations of "race," gender, space, and place, the urban underclass concept shapes contemporary racist and sexist discourses and policies. It severely limits our understanding of the causes, consequences, and remedies of poverty by neglecting the majority of the poor, including people from different "races," the working poor, and people living outside of inner cities, and the processes by which people move into and out of poverty. By focusing on the moral attributes of one "race" of poor people, it promotes cultural and/or behavioral explanations of poverty, thereby allowing relations of power and inequality to be ignored. In the end, by promoting racism and sexism and defining poverty by unemployment, it obscures the connections among many poor people—connections that could form the basis for political action.

THE POVERTY DEBATES: THE FEMINIZATION OF POVERTY

The most visible feminist intervention in the public debates about poverty and welfare reform is in the form of the feminization-of-poverty thesis. Though less pernicious in terms of its political implications than the urban underclass thesis, the feminization-of-poverty thesis, as Baca Zinn (1990) has argued, essentializes gender by not recognizing that different structures of inequality give rise to different kinds of constraints and survival strategies.

The term "feminization of poverty" was coined by Diana Pearce (1979) to highlight the fact that poverty disproportionately affects women and their children. A number of explanations has been put forth to explain this trend, including family structure, the welfare system, and women's disadvantaged position in the labor force (for reviews see Goldberg and Kremen 1990; Kodras and Jones 1991; McLanahan, Sørensen, and Watson 1989; Schram 1995). Although it is clear that women are disproportionately impoverished (McLanahan, Sørensen, and Watson 1989; Pearce 1990; Schram 1995), women's poverty cannot be explained solely by gender but must take into account processes of "race" and class (Baca Zinn 1990). For example, African-American women are likely to be impoverished regardless of marital status because of the disadvantaged position of African American men in the labor market (Baca Zinn 1990; Jones 1985).

The feminization of poverty literature has neglected the geographic variability of poverty (for a critique, see Kodras and Jones 1991) and the way that sociospatial processes contribute to poverty. By focusing only on gender and ignoring the spatiality of poor women's lives, the feminization-of-poverty thesis cannot capture the reality or complexity of poor people's lives, nor can it provide an effective academic or political critique of the urban underclass thesis or the repeal of welfare.

Feminist academics and activists did organize against the repeal of welfare, but there was not widespread opposition by feminists or women.[5] The message used to gain support—that "a war against poor women is a war against all women"—

failed to mobilize large numbers of women and feminists.[6] Gwendolyn Mink (1998a, 1998b), a feminist scholar/activist, argues that it is precisely the ways in which "race" and class intersect with gender to shape women's lives that explains why most white and middle-class feminists supported welfare reform, particularly the mandatory work requirements: "The fact that women are positioned divergently in the nexus among caregiving, wage earning, and inequality separated feminists from one another on the welfare issue and separated employed middle-class feminists from mothers who need welfare" (1998a, 61). Middle-class feminists emphasize waged labor as a means of achieving equality and independence, but working-class women and women of color have often viewed waged labor as a source of inequality. Clearly, women's identities as workers and mothers are constructed by a multiplicity of interconnected (and spatially constituted) power relations. Any successful mobilization against welfare reform or, more generally, poverty will need to begin from this starting point.

IDENTITY AND THE SURVIVAL STRATEGIES OF WORKING POOR WOMEN

I have critiqued the concepts of urban underclass and feminization of poverty as conceptual frameworks for understanding poor women's everyday lives—or, more generally, poverty and the workings of the political economy—as well as bases for political organizing against welfare reform and poverty. I now draw on my research with working poor women in Worcester, Massachusetts, to illustrate how a nonessentialist analysis of identity and space helps to make sense of women's everyday experiences of poverty.

In 1991, I conducted in-depth interviews with 26 African American and 27 European American low-waged women with children living in Worcester.[7] Worcester, a classic Frostbelt city, continues to experience economic restructuring similar to those of other old industrial centers in the United States. Research has shown that Worcester has high levels of occupational sex segregation and wage disparities (Hanson and Pratt 1991, 1995). These economic trends have had numerous effects in Worcester that have hurt families headed by women and African Americans (Gilbert 1998). According to U.S. census data, in 1989, 31 percent of families with children under the age of 18 in Worcester were headed by women, as compared to 11 percent nationally; nearly 57 percent of female-headed households in Worcester in 1990 were below the poverty line (U.S. Census Bureau 1990). Though only 5 percent of the population of Worcester is African American, their families are disproportionately affected by poverty: 33 percent of African Americans fell below the poverty line, as compared to 16 percent of white families.

Although much of the public and academic discourse about poverty is focused on women receiving public assistance, many employed women are no more financially secure than they would be if they had received welfare benefits (Spalter-Roth et al. 1993). Yet an underlying assumption of welfare reform is that poor women with children will become economically self-sufficient through waged work despite the well-documented facts that most women are in sex-segregated occupations with low wages and lack of benefits, that there is still a significant wage gap, and that many women's wages are less than adequate to support a family (Hanson and Pratt 1995; Institute for Women's Policy Research [IWPR] 1995; Jezierski 1995; Kodras and Jones 1991; Reskin and Hartmann 1986). Furthermore, research has determined that although 43 percent of AFDC mothers work substantial hours, they still cannot lift their families out of poverty (IWPR 1995).

Given these data in the context of a welfare reform package that will clearly increase the numbers of working poor women, we urgently need to examine the barriers to and opportunities for working poor women's economic security. How do working poor women ensure their survival and that of their families? I address this question through an analysis of the role of women's personal networks—family, friends, neighbors, coworkers—in serving as one aspect of women's strategies to obtain child care, housing, and employment. I have chosen to focus on women's networks for two reasons. First, by exploring the creation and use of networks as part of women's survival strategies, I counter traditional beliefs that poor women are passive or lazy. Second, by focusing on the role of place-based personal networks in women's attempts to find a job, child care, and housing solution in space, I can examine how the spatial boundedness of women's lives and its consequences vary depending on the women's location within a constellation of power relations. Specifically, I demonstrate how different constellations of identities shape the manner in which women use rootedness—a potential outcome of boundaries—in their survival strategies.

Identities as Mothers, Employees, and Family Providers

Contrary to the urban-underclass thesis, my research suggests that there are many similarities in the daily struggles and survival strategies of African American and white working poor women as a result of their participation in gender and class processes. Interestingly, these similarities are often the result of the spatiality of women's daily lives.

Women's survival strategies and the spatial boundedness of their everyday lives are mutually constituted. Many women, regardless of the presence or absence of a partner, must fulfill the multiple roles of employee, mother, and family provider. Many women experience severe time and space constraints in attempting to meet all of their responsibilities in a society that does not acknowledge or support their multiple roles. Since neither employers nor the state is developing significant policies that recognize this, women's strategies are highly privatized. Thus, poor women's lack of access to resources results in time and space constraints (such as a lack of access to transportation), as demonstrated by two single parents' experiences in attempting to ensure their economic survival. One African American woman described her morning routine after she could no longer afford car insurance: "I wait for the bus for her [a child in first grade] to get picked up. I call a taxi from some place in that area to take the taxi to the daycare provider and from there I would take a bus to work."[8] A white woman described her evening routine as follows:

> Well, it's [first child care place] just five minutes [from work], but in the wrong direction. So I go there and pick her up, and I have to go pick up the other kid which is maybe ten minutes from there [first child care place], and then from there [second child care place] going home is another five minutes. But it would take at least a half hour because you can't just go there and throw the kid in the car as you drive by slowly. You have to park the car, go up the stairs, dress the kid, bring her down the stairs, do the seatbelt, and do the same thing for the next kid.[9]

Many women strategize in response to the time and space constraints by making their employment, child care, and housing decisions in concert.[10] As one African American woman with four children, ages two to twelve years, said, "I wouldn't go too far [to work], I'm having trouble as it is. I need to be there if something happens with the kids—15 minutes max—like where I work now, it takes about 15 minutes to get to any school I might need to."[11] A white woman with one son explained how she had made employment and child-care decisions jointly within the constraints of a bus route. Her son was ten when she made the following arrangements: "I looked for the job particularly because it was within the bus route. . . . The crossing guard at his [her son's] school, took him after school. . . . She'd walk him to the bus stop and put him on my city bus. I would like walk up to the front of the bus and say, "okay, I'm here" and I'd wave to her and he'd get on."[12]

When women cannot strategize in response to the time and space constraints they face in attempting to meet their multiple roles, the results can be devastating. One African American single parent had to quit her job and receive AFDC because of child-care problems. She took a bus to work at 6:30 a.m. in order to be at work by 7:00 a.m. The oldest child, only ten years old, put the youngest children on the bus to the daycare. The bus driver reported her to the Department of Social Services for having such a young child be responsible for the youngest children. Her employer would not change her hours, nor would the union support her. She described her frustration and anguish:

> It hurts . . . because when I stopped working, I had to go to welfare to get them to pay my electric bill and then pay my rent. . . . When I was working . . . I was saving, I had money and everything in the bank. Right now I don't have nothing. . . . She [the social worker] kept calling me telling me things are going to get better. I said, "Things are not going to get better for me because you should be able to talk to the

people for the daycare to come and pick my kids up at 6:00 a.m. you know if you want me to work." I'm the one who wants to work.[13]

The spatial patterns not only reflect women's survival strategies but also affect their job and child-care opportunities. The nature and spatial extent of women's personal networks is closely tied to their restricted daily activity patterns. Such networks play a vital role in determining how women define employment, child-care, and housing opportunities.[14] Most women—African American and white alike—rely heavily on personal contacts to link them to jobs, child care, and housing, and more broadly for economic and emotional support.

Personal networks can be both a resource and a constraint, often simultaneously, on women's economic survival. Women rely heavily on personal contacts to find employment (Gilbert 1998; Hanson and Pratt 1991, 1995), but these channels of information are highly gendered and spatially differentiated (Hanson and Pratt 1995). Women, particularly those in female-dominated occupations, are likely to receive job information from other women and family and community-based contacts, whereas men get job information from other men and work-based contacts. Furthermore, women in gender-typical occupations are more likely than women in gender-atypical occupations to learn about their jobs from women in the local neighborhood. Therefore, though personal networks help women to find jobs, they also can contribute to occupational segregation by sex and connect women to jobs that have lower wages and fewer benefits.

Personal networks also connect women to child-care providers. Most women in my study found their child-care providers through personal contacts, although some women used institutional contacts, the newspaper, or the Yellow Pages. Family members play an important role in connecting women to child care, and, to a lesser extent, so do neighbors and community-based contacts. The method used to find child care affects women's economic survival, because types of child care differ in terms of cost and hours of provision. For example, personal contacts were most likely to lead women to informal child-care arrangements, which can be advantageous, providing inexpensive and flexible child care, or disadvantageous, providing insecure child care that cannot be subsidized by the state because it is not licensed.

Women's identities as mothers, employees, and family providers are reflected in how the spatial boundedness of their lives and their survival strategies are mutually constituted. Furthermore, these identities construct the ways in which spatial rootedness is used in women's survival strategies as well as the consequences of such uses.

Racialized Identities

Although there are striking similarities between African American and white women in their survival strategies, there are also important variances that are the result of processes of "race" or racism.[15] These differences are not the result of a "culture of poverty" but rather of the way power and resources are unequally distributed in society on the basis of "race." Institutionalized and individual racism in the housing and labor markets affect African American women's strategies, whereas white privilege affects white women's strategies.

African American women tend to rely more heavily on personal contacts to link them to jobs, child care, and housing than do white women, who are more likely to use a variety of strategies such as newspapers and telephone books. Furthermore, African American women are much more likely to change jobs with the same employer than are white women, which can sometimes help them avoid encountering racism from the majority society. Personal contacts can perform a screening function by giving women information about employers, landlords, and child-care providers. Personal contacts can also help African American women, for example, by "vouching" for them to an employer.

The kind of personal contacts used by African American and white women often differ. African American women tend to rely more heavily on kin and community-based networks, especially church-related contacts, than do white women. Despite much discussion of the supposed breakdown of the African American family, studies have shown that low-income African Americans rely heavily on the extended family (see, for example, Stack 1974; for reviews, see Benin and Keith 1995; Raley 1995). In fact, the extended family and the church have historically been important institutions in mitigating the effects of living in a hostile and racist society (Billingsly 1968; Gilkes 1985; Jewel 1988).

The differences in African American and white women's strategies to find jobs, child care, and housing can be seen in the spatial extent of their daily activity patterns. African American women are significantly more spatially limited in terms of the journey to work and child care than are white women.[16] The reasons for African American women's spatial boundedness lie in several mutually constitutive processes, which include residential segregation, the "racial" composition of women's networks, and the relationship between women's daily activity patterns and the nature and spatial extent of their networks. Most women make their employment and child-care decisions from a fixed residential location. Because African Americans are spatially segregated in Worcester, these women make employment and child-care decisions from an even more spatially limited residential base than white women. Most African American women I interviewed (69 percent), like most African American women in Worcester more generally (64 percent), live in just 13 census tracts.

The residential segregation of African Americans, however, does not imply that their activity spaces necessarily will be smaller than white women's; other factors help to explain this pattern. African American women are more likely than white women to use personal contacts to find jobs and child care, and personal contacts are more likely to lead women to jobs and child care located closer to home. Furthermore, personal contacts, regardless of type, are more likely to connect African American women than white women to jobs that are closer to home. The level of "racial" segregation of women's networks also contributes to the differences in the spatial boundedness of women's lives. Most of the personal contacts women used to find jobs and child care were of the same racialized group as were most of their child-care providers. Since most African Americans live in just a few areas of the city, the spatial boundedness of their daily lives and the spatial extent of their networks, which are mutually constituted, are limited.

To understand how these differences play out in women's lives, I present here the stories of two women, one African American and one white. Julie Clarkson is an African American, 34 years old, single mother of three children ages 15, 4, and 1 year.[17] She earns $29,120 as a full-time operator for Massachusetts Electric on Southbridge Street in Worcester. She has worked there for years in different jobs. Her most recent job had been posted at her workplace, and she applied for it because it was more money and she was "going crazy" in customer service. Her travel time to work is 30 minutes with child-care trips, and 5 minutes directly.

Julie owns a home in Main South that she bought with her mother. The house was a few doors down from a previous residence. Main South, a compact area in the center of the city, is the neighborhood in which most African Americans in Worcester live. Julie's mother performed the household and child-care responsibilities at no cost while Julie supported the family financially. After Julie's mother died, the children went to an aunt who ran a licensed family daycare also located in Main South. She now has her two youngest children in a formal daycare center located in an African American church. Although she does not attend that church, she found out about the center through her church and receives some help from her own church with child-care costs. Julie prefers formal child care to kin-related child care despite her extensive use of the latter.

Julie's brother and one of his young children now live with her because he cannot afford to live on his own. Julie's brother helps with some of the bills, but does not pool income. Julie takes his child to and from child care, adding another 20 minutes to her journey-to-work.

Elizabeth Johns is a white, 28-year-old, single mother with a four-year-old daughter and a nine-month-old son.[18] She earns less than $10,000 per year as a preschool teacher in Grafton (an eastern suburb), working 32 hours per week with no benefits. She is laid off each summer and collects unemployment. Elizabeth searched for her job through newspapers, employment agencies, and personal contacts including family and friends. She found her job through a white woman friend that she met at childbirth classes who lives in Shrewsbury (another eastern suburb). Her friend's daughter had previously attended the preschool. Her friend saw an ad in the local paper where her mother lives and told Elizabeth about the job.

Elizabeth now travels 60 minutes from home to work, including stops at child care; if she went directly from her home to work, it would take only 20 minutes. Elizabeth's daughter attends a child-care center at a local community college which Elizabeth had previously attended. If she needs more child care, a young woman who used to work in a convenience store across from Elizabeth's house watches her daughter. Her son attends an unlicensed family daycare run by a woman that she knew from high school. Another friend from high school had told her that this woman was a child-care provider in Grafton, where Elizabeth works. She had also called places that she found in the Yellow Pages.

Elizabeth lives in an apartment in Grafton Hill on the east side of Worcester. She found her apartment through the newspaper. She had an extremely difficult time finding a landlord that would rent to her because she receives Section 8 and only pays $14.00 a month in rent.

These two women illustrate how racism intersects with gender and class to shape the spatial boundedness of women's lives and the ways that spatial rootedness is used in women's survival strategies. African American and white women differ in terms of their use of personal networks and the kinds of networks used to attain jobs, child care, and housing. We also see how the nature and spatial extent of women's personal contacts, the "racial" composition of their networks, and residential segregation result in African American women having more spatially limited daily activity patterns than white women (see Figure 3.1).

Identities as Migrants and Long-time Residents

One process that affects women's survival strategies in terms of their use of networks is migration (Hanson and Pratt 1992, 1995). Quite expectedly, family plays a lesser role in migrant women's lives, especially in finding jobs and child care. Women who had migrated to Worcester as adults were more likely to rely on neighbors or on work-based and church-based contacts for the kinds of assistance that require proximity to people, such as finding a job or child care. Migrant women, did, however, depend on kin for financial and emotional support. Long-time residents were more likely to use family members for jobs, child care, and housing; they also rely on community-based contacts, often women with whom they grew up, for emotional support. Whether one migrated to Worcester as an adult or lived in Worcester her entire life has inevitably led to quite different life experiences, problems, and solutions for women of the same racialized group. Someone born outside of Worcester but who had moved to Worcester as a child with her family will have more similar experiences to the child who was born and grew up in Worcester (for example, attending high school in Worcester, having immediate family in Worcester) than a person who migrated as an adult to Worcester.[19]

To illustrate how the process of migration affects women's networks across racialized groups, I present the stories of four women—two long-time residents and two migrants to the Worcester area. These women's life stories illustrate the ways that women's identities as migrants and long-term residents can affect women's use of place-based networks and their survival strategies.

Figure 3.1 Daily Activity Patterns for Women, City of Worcester, 1991

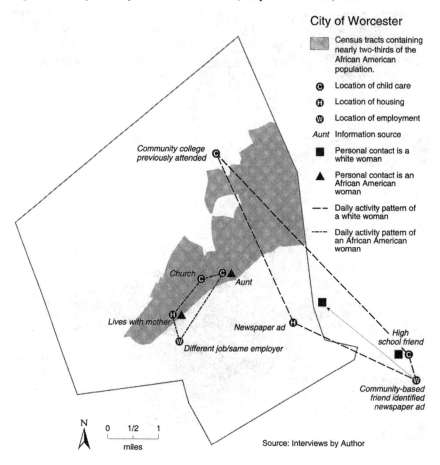

City of Worcester

Census tracts containing nearly two-thirds of the African American population.

ⓒ Location of child care

ⓗ Location of housing

ⓦ Location of employment

Aunt Information source

■ Personal contact is a white woman

▲ Personal contact is an African American woman

— — Daily activity pattern of a white woman

---- Daily activity pattern of an African American woman

Source: Interviews by Author

Patricia Davis is an African American, 40-year-old, single parent of 16-year-old and 7-year-old boys.[20] She was born and raised in the Main South neighborhood of Worcester. Pat lived with the father of her two children for 16 years before she left him. She receives no child support. Pat is a case manager for a social service agency, a job she found through a friend who had once been a neighbor. Pat has networks at work, in the community, and with many relatives:

> I have a lot of contacts in the community. Part of it has been my jobs [in social service agencies] and besides that my mother was in social services when I was a kid so a lot of it is roots and I always use my resources. . . . I have a lot of friends at work. We stay in touch and talk about personal things. It is sort of a women's network. I also belong to a black women's network group. We met every other week for

four years [she has since quit], stress related you know, outside of work. We all grew up together. Our mothers were Eastern Stars or Tripods [two African American women's organizations in Worcester], that is where we got the idea. Our fathers and mothers knew each other. We all lived in the same neighborhood or same side of the city, either east side [Belmont Street] or west side [Main South].

Pat clearly views residential rootedness as a survival strategy. Pat's experiences suggest the kinds of advantages potentially available to a woman who is a long-time resident of Worcester: "In the group I was in we all talked about leaving and how it would be to terminate some place that you grew up and that was really horrendous you know thinking about it. I know the streets, I know where the jobs are, I could pick up the phone and call you. My mom is here. You go to Atlanta or Virginia, you don't have those contacts, you don't have any coping. What do you do to replace the coping? So it's easier to stay here."

Laura Edwards is a white, 37-year-old, single parent of a 16-year-old daughter. She was born and raised in Worcester, in the Greendale area, a northern suburb that is predominately white.[21] After her divorce (when her daughter was 9 months old), Laura used family networks to arrange housing, child care, and employment that allowed her to survive. She moved in with her parents because she "thought it would be easier with the baby" and she only paid 25 percent of the household's bills. Laura's mother was a nurse and told Laura about a job as a medical secretary. For 12 years Laura worked the night shift while her mother worked the day shift in order to provide continuous child care for her daughter. Laura switched to day-time hours when her mother retired and could be home with her daughter during the day. She is now working an additional part-time job taking care of an elderly woman that her mother took care of before she died. Now that her parents have died she relies on an aunt for emotional and emergency financial support.

Tanya Cole is an African American, single parent of a 3 year old.[22] She moved to Worcester from Georgia in 1988 with her husband (who had grown up in Worcester), although she has since divorced him. Tanya is a claims representative for an insurance company, a job she found through the Employment Training program. When she got the job, she lost the subsidized child care provided by the Employment Training program. She left her son with her grandmother in Georgia for four months until she could arrange child care in Worcester, providing an interesting example of the nature and spatial extent of women's networks in survival strategies.

In Worcester, however, Tanya has created a complex network of people from her workplace, neighborhood, and church. A woman at work had suggested that she try the Childcare Connection, and through that agency she found affordable care. One woman took her son for a week when Tanya was seriously ill, indicating that she has friends at work who will help her out in an emergency. Her next-door neighbor has helped in emergencies, although she and the neighbor are not friends. She also found her current residence through a friend from work. In addition to the support from work friends, she relies heavily on her church contacts; her son's godparents belong to her church. She said, "I was always told, and anyplace I go, I have to find and establish a church family, and that's what you do. . . . I'm not going to say all people at church are good, but you know once you establish yourself, I think you get a lot of help." Tanya would go to the church itself and church-based contacts for financial help in an emergency.

Pam Wilson, a white single parent with three daughters aged 15, 13, and 7, came to Worcester from New York in 1986.[23] She was escaping an abusive partner and moved to Worcester because she thought he would never find her there. In her case, migration was a survival strategy. After she arrived in Worcester, she cleaned houses for one month with a woman that she met in the neighborhood until she found a job through the newspaper at a women's shelter. She left her children with neighbors for a few weeks until she could find formal child care. She said, "Even for me it was pretty iffy and risky, but it worked out okay."

Pam lives in a co-operative house in Main South.[24] She has a good friend who lives there who was the first person she met in Worcester. The friend had been a neighbor, and Pam convinced her to try the co-op. They help each other with child minding, and in a child-care emergency she depends on her boyfriend, her boyfriend's father, anyone living in her building, or a few friends. She has always made sure that she knows the people living around her in case there is an emergency—"That's just the way I am—it is a conscious strategy." She has received financial assistance from her boyfriend and her mother who lives in New York. "When you don't have your family nearby, you have to turn to people who aren't related to you. I have no family in Worcester. I meet people through my children and through friends at work." Like Pat, Pam's survival strategies center on building networks. Because Pam migrated to Worcester she cannot rely on family networks for jobs, child care, or housing, but she does receive financial assistance from kin.

The foregoing vignettes demonstrate that women's identities as migrants and long-term residents shape the ways in which rootedness is used in their survival strategies and can be more salient than racialized identities.

Identities as Single Parents

Another process that affects women's strategies is the presence or absence of a partner in the household, and it seems to affect African American and white women differently.[25] There were no significant differences in the networks of African American single parents and African American women with a partner present in the household.[26] This suggests that a racialized identity is more salient for women's strategies than the presence or absence of a partner.

In contrast, white single parents were more likely to have networks than white women with partners present in the household; such networks included those at work and among friends in their neighborhoods. Single parents were more likely to have used personal contacts to find their current residence than were women with partners. Furthermore, single parents were more likely to be involved in community activities. These findings suggest that some white women who are single parents are more likely to establish networks than are some with partners present in the household. Extensive networks are reinforcements that help a single adult to manage all the different roles necessary to ensure the survival of a family. Two white single mothers illustrate this point.

Barbara Graham is a 41-year-old mother of three sons still living at home, ages 16, 20, and 21.[27] She has been a single parent since 1978, when she separated from her ex-husband. Barbara is now a full-time social worker and earns $30,000 a year. She received both partial and full benefits on AFDC from 1971 to 1981 while she was volunteering, working part-time, and attending school. Barbara has established and used many networks—community, family, work, and neighborhood—during her time as a single parent. Barbara has relied heavily on neighborhood networks for both jobs and housing:

> I started out [how she found a job] when I was on welfare and my landlady, who was wonderful, adopted me as her daughter. She belonged to the Model Cities Program and she was chairman of a program called HELP—Health Education and Leadership Planning. She invited me to a meeting one night and again, they gave you a $5 stipend for attending. Well, that represented bread and Pampers okay. There were no food stamps then and there were no commodities or, you know, cheese and butter and all that other stuff, so any little bit of extra you could get from wherever you took advantage of it. Well, little did I know that this is where the networking began. This is where I met other women.

She also relied heavily on family and neighbors for child-care assistance:

> Well, to tell you the truth and just by the grace of God, no I didn't [have child care] because I couldn't afford it. That's when I would just like leave them and I would give [my eldest son] instructions because there was a time that we didn't have a phone, and that really presented a problem, too, because, like, if there was an emergency, who do you call? Then we did have a phone. So it was call Auntie [her sister] if there's an emergency and for the longest time she was pretty close by, so it was either that or have the neighbor listen up or, you know, I took my chances and went to school and they were on their own. And like I say just by the grace of God they had that angel that protected them. . . . They [neighbors] played a key role, oh, they really did you know. And I always lived above somebody. . . . I was there [3-decker on Piedmont Street] 11 years so it was my landlady for a number of years, then she rented out to—and all of her tenants were black—an older woman who again was like a motherly, would kind of watch out for the kids. But the last two people who were there were both single parents and we shared, you know if I had an evening meeting.

Barbara has also created many networks at work and through her community activities; she has used them to find jobs and housing or for emotional support. She co-owns her house with a good friend from a previous workplace.

> We [she and the woman with whom she co-owns her home] were two single parents; our ethnic group is the same—we're both Italian. But I think that the thing that attracted our friendship was we had strong religious beliefs that were like almost the same and we were TCB people, we took care of business, okay. Rena's children came first, my children came first. We didn't do all the luxury kind of things, we took care of necessities first and the luxuries come later, and I think that's why this joint partnership has worked, because of where we both came from. And she was also a welfare mom, you know. The other thing is, um, I'm very much into black people as much as I am into white [her children are biracial] but you have to understand that poverty has no color boundaries, hunger doesn't. So when women are all in that same category, you don't really see, you know you just look at what you need to do to take care of yourself.

Barbara has been extremely involved in community activities, including a housing organization, child-care centers, church activities, and education groups. As she says, she "has utilized her resources."

Jill Miller, age 26, is a single parent of a 7-year-old girl.[28] Working full-time as a secretary, she earns $15,000 a year. Jill has always been a single parent and relied on AFDC for three years while she was in school. Jill lives on a street in Main South that has a number of buildings that are owned co-operatively. She got into the co-op through her brother and paid by "sweat equity." She is also very networked, relying on family, neighbors, and coworkers for financial, emotional, and child-care support. Jill shares many of Barbara's theories about networks: "The only way I think I've survived being single is by being in the co-op. I could have paid $500.00, I mean it's difficult to pay a lot of rent, but I could have done that. I would say it is more of the emotional and learning experience. I mean I didn't know anything about communities. I didn't know how you went to a city council meeting, how you petition for things, [or] how you fix a wall. Being here taught me an incredible amount. This is like one of the best streets in Worcester. It was all of it—emotional, spiritual, financial." Jill has received both child-care support and financial support from her neighbors, including her brother:

> In the recent past I've been in that situation [receiving financial assistance] when I was on welfare and going to school. I was not able to pay the rent. . . . At that point other people chipped in and paid more rent to support mine. . . . I would have ended up in Great Brook Valley [a public housing project]. . . . The other thing about when I said that I wasn't able to pay rent and other people helped, I also did things for them. I did more sweat equity or I did more shoveling or I went and watched the kids, so luckily it was a barter system and [I] had good luck with that.

Jill also gets emotional support from friends at work, because she thinks that "women, especially single women, need that. I mean being a single parent that's the only thing that saves you."

Both Barbara and Jill emphasize the importance of networks, of having a support system, to women who are single parents. They suggest that women have to create support systems in order to actively ensure the survival of themselves and their families, both economically and emotionally. The identity of "single parent" appears to be stronger vis-à-vis a racialized identity for white women than for African American women in terms of the ways in which rootedness is used as a survival strategy.

CONCLUSION

An effective feminist and antiracist critique of the urban underclass and feminization-of-poverty theses requires a geographical analysis based on, to borrow Massey's (1993) phrase, a progressive sense of place (and space). Clearly, space and place play roles in the causes and consequences of poverty in women's everyday lives. However, place and space do not play the roles suggested by environmentally deterministic explanations of poverty that are based on conceptualizations of space as a container and place as a bounded enclosure. Rather, my research illustrates that the spatiality of women's lives is important, for example, in terms of the place-based nature of networks, residential segregation, and the time/space constraints women face in attempting to find a job, child care, and housing solutions.

Poor women's survival strategies are varied and complex, attesting to their strength and ingenuity in extremely difficult circumstances that have been shaped by their participation in such processes as "race," gender, and class. I have demonstrated that women's locations in different constellations of power relationships shape the spatial boundedness of their lives, the ways in which rootedness is used in survival strategies, and the ways in which spatial boundedness and rootedness may be enabling as well as constraining. The shapes of different networks is based upon the performance of different identities. Understanding the similarities and differences in the survival strategies of working poor African American and white women requires a theoretical framework that explores women's participation in multiple, interconnected, and spatially constituted power relations.

The role of place-based networks in women's survival strategies demonstrates that women are agents in the production of geographical boundaries in at least two senses. In a metaphorical sense, women produce boundaries in urban space through the use of networks to create a job-housing-child-care combination that allows them to provide for their families. In a more literal sense, women produce boundaries in urban space through networks whose spatial dimensions outline the meeting places and the work/residential locations of people in networks. Understanding how women participate in the creation of boundaries as well as challenge them, and how such boundaries may be enabling as well as constraining, is an important part of constructing a feminist politics based on coalitions and affinities that acknowledges the diversity of women's experiences.

Nonessentialist conceptualizations of identity and space within an antiracist and feminist theoretical framework provide an analysis of urban poverty that better explains women's everyday experiences than do either the urban-underclass or feminization-of-poverty theses. An analysis of women's locations within constellations of spatially constituted power relations and the salience of different place-based identities also provide the basis for an effective, progressive political agenda. Such an agenda reframes the debate about "welfare reform" more broadly within the mutually and spatially constituted processes of the changing political economy, racism, and sexism and their effects on all poor people. In so doing, it allows for the possibility of organizing poor people across boundaries of "race," gender, employment status, and place while recognizing the distinction of differing experiences. This visionary agenda is being promoted by many radical working-class grass-roots organizations forming across the country today, responding to the vicious attacks on poor people's ability and right to survive.[29] Those of us working to construct a feminist politics grounded in the diversity of women's experiences should join them.

NOTES

This research was assisted by awards from the Social Science Research Council through funding provided by the Rockefeller Foundation and the National Science Foundation (SES-9103501). An earlier version of this chapter appeared as "Identity, Space, and Politics: A Critique of the Poverty Debates" in *Thresholds in Feminist Geography*, edited by J. P. Jones III, H. J. Nast, and S. M. Roberts (1997, 29–45). I would like to thank Kris Miranne and Alma Young for their helpful comments on this chapter and their support. I would also like to thank Sherry Ahrentzen, Glen Elder, Cindi Katz, Audrey Kobayashi, Glenda Laws, Karen Nairn, Laura Pulido, Sue Roberts, Chuck Rutheiser, and Gill Valentine for their helpful comments on earlier versions of this chapter, and Mark Mattson and Jeff McMichael for preparing the figures.

1. I place "race" in quotation marks to indicate that it is a socially constructed category. I use the term "white" to highlight the fact that white people are a "racial" category that promotes white privilege by constructing whiteness as the norm and hence invisible. Simultaneously, white privilege functions by essentializing the "racial" category of black people. Therefore, I use the term "African American" to highlight that "blacks" are an ethnic group as well as a "racial" designation.

2. A number of feminists have argued that accusations of essentialism have created a "chilly climate" in feminist debates because it is sometimes used to silence debate (see, for example, Martin 1994; Schor and Weed 1994). Martin (1994) convincingly argues that white feminist attempts to rectify their previous failures to theorize "race" and class

(among others) have led to the pitfall of "false difference." These problems are not, I believe, inherent to nonessentialist theorizing. It is my intention that the following analysis will illustrate how a nonessentialist conceptualization of "race" and gender is an effective analytical and political tool for feminist and antiracist research.

3. This political rhetoric has been given credibility by mainstream social science research on poverty despite the existence of a substantial literature that critques the underclass thesis and the role of social scientists in perpetuating war on the poor (see, for example, Dujon and Withorn 1996; Handler 1995; Katz 1989; Kelley 1997; Piven and Cloward 1997; Reed 1982; Schram 1995; Williams and Peterson 1998).

4. See Pulido (1997) for a fascinating discussion of the racialization of South Central and East Los Angeles, and residents' challenge of, and participation in, this process.

5. For a discussion of feminist activism against the repeal of welfare, particularly the activities of the Women's Committee of 100, see Boris (1998); Kornbluh (1998); Michel (1998); Mink (1998a, 1998b).

6. For example, the Women's Committee of 100 placed a full-page ad in the *New York Times* on August 8, 1995, that explained why welfare cuts were a women's issue. I am not trying to belittle the efforts of feminists fighting welfare reform (my "signature" is on the ad) nor blame feminists for welfare reform. I am trying (along with others) to figure out ways that we as feminist academics and scholars can join with poor people devastated by welfare reform to build a movement to end poverty in this country.

7. For a more detailed discussion of the data, methods and study area, see Gilbert (1998).

8. Female, interview by author, tape recording, Worcester, Mass., August 27, 1991.

9. Female, interview by author, tape recording, Worcester, Mass., August 9, 1991.

10. For a more detailed discussion of the interrelatedness of women's jobs, child-care, and housing decisions, see Gilbert (1998).

11. Female, interview by author, tape recording, Worcester, Mass., August 13, 1991.

12. Female, interview by author, tape recording, Worcester, Mass., August 5, 1991.

13. Female, interview by author, tape recording, Worcester, Mass., August 26, 1991.

14. For a more detailed discussion of the role of personal networks in women's survival strategies and the ways in which networks can be both a resource and constraint, see Gilbert (1998).

15. For a more detailed discussion of the differences in African American and white women's use of personal networks, the kinds of personal networks used, how networks are a resource and constraint, and the spatial boundedness of their daily lives, see Gilbert (1998).

16. African American women traveled an average of 11.9 miles to their jobs, whereas white women traveled 17.8 miles. African American women commuted fewer miles, including child care (27.1 miles), than did white women (39 miles).

17. All names are pseudonyms. Julie Clarkson, interview by author, tape recording, Worcester, Mass., November 21, 1991.

18. Elizabeth Johns, interview by author, tape recording, Worcester, Mass., July 1, 1991.

19. All of the women defined as migrants had lived less than half their lives (or an average of seven years) in the Worcester (SMA). All of the women defined as nonmigrants had lived more than half their lives (or an average of 33 years) in Worcester SMA. Nearly

74 percent of the nonmigrants had spent their entire lives in the Worcester SMA. One-quarter of the women who were migrants were European American, and one-half were single parents.

20. Patricia Davis, interview by author, tape recording, Worcester, Mass., November 26, 1991.

21. Laura Edwards, interview by author, tape recording, Worcester, Mass., October 10, 1991.

22. Tanya Cole, interview by author, tape recording, Worcester, Mass., October 12, 1991.

23. Pam Wilson, interview by author, tape recording, Worcester, Mass., August 9, 1991.

24. Co-operative housing is a building, usually an apartment building, in which the tenants own the property.

25. Among African American women, there were 13 single parents and 13 women with partners in the household. Among white women, there were 21 single parents and 6 women with partners present in the household.

26. Six of the African American single parents were migrants to Worcester, and six of the African American women with partners were migrants to Worcester.

27. Barbara Graham, interview by author, tape recording, Worcester, Mass., November 3, 1991.

28. Jill Miller, interview by author, tape recording, Worcester, Mass., October 10, 1991.

29. One organization with which I have worked closely is the Kensington Welfare Rights Union, a multiracial organization of poor and homeless men and women based in Philadelphia (Gilbert 1999). For a discussion of a number of other such organizations, see Pulido (1996, 1997, 1998); Kelley (1997); Savage (1998); Gilmore (forthcoming).

REFERENCES

Abramovitz, Mimi. 1996. *Under Attack, Fighting Back: Women and Welfare in the United States.* New York: Monthly Review Press.

Aiken, Susan, Ann Brigham, Sallie Marston, and Penny Waterstone, eds. 1998. *Making Worlds: Gender Metaphor, Materiality.* Tucson: University of Arizona Press.

Baca Zinn, Maxine. 1990. "Minority Families in Crisis: The Public Discussion." In *Women, Class and the Feminist Imagination: A Socialist-Feminist Reader,* edited by Karen Hansen and Illene Philipson. Philadelphia: Temple University Press.

Benin, Mary, and Verna Keith. 1995. "The Social Support of Employed African American and Anglo Mothers." *Journal of Family Issues* 16: 275–297.

Billingsly, Andrew. 1968. *Black Families in White America.* Englewood Cliffs, NJ: Prentice-Hall.

Boris, Eileen. 1998. "Scholarship and Activism: The Case of Welfare Justice." *Feminist Studies* 24, 1: 27–31.

Brewer, Rose M. 1993. "Theorizing Race, Class and Gender: The New Scholarship of Black Feminist Intellectuals and Black Women's Labor." In *Theorizing Black Femi-*

nisms: The Visionary Pragmatism of Black Women, edited by Stanlie Myrise James and Abena P.A. Busia. London: Routledge.

Collins, Patricia H. 1990. *Black Feminist Thought: Knowledge, Consciousness, and the Politics of Empowerment*. London: Routledge.

Dujon, Diane, and Ann Withorn, eds. 1996. *For Crying Out Loud: Women's Poverty in the United States*. Boston: South End Press.

Fincher, Ruth, and Jane Jacobs, eds. 1998. *Cities of Difference*. New York: Guilford Press.

Gilbert, Melissa R. 1997a. "Feminism and Difference in Urban Geography." *Urban Geography* 18: 166–179.

———. 1997b. "Identity, Space, and Politics: A Critique of the Poverty Debates." In *Thresholds in Feminist Geography: Difference, Methodology, and Representation*, edited by John P. Jones III, Heidi J. Nast, and Susan M. Roberts. Lanham, Md: Rowman and Littlefield.

———. 1998. " 'Race,' Space, and Power: The Survival Strategies of Working Poor Women." *Annals of the Association of American Geographers* 88: 595–621.

———. 1999. "From the 'Walk for Adequate Welfare' to the 'March for Our Lives': Welfare Rights Organizing in the 1960s and 1990s." Unpublished manuscript.

Gilkes, Cheryl Townsend. 1985: "Together in Harness: Women's Traditions in the Sanctified Church." *Signs: Journal of Women in Culture and Society* 10:679–699.

Gilmore, Ruth W. Forthcoming. "You Have Dislodged a Boulder: Mothers and Prisoners in the Post Keynesian California Landscape." In *Transforming Anthropology*.

Goldberg, Gertrude S., and Eleanor Kremen. 1990. *The Feminization of Poverty: Only in America?* Westport, Conn.: Greenwood Press.

Handler, Joel. 1995. *The Poverty of Welfare Reform*. New Haven: Yale University Press.

Hanson, Susan, and Geraldine Pratt. 1991. "Job Search and the Occupational Segregation of Women." *Annals of the Association of American Geographers* 81 (June): 229–253.

———. 1992. "Dynamic Dependencies: A Geographic Investigation of Local Labor Markets." *Economic Geography* 68: 373–403.

———. 1995. *Gender, Work, and Space*. London: Routledge.

Hughes, Mark A. 1989. "Misspeaking Truth to Power: A Geographical Perspective on the Underclass Fallacy." *Economic Geography* 65, 3: 187–287.

———. 1990. "Formation of the Impacted Ghetto: Evidence From Large Metropolitan Areas, 1970–1980." *Urban Geography* 11, 3: 265–284.

Institute for Women's Policy Research (IWPR). 1995. *Research in Brief: Welfare to Work: The Job Opportunities of AFDC Recipients*. Washington, D.C.: Institute for Women's Policy Research.

Jewel, Sue. 1988. *Survival of the Black Family*. New York: Praeger.

Jezierski, Louise. 1995. "Women Organizing Their Place in Restructuring Economies." In *Gender in Urban Research*, edited by Judith Garber and Robyne Turner. Thousand Oaks, Calif.: Sage Publications.

Jones, Jacqueline. 1985. *Labor of Love: Labor of Sorrow*. New York: Basic Books.

Jones, John Paul III, Heidi Nast, and Susan Roberts, eds. 1997. *Thresholds in Feminist Geography*. Lanham, MD: Rowman and Littlefield.

Katz, Michael B. 1989. *The Undeserving Poor: From the War on Poverty to the War on Welfare*. New York: Pantheon Books.

———, ed. 1993. *The "Underclass" Debate: Views from History*. Princeton: Princeton University Press.

Keith, Michael, and Steve Pile, eds. 1993. *Place and the Politics of Identity*. London: Routledge.

Kelley, Robin. 1997. *Yo' Mama's Disfunktional! Fighting the Culture Wars in Urban America*. Boston: Beacon Press.

Kobayashi, Audrey, and Linda Peake. 1994. "Unnatural Discourse: Race and Gender in Geography." *Gender, Place and Culture* 1, 2: 225–243.

Kodras, Janet, and John Paul Jones III. 1991. "A Contextual Examination of the Feminization of Poverty." *Geoforum* 22, 2: 159–171.

Kornbluh, Felicia. 1998. "The Goals of the National Welfare Rights Movement: Why We Need Them Thirty Years Later." *Feminist Studies* 24, 1: 65–78.

Martin, Jane R. 1994. "Methodological Essentialism, False Difference, and Other Dangerous Traps." *Signs: Journal of Women in Culture and Society* 19, 3: 630–657.

Massey, Doreen. 1993. "Power-Geometry and a Progressive Sense of Place." In *Mapping the Futures: Local Cultures, Global Change*, edited by Jon Bird, Barry Courtier, Tim Putnam, George Robertson, and Lisa Ticken. London: Routledge.

———. 1994. *Space, Place and Gender*. Minneapolis: University of Minnesota Press.

McLanahan, Sara S., Annemette Sørensen, and Dorothy Watson. 1989. "Sex Differences in Poverty, 1950–1980." *Signs: Journal of Women in Culture and Society* 15, 1: 102–122.

Michel, Sonya. 1998. "Childcare and Welfare (In)justice." *Feminist Studies* 24, 1: 44–54.

Mink, Gwendolyn. 1998a. "The Lady and the Tramp (II): Feminist Welfare Politics, Poor Single Mothers, and the Challenge of Welfare Justice." *Feminist Studies* 24, 1: 55–64.

———. 1998b. *Welfare's End*. Ithaca, N.Y.: Cornell University Press.

Pearce, Diana. 1979. "Women, Work, and Welfare: The Feminization of Poverty." In *Working Women and Families*, edited by K. W. Feinstein. Beverly Hills, Calif: Sage Publications.

———. 1990. "Welfare Is Not for Women: Why the War on Poverty Cannot Conquer the Feminization of Poverty." In *Women, the State, and Welfare*, edited by L. Gordon. Madison, Wis: University of Wisconsin Press.

Piven, Frances Fox, and Richard Cloward. 1997. *The Breaking of the American Social Compact*. New York: New Press.

Pratt, Geraldine, and Susan Hanson. 1994. "Geography and the Construction of Difference." *Gender, Place and Culture* 1: 5–29.

Pulido, Laura. 1996. *Environmentalism and Economic Justice: Two Chicano Struggles in the Southwest*. Tucson: University of Arizona Press.

———. 1997. "Community, Place, and Identity." In *Thresholds in Feminist Geography: Difference, Methodology, and Representation*, edited by John P. Jones III, Heidi J. Nast, and Susan M. Roberts. Lanham, Md.: Rowman and Littlefield.

———. 1998. "Development of the 'People of Color' Identity in the Environmental Justice Movement in the Southwestern United States." *Socialist Review* 96: 145–180.

Quadagno, Jill. 1994. *The Color of Welfare: How Racism Undermined the War on Poverty*. New York: Oxford University Press.

Raley, Kelly R. 1995. "Black-White Differences in Kin Contact and Exchange Among Never-Married Adults." *Journal of Family Issues* 16: 77–103.

Reed Jr., Adolph. 1992. "The Underclass as Myth and Symbol: The Poverty of Discourse About Poverty." *Radical America* (January-March): 21–38.

Reskin, Barbara, and Heidi Hartmann, eds. 1986. *Women's Work, Men's Work: Sex Segregation on the Job.* Washington, D.C.: National Academy Press.

Rose, Gillian. 1993. *Feminism and Geography: The Limits of Geographical Knowledge.* Minneapolis: University of Minnesota Press.

Savage, Lydia. 1998. "Justice for Janitors: Geographies of Organizing." In *Organizing the Landscape: Geographical Perspectives on Labor Unionism,* edited by Andrew Herod. Minneapolis: University of Minnesota Press.

Schor, Naomi, and Elizabeth Weed, eds. 1994. *The Essential Difference.* Bloomington: Indiana University Press.

Schram, Sanford. 1995. *Words of Welfare: The Poverty of Social Science and the Social Science of Poverty.* Minneapolis: University of Minnesota Press.

Smith, Neil, and Cindi Katz. 1993. "Grounding Metaphor: Towards a Spatialized Politics." In *Place and the Politics of Identity,* edited by Michael Keith and Steve Pile. London: Routledge.

Soja, Ed. 1989. *Postmodern Geographies: The Reassertion of Space in Critical Social Theory.* London: Verso.

Spalter-Roth, Roberta, Heidi Hartmann, and L. Andrews, 1993. "Mothers, Children, and Low-Wage Work: The Ability to Earn a Family Wage." In *Sociology and the Public Agenda,* edited by William Wilson. Newbury Park, Calif: Sage Publications.

Stack, Carol. 1974. *All Our Kin: Strategies for Survival in a Black Community.* New York: Harper and Row.

U.S. Bureau of the Census. 1990. Poverty in the United States: 1990: Current Population Reports. Series P-60, 165. Washington, D.C.: U.S. Government Printing Office.

Williams, Rhonda, and Carla Peterson. 1998. "The Color of Memory: Interpreting Twentieth-Century U.S. Social Policy from a Nineteenth-Century Perspective." *Feminist Studies* 24, 1: 7–25.

Chapter 4

Boundaries Cracked: Gendering Literacy, Empowering Women, Building Community

Jennifer E. Subban and Alma H. Young

Literacy is one of the most significant ways in which we make meaning of our everyday experiences and of events in the world(s) around us. And yet, understanding literacy is complicated, since it is a "loaded term" that represents different things to different people (Graf 1995). Thus, literacy needs to be "unpackaged" (Scribner 1988) so that we can understand its multidimensions and see how it is embedded in social, cultural, and political contexts. Giroux (1987) suggests that we unpack the concept by thinking of literacy as cultural politics, highlighting the social, cultural, political, and economic dimensions of life; as liberating remembrances, highlighting the importance of history in the process of becoming culturally literate; and as narrative, alluding to the personal dimension of literacy. In unpackaging literacy, we come to understand how it can be used to maintain the status quo, or to subvert power arrangements and open up opportunities for the dispossessed.

For some, literacy is purely functional, providing students with the academic skills to read, write, and do calculations. These skills are thought to serve as a cognitive toolbox, existing independently of any context. Here, literacy is taken to be neutral, acultural, nonracial, nongendered, and apolitical (Fingeret 1992). Literacy programs based on this approach, however, ignore the underlying issues they are trying to solve and inadvertently blame those lacking literacy skills. They place an added layer of victimization on those already once victimized by the ascribed statuses of race, class, gender, and caste.[1] This concept of literacy serves to maintain the status quo.

Others adopt a cultural approach to literacy, which attempts to bridge the gap between socially neutered definitions of (functional) literacy and the reality within which literacy experiences are grounded. This approach attempts to situate people's literacy practices in the broader social relations that govern them. As Heath observes, "Unless accompanied with cultural knowledge . . . literacy does not lead the writer to make the essential leap from literacy to being literate—from knowing what the words say to understanding what they mean" (1986, 16). But whose reality, whose culture, should be privileged? For some who adopt cultural literacy, it is mainstream culture that must be nurtured, but, as noted by Asante (1991), this view serves to maintain relationships of power that marginalize some communities. Others believe that the literacy process should nurture the indigenous culture because this validates a community and allows a community to define itself, as opposed to being externally defined (Shujaa 1994).

A third approach is critical literacy, which is a response to an increased awareness of the connection between power relations and the literacy experiences of individuals and communities (Freire and Macedo 1986). The purpose of critical literacy is to develop individuals with the ability to analyze and challenge the oppressive nature of society and to facilitate the transformation of that society to a more just, equitable, and democratic one (McLaren 1986). To this end, critical literacy is a struggle for voice, empowerment, and emancipation. It is a process that develops a critical consciousness among learners who become active, knowing subjects in the process of learning how to read their world in order to transform it (Freire and Macedo 1987). Thus there is a recognition that there is a socially constructed context to both the word and the world. Reading the world and analyzing one's experiences in it provide an opportunity to understand one's role in society. At the heart of this literacy experience is the transition from knowing our place in the world to resisting and subverting that place to create one that enhances our living.

Fasheh (1990), among others, suggests that effective resistance and subversion can only take place if one is embedded within a strong community. The relationship of literacy to community building is an intriguing one, one that has been explored much more in the Third World context than in North America.[2] If we accept Bhattacharyya's (1995) definition of community building (or what he calls community development) as the pursuit of solidarity and agency, then we begin to see some of the connections. Solidarity provides a community with a shared identity and code of conduct. Agency "provides the capacity of a people . . . to create, reproduce, change and live according to their own meaning systems, the powers effectively to define themselves as opposed to being defined by others" (Bhattacharyya 1995, 61). Clearly, an ability to "read the word and the world" becomes essential to community building. Thus both (critical) literacy and community building recognize the need to challenge the basis on which knowledge and meaning are constructed. The goals of both include a reconstitution of identity, individual and collective, and a transformation of one's social reality.

Women are often vital to the process of community building. Along with other ethnic-racial groups, African American women's community work has been recognized as a distinctive element in their family roles. Their community work has often been geared toward social change and focused on internal development and external challenge (Gilkes 1994; also see Collins 1991; Spain this volume). Women with low literacy status are curtailed in their ability to be effective community builders, to influence the world and the word governing it. Smith (1987) states that the relations of ruling in (most) societies are mediated by texts, the primary medium of power. Not having access to texts, the women do not have access to one of the most significant means of influence in society. This lack of influence applies to the world beyond the boundaries within which they function as well as to the boundaries that define their particular communities, since the latter are in many ways externally defined.

To a large extent, women are discouraged from knowing "too much." Not having the skills to decipher the codes of text limits what women can come to know. Equally significant is the fact that those outside the world of women are not exposed to the reality of women's lives, their ideas, and their ways of knowing. Such a circumstance is exacerbated for women with low literacy status. These women do not have a vehicle through which they can transport their construction of knowledge and meaning, especially beyond the physical and cultural boundaries of their communities. They are, as a result, not represented in the organization of ruling within their society, or in the systematically developed knowledge that has entered into it (Smith 1987).

The case studies presented below explore the experiences of low-income, African American women who participated in a family literacy program in New Orleans between 1992 and 1996. It examines the multiple boundaries of race, gender, and literacy that impact these women's everyday experiences. It also examines the ways in which these boundaries reinforce each other, often serving to limit women in what they can know. The point of departure is the women's literacy status, which can be seen as a boundary. The chapter brings into focus the dual nature of boundaries, functioning to constrain the women to particular spaces within their urban environment, while simultaneously creating opportunities for the women to define spaces of their own.

THE TOYOTA FAMILIES FOR LEARNING PROGRAM

In 1991, New Orleans was chosen by the National Center for Family Literacy (NCFL) as one of 15 cities in the country to implement a family literacy program. This program was made possible through a grant from the Toyota Motor Corporation. This family literacy program was to represent a new educational model in which family strengths would become the center of curriculum design and implementation. Attention was directed toward helping parents realize their own powers and strengths and their ability to convert these into action. The program was to provide a mechanism and an environment that encouraged critical thinking and problem solving germane to matters in family life. Program administrators measured the growth of the families by their willingness to develop and test various problem-solving alternatives, and to accept their responsibilities as members of a unified group (NCFL 1994).

The Toyota Families for Learning Program (TFFL) focuses on children and parents learning together. Parents who have not completed their high school education return to school with their preschool children and engage in literacy training for a year. In the program, parents are recognized as their children's first and most important teachers. According to NCFL, family literacy programs should help participants (both parents and children) develop a sense of self-worth, promote social interaction, encourage the development of both individual students and the group as a whole, and teach strategies that assist in dealing with everyday stresses. In order to achieve these goals, each program is centered on four integral components. These components include academic learning for parents and preschoolers, discussions among parents on issues of importance to them, structured parent and child interaction, and volunteering around the school and within the community.

In New Orleans the program operates in three public elementary schools, two of which are near public housing developments. The teachers are regular school personnel who have received additional training from NCFL. The program is guided and administered by urban affairs faculty and staff at the University of New Orleans, who have adapted the program to fit the particular needs of the families participating. Each year the program serves approximately 35 families, the majority of whom are considered poor by any government measure. Almost all of the participants are female, African American, young, unemployed, and single heads of household. Over 40 percent dropped out of school between the eighth and tenth grades (Subban 1998). Most have returned to school in order to complete their Graduate Education Diploma (GED). They understand, correctly, that a high school diploma is essential these days to being able to find a job, and they seek to become more economically independent. A few of the participants in our study had completed high school but still felt inadequate in their literacy skills and wanted to enhance them. Others returned to school in order to be eligible to enroll their preschool children in this enrichment program. As we will see later in this chapter, these women's lives are much richer and more complex than these brief descriptions would suggest.

From its inception, the New Orleans program linked family literacy to community building, requiring an expanded definition of literacy. It meant moving beyond literacy conceptions that focus only on learning the functional skills of reading, writing, and arithmetic. Within the framework adopted by TFFL, literacy, like other social phenomena, is recognized as a social construct and thus must be embedded within the participants' social reality. The program subscribes to a definition of literacy based on the interests and needs of this particular community, at this particular time. Hence the New Orleans program defines literacy as a process that is grounded in the cultural and concrete reality of a community. It seeks to develop the human resources and competencies of the community (including but not limited to functional literacy skills), and reconstitutes and/or enhances feelings of self-worth, empowerment and self-acceptance among community members. It nurtures cultural awareness and facilitates networking, communication and the exchange of ideas and experiences, both internally and externally. (Subban 1998, 18)

This definition is reflected in the program philosophy and methods of implementation. For instance, " in TFFL, education is about teaching and learning about ourselves and others, acknowledging that learning takes place both inside and outside the classroom, building and living in community with others . . . it is about action" (Subban, 1998, 167).

LOW LITERACY AS A BOUNDARY FOR WOMEN IN TFFL

By enrolling in the TFFL program, these women made an important decision to overcome what they saw as an impediment to their ability to shape their lives and the lives of their children. That impediment was their low literacy status, which they felt kept them from nurturing their children in the ways they wanted, achieving the kinds of jobs they sought, and establishing the relationships they desired.[3] These women decided to enter the Toyota program in order to improve their literacy levels and, they hoped, their life chances. Despite having made such a momentous decision, many of the women were not without trepidation when they entered the program: Some of the women were anxious about being in a classroom at their age; others feared they couldn't learn; still others worried about what their peers would say about their returning to school.

Much of the apprehension, however, stemmed from remembering the negative experiences they had encountered when they were in school before. As one of the participants explained:

Mr. Johnson! He was the one always told me about my penmanship. Oh, God, I used to hate going to his class cause he used to call me all kinds of, you know, "Here comes the dummy." . . . So he [would] put me down in class and he just talk a lot in front of everybody, "Look at the dummy. Go up to the board." And me and him had it hot and heavy; I throwed a chair at him I was so angry with him one day . . . the man grabbed me, he start to fight me. And I . . . ran home. He was an old man. He was very mean to me. I didn't even care of doing nothing no more.

Despite their anxiety, however, a number of women also expressed their excitement at the prospects it offered. These prospects included getting a GED, learning about computers, having fun and enjoying the company of other adults, learning how to deal with both their children and the community, and changing their life styles.

Functioning at the lower levels of literacy, these women stand on the fringes of city life, having little access to economic and political resources on the one hand, and being limited psychologically, socially, and physically on the other.

Employment

Employment opportunities for women of low literacy status are limited, and in New Orleans are focused primarily within the lower end of the service sector. These jobs are among the lowest paying and typically are devoid of benefit packages. In some instances, these jobs are structured around shift work, as opposed to salaried positions, giving employers the opportunity to schedule shifts of less than 40 hours per week and at varying hours. For employees, shift work requires constant negotiations over child care, transportation, and housing (see Gilbert this volume, chap. 3).

For women in TFFL, their average annual income at the time of participation is less than $10,000 and 74 percent derive some of their income from public assistance. National research shows that 43 percent of adults who function at the lowest level of literacy live in poverty, work an average of 19 weeks per year, and constitute 75 percent of unemployed adults. The average number of weeks worked per year by persons on welfare with low literacy levels is 11. Significantly, over 65 percent of people on welfare who have a high school diploma or GED leave welfare and become self-sufficient within two years (NCFL 1994).

Dependence

Because of their limited opportunities for income, many women of low literacy status find themselves dependent on others and on the state. Some of the women in TFFL reported having to rely on family members, friends, partners, and social workers for such basic literacy functions as reading a child's school report, paying bills, and writing correspondence. They have also had to have assistance with matters such as housing, health care, and public transportation. In other cases, dependence stems from needing financial support from family members, partners, and welfare programs such as Aid to Families with Dependent Children (AFDC) (currently Temporary Assistance to Needy Families, or TANF), Social Security, Medicaid and the food stamps program. Many of the "spousal" relationships that the women enter into are based on the financial support they can garner.

Due to their low literacy status, these women are often frustrated by their interactions with institutions that they encounter as part of everyday life. One such institution is that of the schools in which their children are enrolled. At the heart of this frustration are the negative experiences many of the women themselves had with school, experiences that make them feel that schools never give students a fair break. Such experiences are ever present in the minds of the women as they attempt to advocate on behalf of their children. These women are also astutely aware of the negative perceptions that school faculty and staff have of them, and, lacking the verbal skills to communicate their concerns, they often conduct themselves in ways that confirm the negative perceptions of school personnel.

Schools, however, are not the only institutions that the women encounter. Another institution that often leaves the women feeling powerless is the "welfare office." The literacy status of the women makes them dependent on their case workers for information. Case workers act as the interpreters and conveyors of information on policy decisions and regulations devised by the state. However, the experiences of the women reveal that case workers also function as gatekeepers of information, neglecting to share with their clients information on options they could pursue and on benefits for which they are eligible; sometimes they make decisions for their clients.

Self Worth

An important manifestation of the literacy status of the women in TFFL is their diminished sense of self-worth. Having a low literacy status is very often associated with a sense of worthlessness, the shame of not being able to read, and notions of not having the intellectual capacity to be able to do so. In the words of the women, they often "feel stupid." Yet, self-worth is critical to the women's willingness and ability to engage in the learning process. One woman stated that it took several months before she felt good enough about herself to open up to learning. Before the women are ready to begin that process, they present countless excuses for their lack of participation in classroom activities.

Having a low sense of self-worth is not limited to classroom activities; it often confines the women in other aspects of their everyday lives. The women talk about the effects of their literacy status on their relationships with their children, especially as it pertains to their children's learning, and on their relationships with other family members and partners. One of the most pressing issues for these women is their inability to assist their children's efforts to be successful at school. In response to this situation, some of the women have, on occasion, played down the importance of education—not because they believed it to be true, but because they wanted to protect themselves from having to reveal their low literacy status to their children. The frustration inherent in this reality leads to other circumstances that often result in parent-child relationships that stand in contradiction to the hopes and dreams these parents have for their children.

Leaving school prior to graduation was a major contributor to the negative self-images of the women in TFFL, but leaving school was simply the end of a long road of abuse, neglect, and miseducation for them. Resistance to negative comments and actions of teachers and other adults came in the form of defiance, with-drawal, and attention-seeking behavior—responses that carried over to their adult lives. To cushion the assaults on their sense of self-worth, these women created their own boundaries, detaching themselves from the communities around them. Unfortunately, they also walled themselves off from many social interactions, sometimes even from their own children, in order to protect themselves from ridi-cule. Thus we might argue that a limited literacy status leads to boundaries of isolation. This often translates to a silencing of the self. These boundaries are reinforced for the women by occurring at the intersection of race, class, and gender.

Choice

What quickly becomes apparent from this discussion of literacy status as a boundary in women's lives is the socio-spatial isolation which profoundly im-pacts both the level of access that women have to the major institutions impacting their lives and on the measure of choice that women have in making decisions concerning their own lives and those of their families and communities. For women in the TFFL program, their access and their choices are seriously cur-tailed by their low literacy status, making their efforts to resist, reconfigure, and reconstruct their reality more difficult. And yet these women in TFFL did begin to break the boundaries that constrained them. The decision by the women to participate in the TFFL program represented a significant way to resist their mar-ginalized position in society. Since TFFL's philosophy and structure dictated a literacy experience far different from the schooling they had received in the past, the program brought these women into a greater consciousness of themselves and helped them to become effective agents of change within their lives.

The literacy experiences the women had in TFFL presented a number of op-portunities for them to extend beyond resisting their reality to reconfiguring their lives. As noted before, a fundamental element of the experience was the opportu-nity to develop a sense of community among the program participants. Develop-ing a sense of community in the classroom came, in part, from them recognizing their shared experiences, even the less pleasant ones. Literacy training revolved around the experiences of the women as women, as mothers, as African Ameri-cans, and as poor persons; it provided an opportunity for the women to develop and articulate a common identity. The case study that follows is an example of how the process of community building took place around explorations into the racial logic that governs U.S. society. It shows how this inquiry provided a liter-acy experience that made the women more conscious of the nature of their world and led to both a questioning and a deeper understanding of events in their lives. The political awareness of the women increased, and with that came a demonstra-tion that the more literacy one has, the more likely one is to have visions of the world one wants to have. Without such visions we have no basis for transformation of our world.

LITERACY, RACE, AND WOMEN'S LIVES

We knew from earlier work in African American communities that education (and literacy) was a concern of the residents, especially of parents for their children. Therefore, we thought that TFFL would provide a point of entry for collective work since it encouraged the building of support networks that extended beyond kinfolk. But first it was necessary for the program to strengthen a sense of community by facilitating the ability of participants to recover their voices. One of the most powerful ways that we saw this happen in the program centered on the discussions of language and race, and the growing awareness of how the pervasiveness of the "racial state" limits opportunities. Participants came to understand, as Winant has argued, that "race remains a fundamental organizing principle, a way of knowing and interpreting the social world . . . that it is deeply fused with the power, order and indeed the meaning systems of every society in which it operates"(1994, 2) (also see Omi and Winant 1986). Paradoxically, perhaps, this growing awareness led to a greater sense of solidarity not only among the participants, but also among participants and their teachers (all of whom are African American). This growing awareness, however, did not come without a personal (and collective) struggle, as the examples below will show. The development of solidarity prepares a foundation for agency, since participants are then in a better position to clarify their goals, develop strategies to achieve them, and to act on them using the knowledge, skills, and support networks developed.

Understanding that race is socially and historically constructed (Hacker 1992), we recognize that it is constantly being redefined and contested (Winant 1994). In bringing the conversation on race to the classroom, it was necessary to acknowledge that living in a "racial state" means that we are concerned not just with acts of individual prejudice but also with a mode of rationality that places certain cultures and ethnic groups in a superior position to others. As such, those who are seen as inferior are impacted in ways that minimize solidarity and agency, both individually and collectively. Discussions demonstrated that being in a racial state affects the way we relate to each other and to ourselves, often resulting in relationships of dependency. Thus, the racial state impacts our life choices and life chances. Moreover, we came to see that in the United States, racism is integrally linked to the definition of culture.

The opening each year for this growing awareness of the racial state is a dialogue in the classroom on linguistic domination, for we see "language as the heart of culture, the medium for the production of collective meanings" (Bhattacharyya 1995, 63). Through classroom discussions, the women unpack the power differential of language and begin to see the racial implications. During the process, Standard American English comes to be seen as a dialect that has assumed dominance because it is the language of those who hold power in this country. Participants agree, however, that they prefer black vernacular over Standard English when they are expressing their feelings to each other.

Discussions of this nature provide an opportunity through which participants gain an appreciation of their own language, an important step given that many tend to see it as an ignorant way of speaking—ignorant meaning stupid, unknowing, and sometimes uncultured. Participants come to see that they are more likely to call each other "ignorant" when someone enters their group who speaks Standard English as a main form of communication. The use of the term "ignorant" reflects how they feel about their language and themselves when they are outside of their immediate community, or when a "stranger" enters their group.

The women come to understand that the impact of the hierarchical status of language is far-reaching (Friere and Macedo 1987). For participants of the Toyota program, it affects the expectations they have of themselves, because they know all too well that it is mainstream America which judges their intellect and abilities, and ultimately, it is mainstream America that limits their access to jobs and a decent living wage. The astuteness of participants allows them to see how placing a hierarchy on language disadvantages them. They also usually conclude that while one dialect is essentially no different from another, Standard English has a place in the world they live in and that gaining access to that world may mean accessing that language and, in fact, being bidialectal. In the process, the mindset with which they approach learning Standard English changes from a deficit one to one which recognizes the context of the different situations in which they find themselves. It is the context that helps them decide which dialect to use, not that one dialect is stupid and another not.

Typically, the discussions on language are part of the writing workshops conducted in the classrooms of the adult participants. The workshops take a variety of forms. Most often participants are asked to write about an experience, respond to an event or critical issue, or ask questions about something occurring in the community. Participants share their written pieces with the class by reading them, and the class reciprocates by commenting on the pieces and sharing thoughts that the written pieces trigger for them. The power of this dialogue lies in the fact that the participants come to recognize that they have had similar experiences and that they can share their experiences in a safe environment. Thus, they come to know the impact that some experiences they have not wanted to talk about in the past have on their lives. In short, they get to name their experiences and identify them for what they are. In the process, they build bonds of solidarity with each other.

The pain associated with talking about some of the daily issues that face their communities becomes evident. The impact that racism has had on their lives is especially painful. It is not uncommon for participants to suggest that the class does not need to talk about race. They say things like: we should move on because racism doesn't exist anymore; talking about race means we're advocating hatred; we can't talk about it because we have never experienced racism; we don't want to talk about it because we don't want to know about it (knowing would force us to have to deal with it). Thus, many prefer to handle issues of race by denying its existence or relevance. As one participant anguished: "Because coming up with a slave mentality, we always had a tendency to look down on ourselves. We were under the white race. We were beneath the white race; they were superior. . . . And that would make me feel like I was less than a person." But as participants come to "read the world," they also come to understand the context of their feelings. Acknowledgment that they live within a racial state and that it has affected their lives in concrete ways is one of the milestones that participants pass on the road to self-discovery . . . and to agency.

STORIES TOLD, LIVES REVEALED

One of the stories told belongs to Catalina, who moved from naming racism to recognizing how those dynamics play out in her daily life. She was one of the participants in the Toyota program who was asked to attend an "undoing racism" workshop conducted by a local organization skilled in community organizing (see Young and Christos-Rodgers 1996). She agreed to attend, but once there she felt uncomfortable. Both the mixture of people (professionals, community residents, community organizers, and students) and the language used added to her discomfort. She left before the workshop was finished, saying that she had no reason to talk about racism because she had never experienced it personally. She did, however, agree to a request by program staff that she be part of a planning group at her school to develop a class on racism and the role it plays in our daily lives.

During the process of planning the class, the staff engaged her in dialogue that opened the way for her to recognize her discomfort with the issue of racism. She said that she really knew that it existed, but that she couldn't see it; that talking about it was a waste of time; and, finally, that talking about it could put you in a bad mood, making it hard to smile her way through the pain. She said, "I don't want to feel angry when I look into the faces of white people."

Months later, during a summer internship at a local university, Catalina came to the program staff and stated quite unapologetically that her supervisors at the internship site were behaving toward her in a racist manner. She was very clear about which of their actions showed them to be racist: for example, not looking at her when they spoke, never engaging her in conversation, and underestimating her ability to do the work assigned to student workers. The participant's response raised an important question for the program staff—how to help participants move from naming their experiences, which Catalina could now do, to acting on them so as to create more positive situations for themselves.

The story of Wanda reveals how this was done. A graduate of TFFL, Wanda worked first as a teaching assistant in one of the program sites, and then later as a literacy facilitator in her own adult education classroom at another TFFL site. As a literacy facilitator for the program, Wanda worked along with two literacy AmeriCorps volunteers. Wanda is African American, the two volunteers were white.

When Wanda first joined the program, she had a difficult time talking about race and racism and spent much time drawing attention to the similarities between the races as a way of easing her discomfort. However, in continuing discussions on race in her own classroom, and in her experiences working with the volunteers assigned to her, Wanda was able to gain greater consciousness of her feelings toward race. She started the year saying, "I can't discuss race in my class because I don't know enough about it," but moved on to realize the value of learning more and sharing that knowledge. It was through the sharing of information with the students in her class that she came to see that race impacted all their lives in many different ways.

By assuming a position of authority as literacy facilitator, she was challenged to conduct her own research on how race impacts African Americans, leading her to realize how pervasive racism is and how it limits choices and opportunities. Her position also helped her to understand firsthand the program's philosophy of putting the participant at the center of the program, which means, for example, critiquing the racial state which marginalizes participants within the classroom (either because their knowledge is not privileged, their sense of self-worth is diminished, or cultural differences—languages, actions—are contrary to mainstream expectations). Wanda came to find the words to express what she and others she knew had experienced.

Perhaps what clinched it for Wanda were the reactions of the white volunteers as she changed how the classroom was run. Clearly feeling displaced, they were disgruntled as they realized the norms of their knowledge were no longer at the center. They were very uneasy about not being in control of the situation and having to rely on someone else to direct them. Their discomfort was compounded by the fact that they considered the person directing them to be inferior, academically and culturally. There were also discrepancies between the interpretation of events offered by Wanda and (African American) participants in class and those offered by the volunteers. The volunteers' interpretations were based on cultural values and norms that differed from those of the class participants, and this became more apparent as the consciousness of the class increased. What also became obvious was that there was a gap between the words that the volunteers used (language they had picked up through the program's training sessions) and their actions now that their knowledge was not privileged.

What this experience showed Wanda, and some of the participants, was the kinds of behaviors people exhibit when they feel marginalized. Wanda had moved to the center of the classroom by conceptualizing her role differently than she had previously done: in the old role she had established a relationship of dependence on the volunteers; in the new role, she recognized and accepted her right and responsibility to shape the classroom. The reaction of the volunteers as she moved to this new role informed Wanda's consciousness of the part that racism was playing in the classroom.

The impact of this enhanced consciousness extended for Wanda beyond the program and her classroom. In retrospect, she now connects the dynamics of racism to her lack of achievement when she was in high school. Her schooling conflicted with her cultural knowledge to such an extent that she eventually dropped out before graduation. She now is able to act to influence the experiences of her children at their respective schools, holding teachers accountable for their words and actions. Wanda's commitment to her community is stronger, as evidenced by her interest, ideas, and commitment to perpetuating the knowledge she has gained about herself as an African American woman, and about the history and experiences of African Americans in this country. Her aim is to develop a broader sense of solidarity among African Americans so that they can transform the racial state governing their lives. She has since begun studying at a local university to further her development and achieve the goals she has set for herself.

The TFFL teachers, too, have become more conscious of the racial state through the process of dialogue in their classrooms and in training sessions. The teachers came through a traditional educational experience and now have come to see how those experiences minimized their sense of culture and achievement. Working on race from a critical and cultural perspective provides an avenue for them to explore their own racial realities and to move beyond the limiting perspective of racial dynamics taught them earlier.

Lila, one of the teachers, spent the summer in a writing project for teachers whose theme was "Subvert the dominant paradigm." She was able to explore the racial implications of this theme with her classmates, who had neglected to note the impact of race on the society or on their students. Lila helped her TFFL class think more critically about how race impacts their lives. In one such class discussion, a racial framework was applied to incidents of violence in their community. Students could then see how the criminal justice system is applied differentially to citizens based on race. They began reading the local newspaper more critically. This led to a redefinition of their community, as the students began to debunk some of the stereotypes surrounding black men and crime. They began to look critically at the communities in which they live and the roles they play within them. This discussion also served to strengthen the bonds among the participants and with the teacher. A sense of community was being developed within the classroom.

CONCLUSION

In the stories told, we begin to note how boundaries are broken, how cracks of light are revealed, as individuals become more literate and their visions expand.

Individuals gain the skills and the self-esteem that allow them to begin the journey of critical consciousness, which leads to the possibility of community building. What began as a resistance to illiteracy, of wanting to know more, leads to a reconfiguring of opportunities and the ability to see(k) further. This case demonstrates the dual nature of boundaries: as a space that is isolating as members blind themselves to the outside and seek refuge in the familiar, but also as a space that is empowering as members consciously build community among themselves and others (see hooks 1994).

In resisting their literacy status, the women in TFFL resist more than the label of "illiterate." They resist the limitations that society imposes upon them as young, poor, African American women with low literacy skills. Manifest in the conversations around their decision to improve their literacy status are contradictions they feel between how they want to define themselves and how they are defined by others. Having internalized the negative messages they have received about themselves as "illiterates," as dropouts, and as welfare mothers, they have begun to blame themselves for their positions. But they have aspirations of being good mothers, good providers, and helpful members of the community. What the Toyota program helps them to understand is why these contradictions exist, and it offers a glimpse of how the contradictions can be confronted. In many instances, this increased awareness lifts a burden of self-blame, infuses a new sense of self-pride, and leads to a greater willingness to act collectively. They come to understand that there are new possibilities for personal and collective living. The Toyota program seeks to nurture community within these women's social networks as the context for motivating, empowering, and sustaining them in their preparation for social change. In learning how to give voice to their experiences of oppression, these women are better able to release their creative energies and help sustain resistance and envision alternatives.

NOTES

During the time period discussed in this chapter, Jennifer Subban and Alma Young served as Program Manager and Program Director, respectively, of the Toyota Families for Learning Program in New Orleans. Young is an African American; Subban is a woman of color from South Africa.

1. In Bombay, women interviewed on questions of literacy said that being literate was seen as a way of validating not experience, but existence itself. Persons considered illiterate wear this as a marker of identity. In many cases, this aspect of their being subsumes all others as the "language of literacy continues to be negative, accusatory, devaluing the personhood of individuals on the basis of certain skills considered vital for decent human existence" (Samant 1996, 4).

2. See discussion on Gender and Development (GAD) in Moser (1993).

3. The National Institute for Literacy has established five levels of literacy to measure the functional levels of men and women in the United States. They range from basic skills

at the first level, to symbol analysis at the fifth level. Persons functioning at the lowest literacy level are unable to read/interpret information on a job application, a medicine bottle, a Social Security form, or a lease agreement. They cannot help their children with homework, follow travel directions, or calculate grocery costs. These are basic functions that most people take for granted, and yet there are millions of poorly literate individuals in the United States (see Subban 1998).

REFERENCES

Asante, M. K. 1991. "Multiculturalism: An Exchange." *American Scholar* 60: 267–276.

Bhattacharyya, Jnanabrata. 1995. "Solidarity and Agency: Rethinking Community Development." *Human Organization* 54, 1: 60–69.

Collins, Patricia Hill. 1991. *Black Feminist Thought: Knowledge, Consciousness, and the Politics of Empowerment*. New York: Routledge.

Fasheh, Munir. 1990. "Community Education: To Reclaim and Transform What Has Been Made Invisible." *Harvard Educational Review* 60, 1: 19–35.

Fingeret, H. A. 1992. *Adult Literacy Education: Current and Future Directions: An Update*. U.S. Department of Education, Information Series No. 355. Columbus, Ohio: National Center for Research in Vocational Education.

Freire, Paulo, and Donald Macedo. 1987. *Literacy: Reading the Word and Reading the World*. South Hadley, Mass.: Bergin and Garvey.

Gilkes, Cheryl Townsend. 1994. " 'If It Wasn't for the Women . . .': African American Women, Community Work, and Social Change." In *Women of Color in U.S. Society*, edited by Maxine Baca Zinn and Bonnie Thornton Dill. Philadelphia: Temple University Press.

Giroux, Henry. 1987. "The Hope of Radical Education: A Conversation with Henry Giroux." *Journal of Education* 170: 91–101.

Graf, H. J. 1995. *Labryinths of Literacy*. Pittsburgh: University of Pittsburgh Press.

Hacker, Andrew. 1992. *Two Nations: Black and White, Separate, Hostile, Unequal*. New York: Ballantine Books.

Heath, Shirley Brice. 1986. "Literacy and Learning in the Making of Citizens." 1985 Butt Lecture. Reprinted in *Civic Education, Pluralism and Literacy*. A joint publication by AESA News and Comment and the Center for the Studies of Citizenship and Public Affairs, Syracuse University, August.

hooks, bell. 1994. "Choosing the Margin as a Space of Radical Openness." In *Yearning, Race, Gender, and Cultural Politics*. Boston: South End Press, 145–153.

McLaren, Peter. 1986. *Schooling as Ritual Performance: Towards a Political Economy of Educational Symbols and Gestures*. New York: Routledge and Kegen Paul.

Moser, Caroline O. N. 1993. *Gender Planning and Development: Theory, Practice and Training*. New York: Routledge.

National Center for Family Literacy (NCFL). 1994. *The Power of Family Literacy*. Louisville, Ky.: Philliber Research Associates.

Omi, Michael, and Howard Winant. 1983. "By the Rivers of Babylon: Race in the United States." Part 2. *Socialist Review* 72: 35–52.

———. 1986. *Racial Formation in the United States: From the 1960s to the 1980s*. New York: Routledge.

Samant, U. 1996. "Literacy and Social Change: From a Woman's Perspective—Mi Shiknar: I Will Learn." Paper found at *http://ncal.literacy.upenn.edu/products/ili/webdocs/ilproc/ilprocus.htm*.

Scribner, S. 1988. "Literacy in Three Metaphors." In *Perspectives on Literacy*, edited by E. R. Kintgen, B. M. Kroll, and M. Rose. Carbondale: Southern Illinois Press.

Shujaa, Mwalimu J. 1994. "Education and Schooling: You Can Have One Without the Other." In *Too Much Schooling, Too Little Education: A Paradox of Black Life in White Societies*, edited by Mwalimu J. Shujaa. Trenton, N.J.: African World Press, Inc.

Smith, Dorothy E. 1987. *The Everyday World as Problematic: A Feminist Sociology*. Boston: Northeastern University Press.

Subban, Jennifer E. 1998. *Talking from the Inside Out: The Link between Literacy and Community Development*. A Ph.D. dissertation submitted to the University of New Orleans, May.

Winant, Howard. 1994. *Racial Conditions: Politics, Theory, Comparisons*. Minneapolis: University of Minnesota Press.

Young, Alma H., and Jyaphia Christos-Rodgers. 1996. "Conversations of Power: Community Organizing Strategies of the St. Thomas Resident Council, New Orleans." In *Local Economic Development in Europe and the Americas*, edited by Christophe Demaziere and Patricia Wilson. New York: Mansell.

Chapter 5

Black Women as City Builders: Redemptive Places and the Legacy of Nannie Helen Burroughs

Daphne Spain

Because black women are seldom represented in the typical narrative of urban, planning, or architectural histories, their contributions to the major city-building era between the Civil War and World War I have all but disappeared. The idea that women built cities, much less black women, is at odds with conventional wisdom. Yet black and white women made significant contributions to the urban landscape at the turn of the last century through their work in voluntary associations.

The two most important voluntary organizations for black women one hundred years ago were the National Association of Colored Women (NACW), founded in 1896, and the Woman's Convention (WC) Auxiliary to the National Baptist Convention, formed in 1900. These associations drew inspiration from the Social Gospel, an activist theology that applied Christian principles to daily life, and from municipal housekeeping, an ideology that encouraged black and white women to take care of cities as though they were their own homes. Black women volunteers operated independently of, but parallel to, white female volunteers in organizations influenced by the Social Gospel and municipal housekeeping (such as the Young Women's Christian Association (YWCA), the Salvation Army, and the College Settlements Association) to provide temporary refuge for newcomers to the city (Spain forthcoming).

Black women of this era were not architects, real estate tycoons, or construction workers—these occupations were not yet open to women. Instead, black women contributed to the urban fabric by sponsoring the creation of "redemptive places" in which black men, women, and children found respite from harsh conditions in the industrializing city. Members of the NACW and WC created libraries, orphanages, boarding homes for working women, vocational schools, settlements, kindergartens, and playgrounds that buffered black migrants to the city from the worst consequences of racial discrimination. However, many of the places they created no longer exist, which leads to the assumption that black women did not influence the built environment.

These rather ordinary places were redemptive in three ways: they grew out of religious activism; they tried to save the bodies and souls of black migrants; and they rescued black, middle-class, women volunteers from purely domestic pursuits by giving them public identities. Redemptive places were seldom designed specifically for the purpose devised by the volunteers, but instead were buildings and vacant lots adapted from previous uses. Constituting a "voluntary vernacular," they were neither completely private nor totally public; rather, they occupied a "liminal" or threshold space in which marginal populations (like single women looking for work) made the transition from rural roots to city soil. Redemptive places were liminal in two other ways. They existed only as long as there was demand for their services, then evolved into another type of institution or disappeared entirely; and they provided services that fell between private charity and public welfare (Skocpol 1992; Turner 1971).

The purpose of this chapter is to illustrate how the Social Gospel and municipal housekeeping spurred the National Association of Colored Women and the Woman's Convention to create a particular redemptive place, the National Training School for Women and Girls, through the auspices of its founder, Nannie Helen Burroughs. Burroughs, like many other black women, belonged to both the WC (which she also founded) and the NACW.

Burroughs's lifelong struggles for antilynching laws and women's rights reflected the triple challenges of race, gender, and class facing black women working on behalf of cities at the turn of the twentieth century. As blacks, their first crusade was against lynching. As women, they worked for suffrage, fair wages, and recognition from men. Predominantly middle class, they tried to help lower-class blacks become more respectable by focusing on standards for public and private behavior (Lerner 1974). Club women rarely compartmentalized their programs, using similar strategies to address the problems of race, women, and the poor. The strength of the NACW and the WC was that they addressed issues on all three fronts (see White 1993). A united effort was critical, for according to historian Anne Firor Scott, "The problems with which [black women] grappled were so huge and were growing so fast that their accomplishments tended to be swallowed up in a sea of poverty and prejudice. Yet without their work things would have been much worse" (1990, 18).

HISTORIC AND DEMOGRAPHIC CONTEXT

The major era of urbanization between the Civil War and World War I occurred before women entered the design and building professions. At the time, few women worked outside the home and none could vote, seemingly limiting their ability to shape the social, spatial, economic, or political agendas of the city. Yet voluntary associations provided the means by which women made their mark. City growth between 1870 and 1920 was explosive. Urban industries demanded thousands of new workers, and the supply came largely from Europe. An average of 6 million Europeans arrived each decade between 1880 and 1920. By 1920, approximately one-half of the country's urban population was of foreign birth or parentage. Internal migration from farms and small towns (by both blacks and whites) accelerated during the same period, and the majority of America's population lived in cities by 1920 (Hofstadter 1955; Ward 1971, 6, 52, 53).

Blacks began to replace European immigrants among the urban poor as the twentieth century began. Although small numbers of blacks moved out of the South to northern and midwestern cities after the Civil War, the vast majority (90 percent) still lived in the South until 1910. The pace of outmigration accelerated as blacks sought to escape a declining cotton economy and the legacy of slavery, and as northern industries demanded laborers when European immigration was curtailed.

Some firms actively recruited southern blacks. The Pennsylvania Railroad, for example, brought 12,000 black men north to work on their tracks and equipment during World War I. The emerging black media also played a role. The *Chicago Defender* called for a "Great Northern Drive," with May 15, 1917, as the "day of exodus" that would deliver blacks from poor living conditions in the South. Such intensive migration, however, fueled racial tensions in the North over jobs and housing, and race riots erupted in St. Louis in 1917 and in Chicago in 1919 (Farley and Allen 1987, 109–115).

This demographic context is relevant to the history of voluntary organizations through which women built redemptive places. White organizations such as the YWCA began in northern and midwestern cities when European immigration was at its peak and before black migration from the South reached significant numbers. Thus the most visible urban poor at the turn of the century were white ethnic immigrants. The National Association of Colored Women and the Woman's Convention emerged in both southern and northern cities as blacks began the great migration off farms. Blacks soon became the most visible urban poor, with racial discrimination exacerbating the need for services. By the beginning of the twentieth century, the YWCA served a predominantly white clientele, and the NACW and WC served blacks.

THE SOCIAL GOSPEL AND MUNICIPAL HOUSEKEEPING

Social and economic disruptions following the Civil War convinced Protestant clergy to shift their emphasis from saving individuals to addressing social problems caused by rapid industrialization, urbanization, and extensive immigration.

Though the Charity Organization Movement of the eighteenth century attributed poverty to the sins of individuals and blamed the poor for their squalid living conditions, the Social Gospel held society accountable for creating slums that trapped the poor.

Combining a criticism of conventional Protestantism with a program of progressive reform, advocates of the Social Gospel identified cities as their biggest challenge. Ministers preached that cities were the centers of crime and vice and needed the Christian message more urgently than rural areas. Institutional churches like the Salvation Army and settlements like Chicago's Hull House were the redemptive places in which this interdenominational evangelical work was carried out among whites (Bender 1975, 11; Hofstadter 1955, 175; Hopkins 1967).

Although most historians have focused on the activities of white ministers in the North and Midwest, the Social Gospel also flourished among blacks and in the South. In 1901 a Baptist minister established Bethel Institutional Church in Jacksonville, Florida, that operated a kindergarten, cooking school, and night school; it also created the Afro-American Life Insurance Company. At about the same time, in Washington, D.C., the Shiloh Church and the Nineteenth Street Baptist Church opened daycare centers and clinics for the poor (Higginbotham 1993a, 174).

One of the most famous black Social Gospel efforts was launched in 1900 by an African Methodist Episcopal (AME) minister. Reverend Reverdy Ransom opened Chicago's Institutional Church and Social Settlement at 3825 South Dearborn Street with an auditorium seating 1,200, a dining room, a kitchen, and a gymnasium. The Settlement sponsored a daycare center, kindergarten, mothers' and children's clubs, print shop, sewing and cooking classes, an employment bureau, and a penny savings bank. Some of the white progressive reformers with whom Reverend Ransom worked included Jane Addams of Hull House, Mary McDowell of the University of Chicago Settlement, Social Gospel minister Shailer Mathews, and the lawyer Clarence Darrow (Luker 1991, 174; Woods and Kennedy 1911). These multiple functions were the reason W.E.B. DuBois observed that black churches were "for the most part, curiously composite institutions, which combine the work of churches, theaters, newspapers, homes, schools, and lodges" (Higginbotham 1993a, 173).

The Social Gospel was not the only route to public activity open to black women at the turn of the last century. The secular ideology of municipal housekeeping helped women to justify their participation in city affairs. It was a logical extension of a woman's duties to her family and home, because it emphasized her responsibilities for clean streets, clean sidewalks, and clean air. Civic improvement was defined as "larger housekeeping" and women as naturally the "city's housekeepers" (Hoy 1995). This domestic imagery invited all women to understand the city as a place they could shape. Women who ascribed to principles of municipal housekeeping often endorsed the Social Gospel as well, so that the Social Gospel and municipal housekeeping served as complementary sacred and secular rationales for women's involvement in public life.

THE NATIONAL ASSOCIATION OF COLORED WOMEN

The work of the NACW was a "special kind of municipal housekeeping, carried out with limited resources, which meant that the women themselves did a great deal of hands-on labor in their projects" (Scott 1991, 148). The club's motto, "Lifting as we climb," reflected its mission to improve the status of the entire race as its members climbed the socioeconomic ladder. Their goal was "raising to the highest plane the home life, moral standards, and civic life of the race" (Davis 1934, 5, see also 14, 86). By 1914 the NACW had 50,000 members in more than 1,000 clubs (Shaw 1991). These women were an educated elite, typically married to professional men, who defined their duties as acknowledging their "weak sisters," having compassion for their "inferiors," and helping "waifs and strays of the alley come in contact with intelligence and virtue" (Hine 1990b, 31). Their outreach took form in the built environment. The NACW sponsored homes for the aged, for working women, and for unwed mothers; hospitals and clinics; kindergartens; libraries; and settlement houses.

The NACW was founded in 1896 as a response to a slanderous attack on black womanhood. The President of the Missouri Press Association, James W. Jacks, wrote a letter in defense of lynching to English abolitionists in which he stated that most colored women in the United States were "wholly devoid of morality and that they were prostitutes, thieves, and liars." The English abolitionists sent a copy of Jacks's letter to the editors of *Woman's Era*, the newsletter of Boston's New Era Club organized by Josephine St. Pierre Ruffin in 1893. Ruffin had been contemplating a national convention for black clubwomen, and Jacks's accusations fueled her determination (Wesley 1984, 28).

As Ruffin was organizing the New Era Club, Mrs. Helen Cook was forming Washington D.C.'s Colored Women's League, which was formally incorporated in 1894. A parallel organization to the New Era Club, the League's mission was to document the status of blacks and to promote their progress. One of their first projects was a night school, soon followed by a kindergarten and day nursery. Kindergartens had been the original priority for the New Era Club, suggesting that clubwomen recognized the importance of educating the next generation as well as of providing daycare for working mothers.

Another contributing factor to the birth of the NACW was black women's exclusion from the 1893 World's Columbian Exposition in Chicago. The Columbian Exposition was *the* defining event in architectural and planning histories. It showcased the work of famous architects (Chicago's own Daniel Burnham; Peabody and Stearns of Boston; and McKim, Mead, and White of New York City) and was a template for the City Beautiful Movement. White women had difficulty joining men in preparations for the Fair and had to settle for representation through a Board of Lady Managers composed of women's clubs members. Black women found it impossible to participate because eligibility for the Board of Lady Managers was determined by organizational affiliation, not awarded to individual persons (Weimann 1981).

Hallie Q. Brown, a graduate of Wilberforce University, had lobbied most actively for black women's inclusion in the Fair. In a letter to one of the Lady Managers protesting the absence of black women from exhibits in the Woman's Building, Brown observed that "if the object of the women's department of the Columbian Exposition is to present to the world the industrial and educational progress of the bread-winners, the wage-winners, how immeasurably incomplete will that work be without the exhibit of the thousands of colored women of this country" (Wesley 1984, 27). Brown's lobbying failed, but it strengthened her resolve to form a national organization for black women.

Various regional associations of black women's clubs emerged during the early 1890s and finally united under the umbrella of the NACW in Washington, D.C., in 1896. Mary Church Terrell of the Colored Women's League was elected president of the new organization after receiving the majority of votes from 73 delegates representing 5,000 members from 25 states. Thus did black women create an organizational structure similar to that of the racially exclusive General Federation of Women's Clubs (GFWC), founded in 1892 to coordinate the activities of thousands of white women's clubs.

Relations between the NACW and GFWC were strained from the start. At its 1898 conference, the GFWC declined "fraternal greetings" from the NACW, and at its conference in 1900 it refused to accept Josephine St. Pierre Ruffin as a representative of her New Era Club. Although Ruffin eventually was admitted as a representative from the white New England Federation of Women's Clubs, of which she was also a member, the damage was done (Hine 1990a; Wesley 1984, 39–44). The NACW and GFWC remained independent organizations, largely replicating each others' efforts to provide redemptive places that addressed the needs of the poor.

Nannie Helen Burroughs's name began to appear in records of the National Association of Colored Women's conference proceedings in 1906. She gave antilynching speeches, raised money to save the Frederick Douglass home, served as a regional president, and directed pageants at important NACW events. In 1928 Burroughs attended the dedication of the new NACW headquarters in Washington, D.C. (Wesley 1984). Before Burroughs became active in the NACW, however, she had formed an organization that vigorously promoted the Social Gospel agenda: the Woman's Convention Auxiliary to the National Baptist Convention.

THE WOMAN'S CONVENTION

The Woman's Convention (WC) Auxiliary to the National Baptist Convention emerged in 1900 in response to a speech Nannie Helen Burroughs delivered that was titled "How the Sisters are Hindered from Helping," given at the Baptists' annual conference in Richmond, Virginia. Burroughs, only 21 at the time, proclaimed that black women had been unequal members in the church for too long and that this discrimination had fueled their "righteous discontent" with their status. Burroughs's speech galvanized more than 1 million black women who had been active in church work at the local and state levels— the largest collectivity of black women in America (Higginbotham 1993a, 150). Her speech outlined the impediment to women's equal participation in the church. She proclaimed a "righteous discontent" on the part of black Baptist women and predicted a dynamic role for black women in the years to come (Higginbotham 1993a, 150).

As a leader of the WC, Burroughs also endorsed municipal housekeeping. She reminded women that "as a practical part of our Home Mission work, we urge the women here to give more attention to civic improvement. . . . Clean out the rubbish; whitewash and put things in order. . . . This is the only practical way to show that education and Christianity are counting in the development of the race" (Higginbotham 1993a, 202).

Burroughs was a strong advocate of community reform, endorsing the creation of a Social Service Committee in her 1912 annual report to the Woman's Convention. The 1913 manifesto of the WC listed at the top of "What We Want and What We Must Have": "Well-built, sanitary dwellings . . . and streets that are paved and kept just as clean as others in the town are kept" (Higginbotham 1993, 203, see also 222, 276). The WC agenda clearly had been influenced by the NACW. Delegates to the 1904 NACW conference had resolved that "the women of our association prepare themselves by the study of civil government and kindred subjects for the problems of city, state and national life, that they may be able to perform intelligently the duties that have come to some and will come to others in the natural progress of the woman's suffrage question" (Wesley 1984, 63).

BLURRING THE BOUNDARIES

Black women's church and club work were so intertwined during the late nineteenth century that it is difficult to separate their activities into religious and secular categories. This complexity "precludes attempts to bifurcate black women's activities neatly into dichotomous categories such as religious versus secular, private versus public, or accommodation versus resistence" (Higginbotham 1993a, 17). This lack of boundaries, however, made the NACW and WC more effective than if they had operated independently of each other.

Women's church societies had long been a training ground for leadership and organizational skills; they also had been agents of self-help in the black community, providing schools and social services. Leaders of the NACW acknowledged their debt to the church. In 1900, Chicago author and founding member of the

NACW Fannie Barrier Williams stated that "the training which first enabled colored women to organize and successfully carry on club work was originally obtained in church work. These churches have been and still are the great preparatory schools in which the primary lessons of social order, mutual trustfulness and united effort have been taught"(Higginbotham 1993a, 17).

Strong ties bound the National Association of Colored Women and the Woman's Convention. The NACW held its founding convention at the Nineteenth Street Baptist Church in Washington, D.C., and several leaders of the WC also held offices in the NACW. Members of the NACW and the WC attended each others' annual meetings to report on their respective activities, and delegates to the WC often invoked the NACW's motto, "Lifting as we climb." The NACW, despite its secular constitution, included departments on church clubs, evangelical work, and religious work along with those on domestic science and temperance. One of the clearest examples of collaborative effort came when local branches of NACW clubs contributed money to the National Training School for Women and Girls, which was technically controlled by the WC, but was also supportive of NACW goals of racial uplift (Higginbotham 1993a, 182, 183).

Black women relied on the socially acceptable NACW and WC rather than the more radical Suffrage Movement to press their claims for citizenship. Most black clubwomen, like most white women of the day, supported women's traditional sphere and feared that voting would "unsex" a woman. Black women, though, were in an even more delicate position than white women; some black women believed that if they lobbied for suffrage for themselves, they risked diminishing one of the few sources of power black men had (White 1993). Among NACW members supporting women's suffrage were Josephine St. Pierre Ruffin, Mary Church Terrell, and Hallie Q. Brown (Hine 1990b, 38). Most outspoken of all was Burroughs, who challenged WC members in a 1912 speech to mobilize because "if women cannot vote, they should make it very uncomfortable for the men who have the ballot but do not know its value" (Higginbotham 1993b, 203).

NANNIE HELEN BURROUGHS

Born in rural Virginia in 1879, Nannie Helen Burroughs moved to Washington, D.C., with her mother when she was a child. By the time Burroughs died in 1961, she had founded the Woman's Convention, become an officer in the National Association of Colored Women, established the National Training School for Women and Girls, organized a union for domestics, and been a national speaker for the Republican Party. The stories of these voluntary associations and this remarkable woman add to our knowledge of the roles race and gender played in building the industrializing city.

Burroughs's accomplishments were atypical for a black woman of her day, but then so were her origins. Although she was the granddaughter of slaves, her father attended college and was an itinerant preacher. Her mother moved to Washington, D.C., without her husband to find work for herself and schools for Nannie Helen and her sister (who died in childhood). Nannie Helen Burroughs attended the Colored High School and joined the Nineteenth Street Baptist Church. She developed oratorical skills in school and in church that made her an extremely effective crusader throughout her life (Higginbotham 1993b).

After graduation, Burroughs was denied a position she coveted as assistant to her former domestic science teacher, ostensibly because of her dark skin color and lack of social connections. This disappointment shaped Burroughs's lifelong commitment to creating opportunities for poor black women. Before finding her niche with the National Training School, Burroughs organized a women's industrial club in Louisville that offered evening classes in bookkeeping, sewing, cooking, and typing. She was living in Louisville when she made the trip to the National Baptist Convention and delivered the speech that gave birth to the Woman's Convention (Higginbotham 1993b).

Another organization in which Burroughs became active in the 1920s was the Republican Party. Concerned that blacks were defecting from the party of Abraham Lincoln, Burroughs and other clubwomen formed the National League of Republican Colored Women in 1924. Her high profile in that group earned her a place on the speaker's bureau of the Republican National Committee (Higginbotham 1993b).

Nannie Helen Burroughs spoke to—and for—thousands of black women about the importance of racial and gender equality at the same time Booker T. Washington and W.E.B. DuBois were debating whether black progress depended on vocational education for the masses or on the cosmopolitan example set by the most "Talented Tenth" of the race. Burroughs rejected DuBois's emphasis on the Talented Tenth. She believed that "teachers, preachers, and 'leaders' cannot solve the problems of the race alone. The race needs an army of skilled workers, and the properly educated Negro woman is the most essential factor" (Higginbotham 1993a, 212).

Burroughs had a radical understanding of the conflict of interest between black women workers and white middle-class women. During debates over the Nineteenth Amendment, Burroughs advocated the unionization of domestics because "the women voters will be keen to see that laws are passed that will give eight hours a day . . . to women in other industries, but they will oppose any movement that will, in the end, prevent them from keeping their cooks and house servants in the kitchen twelve or fifteen hours a day" (Higginbotham 1993a, 218). Burroughs proceeded to launch the National Association of Wage Earners in 1920 to improve living and working conditions for domestics; members of the NACW and the WC were on its governing board. The National Association was shortlived, however, and disbanded by 1926 (Higginbotham 1993a, 219).

Nannie Helen Burroughs occupied a pivotal position within the WC, one that helped her make connections to the NACW and allowed her to mobilize both organizations to support her vocational school. Burroughs's greatest achievement was the National Training School for Women and Girls, a redemptive place she created for women who were new to Washington, D.C.—just as her mother had been two decades earlier.

NATIONAL TRAINING SCHOOL FOR WOMEN AND GIRLS

Burroughs opened the National Training School for Women and Girls in 1909 with thirty-one students in a dilapidated, eight-room farmhouse outside Washington, D.C. The curriculum and discipline of the National Training School attempted to professionalize domestic service by offering vocational courses in housekeeping, laundering, household administration, and dining-room management.

The school was located in a community called Lincolnville that had fewer than a dozen houses and no paved streets, water, or electric lights. The purchase price of $6,500 was funded almost entirely by donations from blacks, mainly through the Woman's Convention. Whites were solicited for donations after the first buildings were constructed, but at no point did the school's existence depend on white funding. Students lived, learned, and worked at the school. Burroughs required the girls to fetch coal from the bottom of the hill (where it was dumped by a freight train) and to tend to the garden, pigs, and chickens (Hayes 1997).

Burroughs opened the combination boarding home and vocational school because she recognized that "two-thirds of the colored women must work with their hands for a living, and it is indeed an oversight not to prepare this army of breadwinners to do their work well" (Hine 1990a, 75). The school's motto was "Work. Support thyself. To thine own powers appeal." Equal emphasis was given to good conduct, manners, and dress. Burroughs noted in 1912 that several girls failed to get their diplomas because of untidiness and careless attire (Higginbotham 1993a, 216, 293).

The National Training School, like the NACW and WC, recommended domestic virtue as an avenue of acceptance into white society. It encouraged students to be clean and orderly to combat racial stereotypes that blocked their upward mobility. These organizations adopted Booker T. Washington's "Gospel of the Toothbrush," a docrtine that he subscribed to the lessons in personal cleanliness promoted by his alma mater, Virginia's Hampton Institute (Hoy 1995, 89). Not surprisingly, given the similarity of their educational philosophies, Burroughs was known among her contemporaries as the "female Booker T. Washington" (Higgenbotham 1993a, 211).

One of the reasons the school was located in Washington was the large number of black female migrants there and the opportunities for employment with government officials. Burroughs fought to redefine domestic service as skilled rather than menial labor, urging women to do "ordinary things in an extraordinary way." Burroughs thought that liberal arts education for the majority of blacks was in the distant future, and her pragmatism translated into the homily that "until we realize our ideal, we are going to idealize our real" by insisting that "first-class help must have first-class treatment" (Higginbotham 1993a, 211; Hine 1990a).

A model house at the school was named after benefactor Maggie Lena Walker, the first black woman bank president (of the Penny Savings Bank in Richmond, Virginia). This "practical house" offered instruction in food preparation, cleaning, answering the doorbell and telephone, and other tasks most employers expected. Soon a laundry and several other buildings supplemented the original farmhouse and barn. Students also could take classes in missionary work, nursing, bookkeeping, and nontraditional subjects like printing, barbering, and shoe repair (Higginbotham 1993a, 215; Hine 1990a, 220).

Converting the original farmhouse and barn into a school was typical of the voluntary vernacular style of redemptive places. The school was redemptive in the sense that it occupied a threshold between public and private space. Some parts were reserved for personal activities like sleeping and tending the garden. Other parts were classrooms in which professional behavior was expected. This liminal element was part of the school's strength. It introduced students to the delicate balance between public and private behavior expected of domestic servants. Finally, the school furthered Nannie Helen Burroughs's public reputation at the same time as it prepared its students for urban employment. Burroughs's presidency of the National Training School for its duration was her central identity.

The National Training School closed during the Depression. By then the school had granted the equivalent of high school and community college degrees to more than 2,000 black women from the United States, Africa, and the Caribbean (Higginbotham 1993b). This relatively short lifespan is one characteristic of redemptive places: they emerge to fit the needs of marginal populations in transition, then disappear or evolve into another type of institution as the times demand. The National Training School, for example, re-opened as the National Trades and Professional School for Women in 1934, was closed in 1961 with Burroughs's death, and re-emerged in 1964 as the Nannie Helen Burroughs School, a private Christian elementary school for black students (Hayes 1997).

These two nationwide voluntary associations of black women cosponsored a vocational school in Washington, D.C., that taught poor black women skills for urban life, provided them with a temporary home, and promoted the public career of its founder, Nannie Helen Burroughs. Burroughs was a lifetime member of both the National Association of Colored Women and the Woman's Convention of the National Baptist Convention, organizations based on the Social Gospel and municipal housekeeping. Together the organizations created redemptive places for blacks comparable to those created for whites by female volunteers in the YWCA, the Salvation Army, and the College Settlements Association.

As the black population became increasingly urbanized, black women's organizations relied more on municipal housekeeping and less on the Social Gospel as the enabling ideology for their good works, just like white women's organizations. The NACW continued to collaborate with the WC to achieve their common goals for "uplift of the race," blurring the boundaries between secular and religious work among black female volunteers well into the twentieth century.

Burroughs was a remarkable woman. She set an example for the legions of typical volunteers who constituted the rank and file of the NACW and WC. Like many of them, she was urban middle class, one step removed from rural roots. Her religious faith, commitment to racial uplift, and dedication to women's equality took material form in the National Training School for Women and Girls. Nannie Helen Burroughs's name stands for the thousands of anonymous volunteers who have improved the lives of others as they have created public roles for themselves. Burroughs established the National Training School, but she could not have sustained it without support from the NACW and WC.

The National Training School for Women and Girls was a redemptive place because of its religious origins and its dual ability to save both poor and middle-class women from the prescribed roles of their day. Members of the National Association of Colored Women and the Woman's Convention had a vision of a better urban life for blacks, a vision they implemented by minimizing boundaries between the two organizations. Black women's voluntary work at the liminal edge between the public and private sectors helped shape a more humanitarian city for immigrants. Their story is a reminder that middle-class black women, lifting as they climbed, built bridges to the city for succeeding generations of their sisters.

REFERENCES

Bender, Thomas. 1975. *Toward an Urban Vision: Ideas and Institutions in Ninetenth Century America.* Lexington: University of Kentucky Press.

Davis, Elizabeth Lindsay. 1934. *Lifting as They Climb: The National Association of Colored Women.* Ann Arbor, Mich.: University Microfilms International.

Farley, Reynolds, and Walter Allen. 1987. *The Color Line and the Quality of Life in America.* New York: Russell Sage Foundation.

Hayes, Shirley G. 1997. President of Nannie Helen Burroughs School, Inc. Personal interview, August 19.

Higginbotham, Evelyn B. 1993a. *Righteous Discontent: The Women's Movement in the Black Baptist Church 1880–1920.* Cambridge: Harvard University Press.

———. 1993b. "Nannie Helen Burroughs." In *Black Women in America: An Historical Encyclopedia,* edited by Darlene Clark Hine. Brooklyn, N.Y.: Carlson Publishing.

Hine, Darlene Clark. 1990a. "We Specialize in the Wholly Impossible: The Philanthropic Work of Black Women." In *Lady Bountiful Revisited: Women, Philanthropy, and*

Power, edited by Kathleen D. McCarthy. New Brunswick, N.J.: Rutgers University Press.

————. 1990b. "National Movements and Issues: Women, Race, and the National Association of Colored Women, 1890–1910." In *Black Women in United States History,* edited by Darlene Clark Hine. Brooklyn, N.Y.: Carlson Publishing.

Hofstadter, Richard. 1955. *The Age of Reform: From Bryan to FDR.* New York: Alfred A. Knopf.

Hopkins, Charles H. 1967. *The Rise of the Social Gospel in American Protestantism, 1865–1915.* New Haven: Yale University Press.

Hoy, Suellen M. 1995. *Chasing Dirt: The American Pursuit of Cleanliness.* New York: Oxford University Press.

Lerner, Gerda. 1974. "Early Community Work of Black Club Women." *Journal of Negro History* 59: 158–167.

Luker, Ralph E. 1991. *The Social Gospel in Black and White: American Racial Reform, 1885–1912.* Chapel Hill: University of North Carolina Press.

Scott, Anne Firor. 1990. "Most Invisible of All: Black Women's Voluntary Associations." *Journal of Southern History* 56: 3–22.

————. 1991. *Natural Allies: Women's Associations in American History.* Urbana and Chicago: University of Illinois Press.

Shaw, Stephanie S. 1991. "Black Club Women and the Creation of the National Association of Colored Women." *Journal of Women's History* 3: 10–25.

Skocpol, Theda. 1992. *Protecting Soldiers and Mothers.* Cambridge, MA: Harvard University Press.

Spain, Daphne. Forthcoming. *How Women Saved the City.* Minneapolis: University of Minnesota Press.

Turner, Victor. 1971. "Variations on a Theme of Liminality." In *Secular Ritual Cities and Immigrants: A Geography of Change in Nineteenth Century America,* edited by Sally F. Moore and Barbara G. Myerhoff. Amsterdam: Van Gorcum, Assen.

Ward, David. 1971. *Cities and Immigrants: A Geography of Change in Nineteenth Century America.* New York: Oxford University Press.

Weimann, Jeanne Madeline. 1981. *The Fair Women: The Story of the Woman's Building, World's Columbian Exposition, Chicago 1893.* Chicago: Academy.

Wesley, Charles H. 1984. *The History of the National Association of Colored Women's Clubs: A Legacy of Service.* Washington, D.C.: National Association of Colored Women's Clubs.

White, Deborah Gray. 1993. "The Cost of Club Work, the Price of Black Feminism." In *Visible Women: New Essays on American Activism,* edited by Nancy A. Hewitt and Suzanne Lebsock. Urbana and Chicago: University of Illinois Press.

Woods, Robert A., and Albert J. Kennedy, eds. 1911 (1970). *Handbook of Settlements.* New York: Arno Press.

Chapter 6

Women "Embounded": Intersections of Welfare Reform and Public Housing Policy

Kristine B. Miranne

Since the passage of the Personal Responsibility and Work Opportunity Reconciliation Act (PRWORA) in August 1996, the implementation of its various tenets has become a high priority for individual states charged with responding to this federal mandate.[1] Concurrently, and with much less fanfare, there has been a system of parallel reforms addressing the assisted housing needs of the same population impacted by this welfare legislation, primarily poor, single, female heads of household and their children. It has been argued that changes in welfare provision may negatively impact the housing stability of current welfare recipients and their families (Nichols and Gault 1999; Sard and Daskal 1998). Philosophically, this is problematic, as the ability to obtain adequate shelter, like the need for food, clothing, and medical care, should be at the center of welfare programs (Mulroy 1995).

The U.S. welfare state is often described as a myriad of social insurance and assistance programs directed toward providing income protection to victims of unemployment, disability, industrial accident, retirement, death of the family breadwinner, or extreme poverty. Housing assistance, in the form of subsidized rent (and utilities), is also an integral part of social service provision. From a practical standpoint, federal expenditures on general welfare programs-Temporary Assistance to Needy Families (TANF) and Supplemental Security Income (SSI)—are essentially the same as those for the U.S. Department of Housing and Urban Development (HUD) on shelter assistance for the poor (Newman and Schnare 1990). The fact that welfare programs embody a significant shelter component is one that has been ignored during the development and implementation of both housing and welfare policy reforms. Beneficiaries of the new welfare legislation may be presented with new opportunities as policies and programs are revised, but more likely they will face new challenges in their ability to care for themselves and their families.

Although the provisions of welfare and public housing services are administered by separate federal, state, and local agencies, both sets of reforms intersect in many ways.[2] Poor women and their families stand at these intersections, and in doing so occupy "in-between-spaces" (see De Lauretis 1987). The research question herein looks to these intersections as a way to reveal how poor women are "embounded." Embounded refers to how women are isolated when the state revamps policies while also withdrawing resources. The situation becomes even more complex for women who are both residents of public housing and recipients of welfare assistance. These women find their physical and social places to be contested, fluid, and uncertain. Their enclaves are further defined by sociospatial relations and practices of power and exclusion that result in constituted and multiple boundaries (McDowell 1999). As members of two distinct yet overlapping categories, women find themselves burdened with an identity tied to a specific locale; one which is laden with negative connotations. Yet even when faced with draconian changes in social service provision systems, women do cross, resist, maintain, and reconfigure the physical and socially constructed boundaries they encounter.

RESTRUCTURING OF SOCIAL POLICY

State change has occurred primarily by way of three strategies: devolution, privatization and dismantling (Kodras 1997). Devolution, a transformation internal to the state that alters the scale of government responsibilities, is at the center of virtually all U.S. social policy reforms. Defined as the transfer or decentralization of government functions from higher to lower levels of the federal hierarchy, "devolution redefines government responsibilities for regulating civil society, transfers authority across levels and administrative units of government, redraws the map of government costs and benefits, and changes accessibility and entitlement to government services" (Kodras 1997, 81). The federal government retains the authority to set the direction of how social policy will be developed, but at the same time government reserves the right to require that individual states develop their own set of social policies and programs within the scope of federal mandate. Devolution of the welfare state is also inherently a spatial process of change, as the uneven development of different local states generates various responses to devolution based on local needs, perceptions, and abilities. For example, access to housing assistance is uneven: in Massachusetts, 51 percent of welfare recipients reside in public or assisted housing as compared to 32 percent in Indiana (Nichols and Gault 1999, 8).

In turn, privatization refers to the transfer of governmental functions to commercial firms and nonprofit organizations. Specific to welfare reform, policymakers have encouraged the process of privatization by providing mechanisms within the language of the bill that facilitate participation by private and nonprofit concerns. There is a precedent for the substitution of components of the public sector by private operations. For example, the federal government established quasigovernmental corporations (such as the U.S. Postal Service and Amtrak). Private contractors have been used to construct the interstate highway system and other pieces of the public infrastructure. Subsidies and the use of vouchers (such as food stamps and Section 8 rent vouchers) are spent in the commercial sector (Kodras 1997). Privatization is also a spatial process mirrored in the fragmented nature of the nonprofit sector. As the federal government withdraws funding from many social services and privatizes previous governmental responsibilities, a spatial mismatch is created between communities rich in resources and those with critical needs.[3]

Finally, dismantling the welfare state refers to the withdrawal of government functions either through elimination of programs altogether or by reducing funding such that programs are no longer able to accomplish their goals (usually occurs when a governmental function is no longer considered to be appropriate). Meghan Cope (1997) has argued that the result of these processes can be found rhetorically in that states have more "flexibility" as to how they will develop and implement social policies and programs; "the people" will have more direct control over how the poor are managed; and individuals will have to "take responsibility" for their own welfare and that of their children (184). Thus, we see the development of a public discourse that focuses on the assumption that smaller government is more efficient and the presumption that sanctions will encourage individual responsibility.[4] In this way, social policy programs are constructed by denial as much as by a willingness to provide.

What is missing from this discussion, however, is the gendered nature of the welfare state. The character of the welfare state affects women's material situations, shapes gender relations, structures political conflict and participation, and contributes to the mobilization of specific interests and identities (Orloff 1996). Even though many Americans think of women (single mothers) when they think of "welfare," many scholars and policymakers describe these assistance programs as ungendered or examine them as if the gender of those involved is unimportant. Even when the situation of women within the welfare system is noted, gender is not considered to be an organizing principle (Gordon 1990). The very nature of social policies exhibits a double standard of welfare provision for men—social insurance, which is more generous and popular—and for women—public assistance, which stigmatizes and is less generous (see Abramovitz 1992; Gordon 1994; Skocpol 1992).

At the center of these policies is a dominant capitalist-patriarchal ideology based upon the premise that the male position is one of financial primacy and that women and children should depend on the wage labor of a male breadwinner.

There is, however, little recognition of women's increasing presence in the labor market, their inability to access male wages, or their lower income due to higher divorce rates and low child-support payments. There is also no recognition that women are often out of the job market for periods of time because of childbirth, child care, elder care, or other family needs—responsibilities that society expects women to assume. Thus, blaming women for being poor (for example, not having a husband to support them and their children) or characterizing their status as being dependent is only a description of their financial circumstances, not an explanation for their poverty (Spalter-Roth and Hartmann 1993). Yet if women do not have access to male resources that contribute to the cost of child care and also augment low wages, they become increasingly dependent on the state to provide these supplements.

Although sexism is a system of domination, it has never been the sole determinant in the discrimination and oppression that women face. Race, ethnicity, class, and sexual preference contribute to the matrix of domination that women experience and resist—domination that exists on three levels: personal biography; the group level of cultural context created by race, class, gender, ethnicity and sexuality; and at the systematic level of social institutions (Collins 1991, 364). Recognizing the interlocking nature of these identities leads not only to an investigation of the dynamics of these identities but also to an examination of the connections between them (see Miranne and Young in this volume). Investigating the "social construction of race" reveals the complexities of economic, political, and social processes that have produced different options and alternatives for low-income African American, Hispanic, and white women in relation to occupations, sources of income, household structures, and local social networks (Smith and Feagin 1995). Using this concept pulls us away from an essentialist argument that divides individuals into discrete "races" according to physical characteristics that are then associated with certain types of behavior (Peake 1997, 336). This framework is particularly useful when examining the restructuring of welfare reform and public housing policy. In particular, an analysis of the relations between women and the state that places gender and race at the center will reveal the structure and agency within these two public policies.

Restructuring of Welfare Reform

> Just stop for a moment sometime today and think about how much of your daily life is organized around work, how much of your family life, how much of your social life, not to mention your work life. Think about the extent to which you are defined by the friends you have at work, by the sense that you do a good job, by the regularity of the paycheck. (President William Clinton as cited in Backer 1995, 379)

The solidarity of the 104th Congress in passing PRWORA reflects the fear of many Americans that welfare has become the way of life for too many individuals. The welfare system, however, has its own characteristic way of interpreting women's needs as evidenced by the ongoing debate about how welfare should be transplanted with work (see Mead 1992; Murray 1984). Linking personal responsibility with work indicates that policymakers believe it only takes proper guidance and minimal training for welfare recipients to become self-sufficient (or to be no longer dependent on welfare assistance). The above statement by the president reflects an ideology of work that is not part of the world of poor single mothers and their families; women do not organize their lives simply around paid employment; it is but one component of their complex world. For women are economically disadvantaged in the labor market and have a disproportionate responsibility for reproductive labor and caretaking—responsibilities that traditionally make up women's work (Sidel 1986; Tickamyer 1995–1996). Mandating that women place paid work at the center of their existence, with no discussion of the varied aspects of their lives, forces women to redefine the boundaries and intersections of work, family responsibilities, and their relationship with the state.

In the end, the PRWORA philosophy sees placing welfare recipients in a job— not necessarily a good job, or a satisfying job, or one on the first rung of the career ladder but rather, any job—as a solution to women's dependency on the state. There is no emphasis on training or education, except during brief transitional periods (although some states, including Maine and Virginia, are reconsidering this issue and now include higher education as part of their welfare package). Other states are funneling women into temporary (trial) low-wage jobs, with no benefits, which are expected to terminate in a few months. If recipients are unable to find permanent employment at the end of this transitional phase, they are labeled as failures. The time limits on welfare assistance remain in place, whether a woman has been terminated from work or not (Miranne and Young 1998).[5] In addition, there is no indication of where these jobs are to be found. For example, Wisconsin plans to move 53,700 TANF recipients into the labor market, while an additional 2,000 new enrollees will be seeking work each month for the foreseeable future (Miranne and Young 1998). Even if a comprehensive job-creation program is put in place, it is unlikely that recipients will be able to meet the time-limit requirements to find a job before benefits are ended.

When women do enter the job market, there is little evidence that they will find jobs that will allow them to support themselves and their families. The types of jobs that unskilled and semiskilled women are able to secure in the private marketplace not only fail to meet their basic needs, but they often do not produce the necessary human capital (educational and occupational skill levels) nor the social capital (contacts) needed to obtain better employment. Low-wage jobs often require working at odd hours, do not guarantee a reliable number of hours of work per week, and are subject to frequent layoffs (Edin 1995). Research on single mothers' work histories reveals that many can recount varied experiences in moving from one low-wage job to the other—seeking better wages, more hours, better benefits, more convenient transportation, better circumstances for child care—yet rarely, if ever, improving their earning level in the long term (Edin 1995; Miranne and Young 1998; see Gilbert in this volume). Underlying the discussions of workfare is a preoccupation with individual responsibility as seen by the use of the phrase "dependency to self-sufficiency" within the welfare legislation itself. Interestingly, policymakers provide no definition of self-sufficiency but note that it is obtained through work, that it includes independence from welfare, and that it strengthens families. Rephrased, a poor woman is or is not economically sufficient, she either has or has not the sufficient earned income, and she either is or is not receiving public assistance (Miranne and Young 1998). Yet an analysis of poverty that begins and ends with family structure and marital status does not address the issue that an overwhelming number of poor single mothers who are now in poverty were poor before they became mothers (Amott 1990). Policies that emphasize the strengthening of family life and increasing self-sufficiency clearly reflect misgivings about social reproduction among the poor—families headed by women are weak and disorganized, if not dysfunctional (see Ritzdorf in this volume). Women find themselves caught "in a triple bind: criticized for lack of labor market activity; criticized if work interferes with reproductive work; and criticized for accessing state aid when any of these other activities break down" (Tickamyer 1995–1996, 11).

Although it may be too early to pronounce the success or failure of the recent welfare reform strategies of devolution, privatization, and dismantling, it is apparent that these shifts in policy development and implementation have ignored the complexities of the spatiality of women's poverty and welfare policy. Policy debates tend to occur far from the economic, political, and geosocial spaces occupied by welfare recipients and their families and for the most part have been aspatial in that they ignore the implications of spatial variation. The refusal to recognize these implications can be seen in the geographic disparities of programs and benefits. For example, women residing in the deep south have historically received less benefits than women in other states. Part of this is due to the lower resources of state governments in this region, but these states have also been aggressive in rapidly withdrawing resources under the auspices of the newest welfare reform. This circumstance is heightened by the tensions and contradictions played out between the public functions of welfare and the private lives of women. Poor women at the margins of welfare policies, women who are the primary beneficiaries of social programs, are enmeshed in a gendered and racialized spatiality not of their own choosing. What remains to be seen is how they will be able to negotiate their way around and through the "emboundedness" that occurs as a result of devolution, privatization, and the dismantling of the welfare system.

Restructuring Public Housing Policy

The U.S. Department of Housing and Urban Development sponsors three housing-assistance programs: public housing, tenant-based Section 8 rental assistance, and project-based Section 8 assistance. Public housing developments are owned and operated by local public housing agencies (LHAs) and typically consist of multiple buildings inhabited by individuals who are eligible for the program (income being the primary criterion).[6] The tenant-based Section 8 program provides recipients with vouchers that can be used in the private rental market. HUD's project-based vouchers allow eligible families to live in rental units in the private market that have been subsidized by HUD. These buildings are owned by private and nonprofit organizations contracted by HUD to provide housing (Nichols and Gault 1999, 3). In 1996, approximately 2.1 million families with children received housing assistance. About 83 percent of these families received some income from AFDC/TANF in 1996. In addition, 26 percent lived in traditional public housing, 49 percent received tenant-based vouchers and certificates, and 25 percent lived in project-based Section 8 housing (Sard and Daskal 1998, 110).

Public housing has had a controversial history, beginning with the enabling Wagner-Steagall Act of 1937. Originally intended to clear slums, alleviate unemployment caused by the Depression, and provide housing for low-income renters, the program was a federal mandate directed toward assisting poor families despite opposition from business and real estate interests (Spain 1995, 357). In the beginning, eligibility criteria clearly favored married couples: "The immediate purpose of public housing is to raise the living standards of typical *employed* families of very low income, who are independent and self-supporting. . . . Public housing is designed to improve the condition of millions of working families who have reasonably steady jobs and reasonably steady but inadequate earnings" (Spain 1995, 363; emphasis in the original).

With the Housing Act of 1949, however, LHAs faced a situation that combined massive slum clearance with expanded funding for public housing construction. In turn, construction was now tied to eligibility criteria that selected only those with the lowest incomes who had also been displaced by government action (Hartman 1963). By 1955, the National Association of Housing and Development Officials (NAHDO) stated that problem families (those lacking monogamous values and leading "unregulated lives"; hence female-headed) had replaced traditional families in public housing. By the 1960s, HUD was banned from excluding any applicant due to "moral character." Income from tenants, paid to LHAs, was substantially reduced with the passage of the Brooke Amendments of 1969 and 1971, which limited rent to no more than 25 percent of a family's income. Housing legislation during the 1970s and 1980s, however, was geared toward bringing an income mix back to public housing developments by actually discouraging low-income families from applying; at the same time, it brought public housing construction to a virtual halt (Spain 1995, 363–364).

When the Housing and Community Development Act of 1987 gave preference for public housing to those on waiting lists who had substandard (or no) housing and/or to those paying 50 percent or more of their income for rent, it became apparent that it would be even more difficult for LHAs to create mixed-income developments—a goal that HUD and LHAs have harbored for the past few decades. Nationwide, 7 out of 10 families with extremely low incomes and without housing subsidies spend more than half of their income on rent, indicating a great need for affordable housing. The pool of applicants for public housing—in spite of the physical isolation, condition of the units, or concern for the social structure of the public housing developments—reflects the demand for housing assistance. Yet, in 1996, only 29 percent of welfare recipient families received housing assistance, and many of those had been on the waiting lists for years (Nichols and Gault 1999, 6–7).

The convergence of race, class, and gender has resulted in patterns of residential segregation for economically marginal populations residing in public housing developments. Today, there is no place within contemporary America, with the possible exception of prisons and certain types of hospitals, that stigmatizes individuals in as many debilitating ways as does public housing (Vale 1996). The transition over the years of public housing populations can be attributed to a combination of direct government policies (eligibility criteria, site decisions, and welfare regulations) and default government policies (lack of child support enforcement, women's limited access to military benefits, and lack of a national family policy) (see Spain 1995 for a comprehensive discussion outlining how public housing sites have become gendered spaces due in no small part to these policies.)

In 1995, HUD released the *Reinvention Blueprint*, a sweeping set of initiatives aimed at ameliorating distressed public housing. Designed to help residents living in severe distress as well as to improve the actual physical conditions of the sites, buildings, and units of the developments, these reforms encompass a wide range of both social and physical characteristics. Arguing that the purpose of public housing is to provide homes and a safe living environment while promoting self-sufficiency, HUD is also undergoing a system of devolution, privatization, and dismantling. The agency has consolidated its former 60 programs into three major funding streams. The agency's block grants will become more general as specific grant-in-aid programs and federal initiatives are absorbed. More responsibility is being shifted to LHAs, which are encouraged to submit plans for the renovation and redevelopment of their local public housing sites (Bratt and Keyes 1998). Partnerships with private and nonprofit investors are sought for the construction of owner-occupied houses and rental units that will most likely be offered to working-class families before welfare recipients.

Public housing reform, like welfare reform, is driven by a dissatisfaction with policies seen to create long-term dependency:

Low- and moderate-income families should have greater power to make decisions about their lives, and government should support their quest for self-sufficiency. Public and assisted housing rules that have locked families into substandard housing have impeded their ability to move to self-sufficiency. . . . [Thus, one of HUD's key goals is to make] affordable housing serve as a starting point for families working toward stability and self-sufficiency by emphasizing work, education and security. (Bratt and Keyes 1998, 296; emphasis in the original)

HUD has thus "raised the bar" for the residents of public housing developments and users of its voucher programs by emphasizing self-sufficiency—a concept closely entwined with welfare reform for those individuals who are recipients of both systems of service provision.

As part of its efforts to reinvent itself, HUD appears to be articulating three basic public housing goals: (1) local housing authorities are to increase the mix of incomes in public housing to attract and retain a larger working population; (2) opportunities are to be made available for higher income public housing residents who wish to become homeowners; and (3) public housing must still serve the nation's neediest households. Under the federal umbrella of devolution, local public housing authorities are being encouraged to undertake urban revitalization efforts that allow for maximum flexibility as they determine the initiatives most likely to be successful within their own communities. Issues to be addressed include high density, crime, poor structural design, and oppressive social and economic conditions. Other than the costs of renovation and construction, housing officials are also required to find funds that can be used for a variety of services and resident programs. Partnerships are to be built that include state and local governments, neighborhood organizations, businesses, nonprofit corporations, social service agencies, and public housing residents. Thus, public housing authorities are to become developers of affordable housing, rid their communities of less viable housing, and rebuild their public housing developments to include opportunities for homeownership, rental housing, and even commercial use. In this manner, public housing developments will become part of the solution for community (re)development of cities as opposed to being one of the problems.

Although all of these strategies are laudable in their own right, there is an inherent conflict; with the exception of the Federal Housing Administration (FHA) and the Veteran's Administration (VA) programs, federal housing programs are essentially women's programs. More than 80 percent of nonelderly public housing residents live below the poverty line. Female-headed households now constitute 85 percent of the families with dependent children in public housing, but in some cities this number exceeds 95 percent. It has been estimated that nationwide, there is no full-time wage earner in 76 percent of all public housing households (National Commission 1992). In fact, public housing's rates of unemployment-per-acre are probably higher than for any other kind of community in the United States (Vale 1996).

The extent to which women of diverse racial backgrounds are unable to find adequate private shelter, and therefore depend on public housing, is a bitter comment on the prevalence of women's poverty—women are segregated in public housing because they are too poor to live anywhere else. The developments they reside in are often sited within areas of concentrated poverty that are also spatially (and socially) segregated from the rest of the community (Massey and Denton 1993). Yet it is the permanence of public housing as a community resource for the poor, in addition to the stability of local public housing authorities, that is one of its most salient attributes (Bauman 1994). The changes made to the physical layout of public housing developments, in conjunction with new eligibility criteria, signal the end of this important state resource for a large number of women and their families.

Similar to welfare reform, public housing reform has failed to recognize the spatial variation that exists within and among public housing developments. The rhetoric of both sets of reforms is often directed in a pejorative fashion, with little regard for varying contexts (Tickamyer 1995–1996, 16). Residents of public housing *are* set apart from what is considered to be the mainstream. These boundaries are not trivial. Poor women and their families have been bounded by the geographical constructs of their neighborhoods, by the larger community, and by social service providers (welfare workers, food stamp employees, and personnel in health clinics) that cater to a specific clientele who are marked by their use of such services. Spatial pressures include crowding, segregation, high crime rates, deterioration of public services and infrastructure, an overabundance of low-wage labor, and the mismatch in urban areas between the location of housing and employment opportunities. Even as the state and private interests have worked to isolate public housing residents, women's use of space, and identity with place, will determine how they negotiate boundaries put in place by changes in public housing policies.

THE INTERSECTIONS OF WELFARE REFORM AND PUBLIC HOUSING POLICY

Welfare reform and public housing reform are interconnected in several ways. First, housing legislation now provides subsidies for individuals moving from welfare to work to help them pay their housing costs. The majority of families currently receiving housing assistance pay 30 percent of their incomes for housing. If a family's income changes because of a recalculation in welfare benefits or increased earnings from work, their rent is adjusted accordingly. The Quality Housing and Work Responsibility Act of 1998 (QHWRA), however, allows local housing authorities to disregard increases in welfare recipient earnings for at least 12 months, thus allowing families to keep more of their earned income (Nichols and Gault 1999). By the same token, families who have their income reduced due to welfare sanctions, primarily because of violations of economic self-sufficiency requirements, will not be able to have their rents reduced. If these families, predominantly single, female-headed households, are not able to replace their lost income, they are at risk of losing their housing through nonpayment of rent (public housing managers do evict tenants for failure to meet their rent obligations, even if the families are without income).

Second, new HUD regulations are actually contributing to housing shortages experienced by poor women and their families. QHWRA allows housing authorities to grant housing assistance to families with incomes greater than 30 percent of the area median income. Section 8 vouchers and other forms of housing assistance that might have gone to welfare recipients may be given to others with higher income levels. Although HUD has included 50,000 new housing vouchers for families who receive welfare assistance, the availability of housing assistance for welfare recipients will continue to fall short of the need (Nichols and Gault 1999).

HUD is also facing an enormous cost, $20 billion, associated with the renewal of Section 8 project-based and tenant-assistance subsidies. Between 1975 and 1983, almost 1 million units of housing were built under the Section 8 program. Private developers were given 20-year contracts that committed HUD to pay the difference between a community's fair market rent and 30 percent of household income. Many of these contracts are due for renewal, and so housing stock previously reserved for low-income families will soon be eligible to be put back on the private market (an estimated 300,000 units nationwide) at rents that will not be affordable for many families living at or below the poverty level unless HUD commits the funds to renew the certificates (Bratt and Keyes 1998).

In the midst of this campaign of privatization and dismantling, aging stock is being demolished and is not being replaced. Approximately 10 percent of the public housing stock, 100,000 units, is currently slated for demolition, often without a unit-for-unit replacement. A case in point is Lexington, Kentucky. The local public housing authority plans to demolish 356 units within the Charlotte Court housing complex. By the year 2000, this site will contain 92 single-family, owner-occupied homes. The demolition and rebuilding (which includes building 198 more single-family homes throughout the city) has a price tag of approximately $30 million, including $19.2 million under the 1993 Urban Revitalization Demonstration Act, known as HOPE VI. It is unlikely that many of the current residents of Charlotte Court will be able to buy homes within the renovated areas; a minimum of $12,500 annual income is required and the average income among current residents is $5,100.[7]

Although displaced residents will be provided with vouchers, they will be of no use if women are unable to locate affordable housing on the private market (Ranghelli 1998). Again, the demolition of Charlotte Court in Lexington, Kentucky, reflects the problems of locating affordable housing. Although there is no limit on the number of units available citywide, there is a cap on the size of Section 8 subsidies based on the number of bedrooms and the neighborhood. Rents less than $500 are not very plentiful. A Charlotte Court resident echoed this sentiment when she recounted having a Section 8 certificate in 1997 but losing it because she could not find a suitable, affordable place in the two-month allotment of time she had to look for a new apartment (Mulvihill 1999).

Vouchers are awarded through a competitive grant process, thus adding to the spatial mismatch between recipients and available housing. The more aggressive and better organized of the LHAs can provide expanded housing assistance, but in other areas, welfare recipients bear the brunt of poor management that is out of their control.

Third, the devolution of welfare reform has created separate sets of rules and regulations, depending on the state of origin. For example, several states (Connecticut, Florida, Rhode Island, and Maryland) count housing subsidies as income when determining eligibility for welfare benefits—the average loss in monthly benefits is $65, which is determined by the type of housing assistance received. State housing agencies, as well as HUD, lose income when families with housing assistance lose benefits since these families contribute a lesser amount in rent than they did prior to the loss in benefits. Proposed legislation in Minnesota that reduces TANF benefits by $100 for families who receive housing assistance will result in an estimated loss of $30 to the housing authorities and a 3 percent increase in their annual budget to cover lost revenues (Nichols and Gault 1999, 3). In another move to secure tenant income, some LHAs are taking steps to attract higher income applicants by supporting the repeal of federal preferences and the ban against "skipping" over applicants with lower incomes. These housing managers are seeking the authority to deny apartments to applicants with annual incomes lower than $10,000 until 60 percent of their residents have incomes above that level. A conservative estimate states that this process will take five years (Castro 1997, 53). The same women who may be turned away from public housing during this time period will be facing the ticking of the five-year welfare clock.

Fourth, many welfare recipients have experienced serious problems with housing stability prior to the passage of the welfare reform legislation. For those women currently seeking to move from "welfare dependency" to "self-sufficiency," securing safe and affordable housing is an important step to accomplishing this goal. The loss of welfare benefits and low wages, however, coupled with a lack of housing assistance and the paucity of affordable housing, dramatically increases the propensity of individuals to move. The degree to which poor women are forced to move depends on several factors, all related to spatiality: available housing, economic conditions, social networks, and so on. For example, a Connecticut study found that almost 50 percent of welfare recipients studied had moved at least twice in the two years prior to the survey (Bloom, Andes, and Nicholson 1998). Often, women and their children find themselves "doubling up" with family or friends until they can acquire enough assets or the income to facilitate another move. Although moving in with others can be considered a coping mechanism, such arrangements are often temporary and lead to overcrowding.

Even when women do secure monies for their own housing, they face gender and racial discrimination within the general public housing arena. We continue to see a federal system of housing that channels households with children into different housing programs, which in turn contributes to the spatiality of women's poverty by denying them the opportunity to choose their own housing and neighborhoods (see Cook, Bruin, and Crull in this volume). Families applying for assistance directly to public housing authorities are sorted into groups, with the more disadvantaged ending up in traditional public housing units. Those families with higher incomes, lower welfare dependency rates, fewest children, and smaller concentrations of female heads are likely to be offered privately owned (but federally subsidized housing).[8] African American and Hispanic women-headed households are also at a disadvantage when they turn to the private market for housing. Many rental and sales housing agents discourage these women and their families from locating in certain areas within cities. For these households, this racial intolerance is intensified by discrimination based on the presence of children.

Lastly, women find themselves "embounded" through their inability to access state resources such as welfare benefits and housing assistance due to the restructuring of social service provision systems. The institutional relationships created by categories of gender and race organize the power relations between women and the state as manifested in the welfare system. Women, however, are not passive agents—they recognize the dynamic and volatile nature of these intersections. Therefore, the challenge for women is how to move within the margins, between categories, and how to build connections throughout their communities. Social networks are a critical strategy utilized by women moving between the welfare and public housing systems. In fact, the very existence of these networks is a tribute to women's ability to create opportunities (see Stack 1974; Gilbert in this volume). Networks among women are "a consciousness of kin, an imagery boundary which sets women off in a separate group; and the means by which capacity is built" (Austin 1981, 255). At the same time, poor women are bound to other women who also have reduced resources within otherwise limited locales. Distances caused by isolation of community and the stigma of receiving state benefits may enhance physical and social isolation. Therefore, the challenge will be for women to transcend the intersections among the multiple boundaries of social policies as they work to create new opportunities for themselves and their families.

CONCLUSION

This chapter has revealed how federal devolution, privatization, and dismantling is concurrently transforming welfare policy and public housing policy. Poor women and their families are the ones who will most likely feel the impact of these changes, as they often access welfare and housing assistance concurrently. Thus, a majority of the residents of public housing communities face welfare reform measures which will most likely "outpace the health-care reforms, job-training initiatives, and child-care provisions that are needed to make employment an achievable and economically viable alternative for those who rely on income from welfare programs" (Vale 1997, 159). In the long run, these changes in the provision of welfare will inevitably create an even greater demand for housing assistance. At their current level, welfare grants do not enable women and their children to secure safe and affordable housing on the private market. Cuts in the level of welfare payments will increase the numbers of individuals needing housing assistance as well as the amount of housing assistance each family will need (Castro 1997).

Although there is fault with a welfare reform ideology that focuses on the individual as the root cause of poverty and dependency, the current policy arena is not likely to shift its emphasis in the near future. When welfare rolls do not decrease as quickly as policymakers and administrators anticipate, when women slip in and out of work, or when women are not able to be gainfully employed at the end of the imposed time limits, welfare recipients themselves are likely to be blamed for their inability to move from welfare to work (Miranne and Young 1998). Residents of public housing developments will still be blamed for the conditions that exist within these spaces (crime, teen pregnancies, poverty)—an assumption that directly links all public housing residents to society's ills.

As women interact with these systems of social provision, they begin to see how social organization and language reinforce each other within their experienced space. The rhetoric of state policies creates isolation from resources through federal devolution, thus "embounding" women. Women, in turn, create shelters from immediate dangers while they work to create new social and physical spaces. It is important to note, however, that women may share the same space but not the same experiences. The multiplicities of their lives, as determined by race, ethnicity, gender and class, require that we realize the unique nature of these relations.

Finally, there are important questions that must be asked: How do poor women envision an equitable welfare and public housing system? How will they be active agents from the margins of two systems of social service provision that currently are so important to their survival? How can poor women create new spaces, new boundaries, new intersections that allow them to maximize opportunities? And, how do we frame policy reforms within the concept of emboundedness; one which reveals the multifaceted nature of poor women's lives from their perspective? Only by framing our inquiries in this way will we begin to understand fully how women negotiate the boundaries of their lives.

NOTES

1. The federal guarantee of support is no longer in place, since Aid to Families with Dependent Children (AFDC) has been replaced with a state block-grant system. The lan-

guage of PRWORA is reflective of the assumption that work and the receipt of welfare are mutually exclusive, as the legislation limits the time period for eligibility; denies benefits to children born while their mothers are receiving welfare benefits; and demands that women with young children enter the workforce, regardless of what types of jobs are available (Miranne 1998).

2. HUD administers more than 60 separate housing programs; before welfare reform, different federal agencies administered more than 80 welfare programs (Bratt and Keyes 1998, 797).

3. Katherine Amato-Von Hemert and I are conducting an investigation of antipoverty strategies employed by urban and rural churches in response to welfare reform and the poverty within their communities (churches in rural Colorado, Georgia, and Kentucky and in Los Angeles). Preliminary results indicate that access to resources, availability of time, number of staff and volunteers, and anticipated results of their efforts vary greatly by locale.

4. In 1995, I conducted several focus groups comprised of women who were also welfare recipients. Although they were responding to questions about a pilot program preceding PRWORA, they were quite aware that their activities were being heavily monitored and that sanctions would be the "carrot and the stick." As stated by one respondent: "It's easier to get cut off than get the benefits in the first place. . . . [They] sanction you for this . . . sanction you for that . . . that's the word they use . . . they cut you off. It [welfare] has some benefits but it's more fearful" (Miranne 1998).

5. This time frame is critical because recipients can only rely on public assistance for a total of five years over the course of their lifetime. Unskilled and semiskilled women continuously move in and out of the labor market due to their reproductive responsibilities and so are often the first ones to lose their jobs in times of economic adversity. In the past, welfare assistance has been a resource during this transitional phase between jobs. Many women will find themselves without access to benefits even though they may have been employed sporadically over this period of time.

6. I use the term "housing developments" as opposed to "projects." The latter conjures up images of housing for "broken families" and "poor people," primarily single, female, heads of households and their children, and deviant behavior.

7. Personal interview with Austin Simms, Director of the Lexington-Fayette Urban County Housing Authority, March 1988.

8. It is estimated that 72 percent of all public housing households with children are African American, compared with 44 percent in the certificate and voucher programs and 45 percent in privately owned, assisted stock (Newman and Schnare 1993, 424–425).

REFERENCES

Abramovitz, Mimi. 1992. *Regulating the Lives of Women*. Boston: South End Press.
Amott, Teresa. 1990. "Black Women and AFDC: Making Entitlement Out of Necessity." In *Women, the State, and Welfare*, edited by Linda Gordon. Madison: University of Wisconsin Press.
Austin, June Pankvich. 1981. *Poor Women's Sorority: Social Life Among Women in Low-*

Income Public Housing. Ph.D. dissertation. Ann Arbor: University Microfilms International.

Backer, L. C. 1995. "Welfare Reform at the Limit: The Futility of 'Ending Welfare as We Know It.' " *Harvard Civil Rights—Civil Liberties Law Review* 30: 339–405.

Bauman, John R. 1994. "Public housing: The Dreadful Saga of a Durable Policy." *Journal of Planning Literature* 8: 347–361.

Bloom, Dan, Mary Andes, and Claudia Nicholson. 1998. *Jobs First: Early Implementation of Connecticut's Welfare Reform Initiative.* New York: Manpower Demonstration Research Corporation.

Bratt, Rachel G., and Langley C. Keyes. 1998. "Challenges Confronting Nonprofit Housing Organizations' Self-Sufficiency Programs." *Housing Policy Debate* 9: 795–824.

Castro, Katherine. 1997. "Welfare Reform: How the New Law Affects LHAs." *Journal of Housing and Community Development* 54: 42–53.

Collins, Patricia Hill. 1991. "Learning from the Outsider Within: The Sociological Significance of Black Feminist Thought." In *Beyond Methodology: Feminist Scholarship as Lived Research,* edited by M. Fonow and J. A. Cook. Bloomington: Indiana University Press.

Cope, Meghan. 1997. "Responsibility, Regulation, and Retrenchment: The End of Welfare?" In *The State Devolution of America: Implications for a Diverse Society,* edited by Lynn Staeheli, Janet E. Kodras, and Colin Flint. Thousand Oaks, Calif.: Sage Publications.

De Lauretis, Teresa. 1987. *Technologies of Gender: Essays, Films, and Fiction.* London: Macmillan.

Edin, Kathryn. 1995. "The Myths of Dependence and Self-Sufficiency: Women, Welfare, and Low-wage Work." *Focus* 17: 1–9.

Garber, Judith, and Robyne Turner, eds. 1995. *Gender and Urban Research.* Thousand Oaks, Calif.: Sage Publications.

Gordon, Linda, ed. 1990. *Women, the State, and Welfare.* Madison: University of Wisconsin Press.

———. 1994. *Pitied but Not Entitled: Single Mothers and the History of Welfare.* New York: Free Press.

Hartman, Chester. 1963. "The Limitations of Public Housing: Relocation Choices in a Working Class Community." *Journal of the American Institute of Planners* 29: 283–296.

Kodras, Janet E. 1997. "Restructuring the State: Devolution, Privatization, and the Geographic Redistribution of Power and Capacity in Governance." In *The State Devolution of America: Implications for a Diverse Society,* edited by Lynn Staeheli, Janet E. Kodras, and Colin Flint. Thousand Oaks, Calif.: Sage Publications.

Massey, Douglas, and Nancy A. Denton. 1993. *American Apartheid: Segregation and the Making of the Underclass.* Cambridge: Harvard University Press.

McDowell, Linda. 1999. Gender, Identity and Place. Minneapolis: University of Minnesota Press.

Mead, Lawrence. 1992. *The New Politics of Poverty.* New York: Free Press.

Miranne, Kristine B. 1998. "Income Packaging as a Survival Strategy for Welfare Mothers." *Affilia* 13: 211–232.

Miranne, Kristine B., and Alma H. Young. 1998. "Women: 'Reading the World': Challenging Welfare Reform in Wisconsin." *Journal of Sociology and Social Work* 25: 155–176.

Mulroy, Elizabeth A. 1995. *Newly Uprooted: Single Mothers in Urban Life.* Westport, Conn.: Auburn House.

Mulvihill, Geoff. 1999. "It May Not Be the Best Place, But Is There Another One Available?" *Lexington Herald-Leader*, March 18.

Murray, Charles. 1984. *Losing Ground: American Social Policy, 1950–1980.* New York: Basic Books.

National Commission on Severely Distressed Public Housing. 1992. *Final Report.* Washington, D.C.: U.S. Government Printing Office.

Newman, Sandra, and Ann Schnare. 1990. "Integrating Housing and Welfare Assistance." In *Building Foundations: Housing and Federal Policy*, edited by Denise DiPasquale and L. Keyes. Philadelphia: University of Pennsylvania Press.

———. 1993. "Last in Line: Housing Assistance for Households with Children." *Housing Policy Debate* 4: 417–456.

———. 1997. ". . . And a Suitable Living Environment: The Failure of Housing Programs to Deliver on Neighborhood Quality." *Housing Policy Debate* 8: 703–741.

Nichols, Laura, and Barbara Gault. 1999. *The Effects of Welfare Reform on Housing Stability and Homelessness: Current Research Findings, Legislation, and Programs.* Washington, D.C.: Institute for Women's Policy Research.

Orloff, Ann. 1996. *Gender and the Welfare State.* Institute for Research on Policy, Discussion Paper no. 1082–96.

Peake, Linda. 1995. "Toward an Understanding of the Interconnectedness of Women's Lives: The Racial Reproduction of Labor in Low Income Areas." *Urban Geography* 16: 415–432.

———. 1997 "Toward a Social Geography of the City: Race and Dimensions of Urban Poverty in Women's Lives." *Journal of Urban Affairs* 19: 335–371.

Ranghelli, Lisa. 1998. *The Immediate Crisis in Public and Assisted Housing: More Than a Million Affordable Homes Are At Risk.* Washington, D.C.: Center for Community Change.

Sard, Barbara, and Jennifer Daskal. 1998. "Housing and Welfare Reform." *Social Legislation Bulletin* 35.

Sidel, Ruth. 1986. *Women and Children Last: The Plight of Poor Women in Affluent America.* New York: Viking.

Skocpol, Theda. 1992. *Protecting Soldiers and Mothers: The Political Origins of Social Policy in the United States.* Cambridge: Harvard University Press.

Smith, Michael P., and Joe R. Feagin. 1995. *The Bubbling Cauldron: Race, Ethnicity, and the Urban Crisis.* Minneapolis: University of Minnesota Press.

Spain, Daphne. 1995. "Direct and Default Policies in the Transformation of Public Housing." *Journal of Urban Affairs* 17: 357–376.

Spalter-Roth, Roberta, and Heidi Hartmann. 1993. *Dependence on Men, the Market, or the State: The Rhetoric and Reality of Welfare Reform.* Washington, D.C.: Institute for Women's Policy Research.

Stack, Carole. 1974. *All Our Kin.* New York: Harper and Row.

Tickamyer, Ann. 1995–1996. "Public Policy and Private Lives: Social and Spatial Dimensions of Women's Poverty Welfare Policy in the United States." *Kentucky Law Review* 84: 721–744.

Vale, Lawrence. 1996. "Destigmatizing Public Housing." *In Geography and Identity: Living and Exploring Geopolitics of Identity*, edited by Dennis Crow. Washington, D.C.: Maisonneuve Press.

———. 1997. "Empathalogical Places: Residents' Ambivalence toward Remaining in Public Housing." *Journal of Planning and Education Research* 16: 159–175.

Women and Housing Task Force. 1993. *Unlocking the Door II: A Call to Action*. Silver Spring, MD: McAuley Institute.

———. 1996. *Unlocking the Door III: Service-Enriched Housing*. Silver Spring, MD: McAuley Institute.

PART III

CHALLENGING PLANNED BOUNDARIES

Chapter 7

Theorizing Canadian Planning History: Women, Gender, and Feminist Perspectives

Sue Hendler with Helen Harrison

One could write three different histories of city planning, depending on whether one focused on underlying ideas, attempts to realize them, or results of those efforts.

—Burgess, "City Planning"

Frankly, I wouldn't know how to teach 'The History of the [Planning] Profession'. Which history would that be? The heroic story? Or the story of the 'great planning disasters'? The story of the all-wise planner divining the public interest, or the story of planners complicit in racially and sexually discriminatory practices?

—Sandercock, "Making the Invisible Visible"

In the graduate-level planning courses I took more than a decade ago, the history of planning was discussed in one of two ways: utopian models of the physical development of cities, or normative models of decision-making behavior. The identification of our discussions as only a finite number of possible stories one *could* tell about planning history was, to the best of my recollection, absent and, again in the limited context of my memory, none of us students ever thought to pose questions about the history *of* the history we were learning.[1] Indeed, it has only been years later, after listening to conference presentations, participating in the teaching of women's studies, and friendly discussions with colleagues in planning, history, politics, philosophy, and the like, that my interest in these issues has been piqued. In the relatively narrow context of feminist thought and women's contributions to planning scholarship and practice, a number of questions have arisen for me and have become the focus of a new program of research.[2] This research begins to address debates currently raging in the women's/ gender history field(s), as well as in planning. Might one search for a gender, a women's, or a feminist contribution to planning history? A history of *P*lanning (as a profession) or *p*lanning (as a community activity)? And, in a similar vein, city or community building? How would responses to these questions affect subsequent research endeavors? And so on.

This chapter reflects the work I have done, and the place in which I now find myself, with regard to these issues. A frustration for me, as someone known more for her work in ethical theory than in history, has been the atheoretical nature of many of the discussions of planning history I have encountered. My intention in writing this chapter is to contribute to discussions in planning history by mapping the theoretical terrain represented in contemporary work on women and history, especially planning history, and to begin to work toward making Canadian planning history more inclusive in this regard. The nature of this contribution will be partly based on gaps that I have found in planning history within the context of the diversity of discussions about women and history, and I offer suggestions in this regard at the conclusion of this chapter as to the usefulness of filling these gaps.

An outlook such as this—which attempts to find and place pieces that are perceived to be missing in a historical puzzle—appears to be common in feminist work: "The . . . urge of women's history . . . to fill in the empty spaces in those representations of the past in which hardly any or no women appear stemmed and continues to stem, in part, from looking out at the figures in the landscape of one's own world and seeing that half of them are, after all, women. Or the urge is to set the record straight if, in their 'discursive' appearance, the women have been twisted beyond recognition" (Pierson 1991, 84). Filling gaps and, indeed, changing the shape and appearance of the gaps themselves are mandates of feminist work in this regard. The first task, then, is to define the substrate in which these gaps may be found and to begin to identify what the gaps look like. Given my theoretical focus, the gaps to be addressed are those reflecting fundamental choices among different approaches to stories of our past—especially those pertaining to histories of planning in Canada.

Finally, a point of focus in this book is the notion of boundaries. Discussion of planning's many "pasts" highlights the fact that, first, we can identify and create numerous stories of the development of planning as a profession and, second, depending upon which of these stories we choose to pursue, we may place women in a variety of roles in these options. For example, a more inclusive history of planning in Canada could, but need not, seek to understand and comment on the dearth of women in professional societies and their prominence in, essentially, planning advocacy groups. As we shall see, a feminist perspective of these phenomena would differ from a purely women's or gender-history approach to the same issue. This speaks to the idea of boundaries, how such lines frame our theoretical endeavors, and, potentially, how these boundaries can change. Certain concepts and distinctions are central to this discussion, as follows.

HISTORY VERSUS HISTORIOGRAPHY, WOMEN VERSUS FEMINIST

Obviously, [a feminist planning history] . . . has to do more than recover the 'great women' in planning.

—Sandercock, personal communication

"History" refers to any number of stories, chronologies, and activities. Perhaps the only constants are the notion of time and the fact that there is a subject to be examined within the context of time. After this, however, is little in the way of agreement. History can refer to events that have happened *and* accounts of these events (see, for example, Perot 1992). The two may or may not be the same; the absence of objective, historical facts has, to some degree, become accepted among many scholars, particularly those who have leanings toward postmodern, poststructuralist thought. In this context, a historian provides one reading—one interpretation—of a period, a person, an institution, and so on. This reading may be better or worse, depending upon accepted measures of historical scholarship (see, for example, Newman 1991), but ought not be seen as the only possible story that could be told.

What constitutes these stories? Historians differ, too, in answering this question. For example, "while in Linda Gordon's formulation, history is a more or less accurate account of recoverable experiences, for [Joan] Scott *history is the representation that constructs experiences.* Historians write new histories not to relate existing experiences previously unknown but to give new meanings to experiences never before understood in such a way" (Newman 1991, 62; emphasis in original). In the context of planning, an illustration of this distinction might on the one hand be a chronological description of the professionalization of planning, and, on the other, an analysis of this process incorporating ideas of such things as sexism, scientism, and elitism. The latter provides an account of the process of profession building that gives rise to new understandings about the past and, perhaps, guidance for the future. Historiography, the study of written history, helps us to examine these perspectives and provides an arena for debate (see, for example, Leonie Sandercock's 1998 collection of historiographies for planning). Here we can look critically at the history/ies of a particular subject and talk about what makes a given account more or less persuasive or useful. Historiographies of planning have addressed such things as the liberal, heroic character of many views of planning history (see, for example, Burgess 1993) and the invisibility of minorities (and, in the case of women, a *majority*) (see, for example, Sandercock 1998) in most accounts of early planning efforts.

Historiography in many fields other than planning has been critical of the ways in which women and other marginalized groups have been depicted, or not, in traditional histories. As Kelly states, "what feminist historiography has done is to unsettle . . . accepted evaluations of historical periods. It has disabused us of the notion that the history of women is the same as the history of men, and that significant turning points in history have the same impact for one sex as for the other" (1984, 3). Women's history, feminist history, and gender history have, since the 1960s and 1970s, developed literatures related to, for instance, politics, geography, sociology, professions, and literature. Attempts at rectifying omissions or faulty interpretations, however, have also been problematic in that some have been seen as hopelessly theoretical and ungrounded; others have been criticized as atheoretical and uncritical, and still others as merely exacerbating existing problems.

In this regard, Joan Scott (1988) discusses three approaches to women's history. The first describes women's activities in ways similar to how those of their male counterparts have been documented but focuses on "her-story." Women's history (or "her-story") has many potential drawbacks. First, it may end up being part of the chronicling of the "great (white) men" approach to history, except that men have been replaced by "great women." Such an approach is silent on the histories of the masses—both male and female—and fails to shed light on how the individuals under scrutiny managed to achieve their greatness—a question of particular interest to feminist historians. In addition, looking for greatness often causes us to overlook other oppressed groups (such as people of color, people of diverse sexualities, people with disabilities) whose personal characteristics and subsequent oppression or discrimination make greatness all the more elusive. This approach may thus fill a void in conventional histories, but it does not enable us to fill several others. Another potential difficulty is that women continue to be isolated from "history"; their story remains a separate and distinct one that is unrelated to the history of men, or perhaps the history of human beings as a whole. Finally, "her-story" can "conflate . . . the valuation of women's experience (considering it worthy of study) and the positive assessment of everything women said or did" (Scott 1988, 20). For these reasons, so-called her-story is often seen as an important yet potentially flawed, or at least incomplete, approach to including women in stories about our past(s).

Scott's second approach connects women's history with social history—a field of history that emphasizes processes or systems. Social history contributes ideas of method, the importance of relationships, and a window through which one can study marginalized groups by looking at "large-scale social processes" (Scott 1988, 21). At the same time, social history does not have the goal of looking explicitly at women in these processes; gender is not a primary category of analysis. Thus, while her-story is too segregated from history, social history might be overly integrative in nature in terms of being able to fill a void related to women's roles, experiences, and activities (see also Smith-Rosenberg 1985).

The third approach identified by Scott is one that emphasizes gender. It is interesting that history mirrors other fields, in which an interest in women was first manifested by directing one's attention specifically at women and then, later, by examining more closely the broader, more inclusive issue of gender; for example, the international development literature and practice has moved from a WID (women in development) approach to a GAD (gender and development) emphasis (see, for example, OECD 1995). A focus on gender potentially highlights issues of power, social organization and sociopolitical structures. Similar to social history, this approach has been criticized for moving away from a clear focus on women to the more abstract notion of gender (see, for example, Rose 1993; see also Bock 1989). Again, such criticisms can be found in literature other than that in history as well.

Scott and others argue that all three approaches are part of the feminist goal(s) of rewriting history. Scott says that "the radical potential of women's history comes in the writing of histories that focus on women's experiences *and* analyze the ways in which politics construct gender and gender constructs politics" (1988, 27; emphasis in original). Bock, in the context of these and other dichotomies and categorizations, echoes this sentiment when she calls for "the rejection of mutually exclusive hierarchies, and especially either/or solutions, in favour of as-well-as solutions" (1991, 17). What planning historians can take away from this, perhaps, is the need, first, for many approaches to women's/feminist/gender history and, second, for theorized discussions of the role(s) that each of these can play as part, and only part, of a larger "whole."

An alternative to these approaches is history that is explicitly feminist in its orientation.[3] Feminist history may be defined as "historical work infused by a concern about the past and present oppression of women" (Bennett 1989, 253).[4] A central aspect of this work is its political intent. As Iris Marion Young states, "Describing kinds of oppression, the experience of oppression, and the creative agency of the oppressed can help form resistance and envision alternatives" (in Rose 1993, 95). Thus, feminist history contributes to the filling of historical gaps by highlighting the nature(s) and subjects/objects of oppression; further, it has the goal of working toward the eradication of such oppression.[5]

Relationships among these approaches to history are complex. As Rendall offers, "There is clearly no easy equation between [women's history and feminist history]" (1991, 46). To these we could certainly add gender history. However, there are some differences that characterize the three approaches (such as emphases on women rather than on other concepts such as oppression; foci on individuals versus classes, races, and genders), and these differences may become evident in particular histories such as those in planning. Thus, this depiction of women's, gender, and feminist histories serves to remind us that, though sketchy, there are different, yet overlapping, ways of "writing women" into history, and, that both differences and similarities figure prominently as we move from theory to actual planning stories.

I should note, however, that, as Bock (and others) argue, there are clear advantages of moving away from mutually exclusive categories. Indeed, this had been a contemporary subject for debate in feminist theory, in which scholars such as Judith Grant (1993) take issue with the divisive lines drawn by others such as Rosemarie Tong (1998). An approach to this quandary that some writers have taken and that I follow here is that defining, understanding, and appreciating differences is a necessary first step in deriving subsequent commonalities. Masking difference is one of the aspects of "mainstream" scholarship with which many feminists often take exception, and it is not something I wish to do here. I do, though, want to highlight the fact that each approach to history and to planning history can serve a purpose—especially in a field such as planning history, in which women, gender, and feminism have only recently begun to be discussed. The boundaries around this gap in our intellectual work are thus much more defined and much more critical than are the boundaries outlining finer distinctions among efforts to fill this gap.

A final observation from this discussion serves to remind us that history, whether in planning or elsewhere, is a theoretical endeavor that rests on notions of, first, history, and, second, planning (or some other substantive plot to the "story"). Thus, and recalling the words of historian E. H. Carr, history "consists essentially in seeing the past through the eyes of the present and in the light of its problems" (1964, 21); in this case, the problems to be addressed are those pertaining to inclusivity and diversity with an emphasis on sex and gender. Furthermore, and according to Roth, "Theories of history contain or imply a conception or a vision of the political" (1988, 636); among other things, this means that what we choose to write down as history today will affect subsequent generations of, in this case, planners and those of us affected by planning decisions. As I reiterate at the conclusion of this chapter, changing the lines that demarcate history from nonhistory and planning from nonplanning, as well as different theoretical approaches to same, will, eventually, contribute to amended understandings of the nature, composition, and practice of what we call "planning." Having established this basis, we can turn more explicitly to planning history per se.

WOMEN'S PLACE IN PLANNING HISTORY

Women were not the focus of historical discourse as long as history was primarily an analysis of wars which women did not fight. . . , of parliaments in which they did not sit, or of empires that they did not conquer.

—Kleinberg, *Retrieving Women's History*

This quote rings true when one thinks of urban and regional planning. If planning history is about the physical task of building cities, formalized professional organizations, and the conquering of nature, then the absence of women is expected if not desired by men who controlled the professions. Women were, for the most part, not encouraged to do this sort of work, not permitted to engage in the kinds of studies that would have permitted them to become professional planners, not often interested in many of the more physical aspects of planning, and so on. There are, however, clearly many histories of women in planning, ranging from the role(s) they did have in professional planning bodies to those pertaining to grassroots urban reform.[6] And, following the typology of approaches to women's history presented above, there are also stories of women as individuals and in groups, stories of sociopolitical-economic forces, and gendered stories about power that one could tell. Published planning literature, especially in U.S. and British contexts, touches on many of these themes, as follows.

Many discussions of women in planning history have focused their efforts on the women's history or her-story theme of "great women." American work on Catherine Bauer (Birch 1994a; Oberlander and Newbrun 1995) and Mary Kingsbury Simkhovitch (Wirka 1994) are examples. Catherine Bauer worked as a "nonprofessional" urban planner for more than three decades, especially in the areas of housing, urban design, and planning process. She worked with both women and men to advocate for affordable housing, citizen participation in planning, and a multi/interdisciplinary approach to the field. Unlike most planners at the time, she did not have a background in the physical and applied science, and this perhaps enabled her to have a broad, socially oriented view of planning work.

Like Bauer, Simkhovitch worked primarily in housing and urban design. She helped establish settlement houses in Boston that addressed the needs of immigrant and poor women. In Britain, a few women, such as Henrietta Barnett (Greed 1994), were also active in housing, design, and social services. Although biographical sketches can provide insight into the experiences of particular individuals, they are most useful when supplemented by more general social history. Without this broader view, we cannot tell whether these women were simply lucky to achieve their status in an inhospitable environment or were perhaps truly great—as women or as planners.[7] In any event, however, we can say that some women managed to at least blur the boundaries that distinguished between men's and women's work, planning and nonplanning, and professional and nonprofessional endeavors.

In this regard, and apart from tales of notable individuals, are data recording the proportions of women in planning organizations. Such information allows us to go beyond the occasional "great" woman and obtain a glimpse of broader female or gendered participation in professional planning work.[8] In addition, a third indication of women's participation in the profession is their obtaining the often-necessary educational background for subsequent practice in the planning field.[9] Together, these data help to fill in one story of female participation in planning work—a story that tells of women gradually becoming more involved in conventional paths of professional practice: education in a professional program, membership in a professional society, and the like. If we look for another story,

however—one that tells more about the underlying context for women's participation or lack thereof in planning—we need to go beyond raw statistics. In this
regard, and according to Eugenie Ladner Birch, at the turn of the century women
in the United States "consciously claimed certain urban problems as their own"
(Birch 1994b, 473). Early planning efforts sought to clean up diseased and disorderly cities and to improve the quality of life for all citizens. Because of their
association with domestic work, women were believed to be experts in such matters. Thus, their input was considered crucial to the newly emerging field of city
planning, which became a form of "municipal housekeeping." Through their
charitable organizations and reform efforts, women laid the foundations for social services and social welfare, and provided the "head and heart" of planning
(Birch 1994b, 478).

However, it appears that as planning became professionalized, institutionalized, and taken over by men, it became more efficiency minded, land-use oriented
and less overtly concerned with the social aspects of cities. By the 1920s, planning in the Untied States was increasingly the domain of elite men and had lost
much of its connection to communities and their residents. Birch suggests that
"perhaps the diminished attention of social welfare and aesthetic aspects of the
field could be related to the lack of female participation" in the organized planning profession (1994b, 479).

Although such a position and its underlying context might be seen as an over-
simplification, archival materials do support the fact that women had particular
concerns around the more social aspects of city living. Land use was a topic about
which women had strong opinions, but other planning-related issues appear to be
more prominent in their discussions.

The historical interest of women in their, and their children's, needs has been
well-documented (see, for example, Beard 1915). Playgrounds, housing, health,
poverty, substance abuse, and sanitation have long been the purview of women,[10]
and it was a small step to move from concerns for these issues inside the home
to the neighborhood and, indeed, the entire city. This "enlarged form of housekeeping" (Blackie 1909, 129) can be discussed in terms of municipal/state politics, urban reform, or town and country/urban and regional planning. Women
were part of civic improvement committees, comprised women's leagues, and
acted as enthusiastic lobbyists of municipal governments (Beard 1915). Their activities initiated communitywide endeavors, represented the precursors of planning offices, and/or continued as autonomous forces in city building and improvement. They also furthered a fledgling planning "profession": "There is a
new field opening for women as factors in civic improvement. Women have always set the moral and esthetic standard in the community in which they lived,
and when they once get into this new field of making our cities more beautiful—a
field which is really closest to their natural bent, they ought to accomplish won-
ders" (Levinson in Beard 1915, 306).

Even in the context of planning, however, some women went beyond immediate questions of aesthetics, health, sanitation, and poverty and questioned basic issues of governance and property rights: "While speaking of town planning, perhaps we may be allowed to suggest that the Canadian government should pause before selling land so extensively to private individuals, and consider if it may not be well to work schemes of town planning and municipal ownership" (Cadbury 1909, 134).

A speaker at the 1909 International Congress of Women provided a connection between planning issues as perceived by women and the kinds of data regarding female membership in professional activities cited above. She suggested that only female professionals could appropriately address women's issues: "Whilst we have had a continuous and never-ending war with smoking chimneys! How we long for the practical woman architect to arise who will specialize on chimneys, and, perhaps, save the long-suffering housewife from this intolerable and often insurmountable grievance" (Blackie 1909, 127). Her plea moves beyond a call for the inclusion of "women's" issues in planning and broaches the subject of who is doing the planning. Her conclusion appears to be that only women can adequately address such issues and thus represents a call for more women entering the ranks of professional planners. One of her colleagues, Mary Higgs, provides what could be seen as a reason for this relationship between women's issues and female planners: "Out of the real knowledge gained by experience will, I am convinced, spring a flood of light on women's problems" (1909, 124). In other words, once we have more experience attending to women's issues (and who best, perhaps, to gain such experience but women?), we may be better equipped to plan for the resolution of these issues. Extending this analysis could lead one to speculate that traditional feminist emphases on power, oppression, and equity could then become more central to planning endeavors.

This brief review provides an overview of the place(s) of women in, especially, U.S. and British planning history. An impression left from the works cited here is that women have been active in planning-related activities for a long time. Following reductions in their numbers and in their overt power during the days of ardent professionalization, they are now returning to hold prominent and influential positions within the field. Their original interest in planning matters seems to have been linked to their concerns around the home, but their retreat from the profession is more complex. The inability or disinterest of women to obtain the necessary education to pursue planning careers, societal pressures in a postwar environment that emphasized men returning to positions previously held by women, a new interest in planning values not necessarily held by women, and men exercising their power and making choices to which women had to respond are all discussed in the literature. To these one can add women's double burden of work and domestic responsibilities, a lack of female mentors and professional guidance, salary discrimination, the compartmentalization of women's issues as exclusively female, as well as sexism at a more personal level (see Birch 1994b; Leavitt 1980, 1981).

Another factor could stem from early twentieth-century women being dismissed as uninformed members of the private domestic sphere; it might have been deemed necessary by professional planners to establish a distinction between the social-reform concerns associated primarily with women and the political concerns and technical skills associated more with men. In other words, if planning were to be taken seriously as a legitimate profession, it was necessary to extricate from it any vestige of such unprofessional feminine values as citizen forums, social reform, and urban aesthetics. Whether this line of reasoning is overly conspiratorial remains to be seen.

In terms of the distinctions drawn earlier in this chapter, it would appear that women's history is becoming increasingly prevalent in planning circles. Gender history can, perhaps, be seen as underpinning many of the discussions of early planning efforts and organizations, in that what it meant to be female or male is often implied in these stories. Feminist intent is also clear in the writings of Birch, Greed, and others, as there is a drive toward eradicating women's exclusion from planning activities and enhancing the contributions of women throughout the profession. One can also look to these writers to take issue with the very meaning of such terms as "planning" and "profession" so as to make them more amenable to feminist sensibilities.

CANADIAN PLANNING HISTORY/IES

The physical part of town planning is the technique of sociology and though this technique may still be for a time in the hands of men, the philosophic bases of the [planning] movement is throbbing with that social passion which has built up thousands of welfare societies that are the special creation of women.

—Anonymous, "Women'[s] Part in Town Planning"

Hodge's 1998 text, *Planning Canadian Communities*, is standard reading in many planning courses across the country. In it, he distinguishes among three aspects of planning and of planning history: "(1) the principles and purposes for which planning is pursued; (2) the way in which planning is practiced; and (3) the persons and groups who participate in planning activities" (15). Though he acknowledges that public interest in and concern about communities is a long-standing phenomenon, much of his focus appears to lie in the professional planning realm—a phase of planning in Canada that begins with the development of the Town Planning Institute of Canada in 1919. The role(s) of women are left, for the better part, unaddressed apart from references to, first, their having unique perspectives of urban areas and, second, their place in public participation. Especially relevant to this chapter is the absence in Hodge's work of a distinct theoretical basis for his history, although one can glean from his language hints as to his views in this area.[11]

That women were slow to attain significant representation in the Canadian planning profession is clear; even by 1965, almost 50 years after the "birth" of town planning in Canada, women appear to have comprised only 7 percent of total enrollment in Canadian graduate planning programs (Mehak 1983). By 1971, this had increased to 17 percent (Mehak 1983). This mirrors women's participation in architecture, where their numbers grew from 12 percent of graduates in the 1970s to 25 percent in the 1980s (Lemco van Ginkel, 1991). These figures can be compared to women's participation in the larger category of professional work,[12] where their representation hovered between 10 and 17 percent between 1931 and 1971 (Kinnear 1995) and at around 6 percent in 1911 (Lavigne and Stoddart 1977).[13] In 1975, women represented 9.6 percent of total members in the Canadian Institute of Planners (Butler 1975).[14] Recent data in the province of Ontario suggest that women make up about one-third of the membership of the Ontario Professional Planners Institute (OPPI 1994), and it was not until the 1980s that "women began to enter the profession in large numbers" (Sherwood 1994, 21).[15]

Membership in these professional organizations can be compared to that in related, but differently constituted bodies.[16] For example, in the late 1970s, women made up as much as 40 percent of the membership of the Community Planning Association of Canada (CPAC)—equal to about 4,800 members at that time (Good 1994). CPAC complemented the work of the Canadian Institute of Planners and, similar to the American Planning Association in the United States, provided a means for individuals to become part of a planners' community without the added baggage of accreditation, and other factors. This was a group of people interested in planning issues—not necessarily in becoming planners.

Moving beyond the scope of professional and semiprofessional bodies and proceeding to grassroots urban reform in Canada, the picture of women's involvement becomes quite different. Here we see women active at the national, provincial, and municipal levels fighting to have their voices heard in bettering our urban environments.

There are many stories of women's involvement in urban reform and philanthropy in Canada. Collections by Kealey (1979), Strong-Boag and Fellman (1986), and Stephenson (1977) are but a very few examples. In these texts are stories of individual women; groups of women defined by their location, occupation, or class; and women as a separate sex, complete with a separate ideology—first-wave/maternal/domestic feminism. These women directed their considerable energies in much the same direction as did women in the United States; rebelling against a life of dependence some entered the "caring" professions, and others did voluntary work in their communities. The latter involved city beautification, health issues, children's issues, and housing. As these projects became more the purview of professionals, women were displaced and, until recently, largely forgotten.

The absence of women in the Canadian planning profession is undoubtedly due to many of the same phenomena cited earlier as pertaining to the United

States. We know that, because of the lack of adequately trained professionals, Canada had to import planners from Britain and the United States. They thus would have inherited the gender biases from these countries, in addition to those they might already have had. More recently, we know that organizations such as the CPAC contained a great many women—its only semiprofessional mandate, its integrative approach to planning, and its community-based direction may have been attractive to women. What is less obvious, however, is the fact that women were sometimes not given a clear choice in participating in CPAC activities. According to Lin Good (1994), for example, past president of the CPAC, men working at the municipal level wanted to attend "high-power" meetings such as those of the Ontario Good Roads Association, leaving women to the less powerful, more "light-weight" organizations such as CPAC. Thus, women's representation on such bodies may not have been completely of their choosing. Still, it would seem that, though both men and women have taken part in professional and nonprofessional/voluntary planning practices, women have had a more pronounced presence in the latter, whereas the opposite holds true for men. This again speaks to boundaries between sexes and professional/nonprofessional work.

In general, it appears that Canadian planning history, though echoing many of the same themes as its British and U.S. counterparts, clearly has many secrets when it comes to women and their participation in the field. We have much in the way of historical research to do in order to uncover these stories and provide more (and, many would argue, better) interpretations of the development of planning principles and practices in this country. With so much in the way of possibilities, deciding on the kind of story to tell becomes a compelling first step in any such endeavor. Women's history projects and discussions (such as Good 1975 Wolfe and Strachan 1988), as well as feminist histories (see Wills 1989), have begun to supplement conventional histories of planning in Canada such as that told by Hodge (1998), but there are currently many more questions than answers in this field.

CONCLUSION

The end of any history is a lie in which we all agree to conspire.

         —Atwood, *The Robber Bride*

The final chapter [of this new version of The American Planner*], Eugenie Ladner Birch's superb survey of women's contributions and struggles with the planning profession between 1880 and 1980, remains in place as it continues to fill a void in the literature. Surely, someday soon . . . this chapter will become obsolete.*

         —Krueckeberg, *The American Planner*

Joan Kelly (1984) has argued that men and women experience history differently and cites the example of women not reaping the benefits of the Renaissance as did men. Kelly uses the criteria of regulation of female sexuality (as compared to that of men), women's economic and political roles, cultural roles of women, and ideology about women in assessing how a given event or period in history affects women. What we know to this point in time about Canadian planning history would indicate that the professionalization of planning has not served women well; it has limited their economic and political clout, at least in the "short" term, it has taken away from them an avenue for expressing their reformist ideals, and it reinforced the notion that a woman's role was in the home (or an expanded version thereof). The role(s) of women thus became "bounded" in complex ways—partly perhaps of their own choosing and partly due to forces beyond their control.

Having said this, however, these boundaries are ones that we create for reasons of efficiency, comprehensibility, or academic parlance. As (planning) history is not cast in stone, so too are these boundaries not immutable truths. At the very least, I think, one needs to recall our original intent in discovering untold historical stories in planning—this being to fill a gap in conventional discussions of how planning has come to take on its current form(s).

Turning to the potential uses of the sorts of histories discussed here, I can build on the ideas of Abbott and Adler (1989), who argue that learning planning history can help us to avoid repeating yesterday's mistakes and can help build solidarity and pride in our profession and professional work. History can also be used, they hold, as a tool of analysis that can be employed in both scholarship and planning practice. Perhaps even more pertinent to the notion of boundaries in planning, however, are Beauregard's thoughts on the role of history in planning: "planning histories are simultaneously about the past and the present capacities of planners and . . . by reading planning histories planners are either empowered or . . . disempowered" (1998, 187). He goes on to say, "To produce planning texts that empower, we must do more than recognize voices that have been suppressed and do more than approach planning from below" (195). "Doing more" here involves a writing style and epistemology that acknowledges and accommodates uncertainty, conflict, and complexity. In this regard, I do not wish, in this chapter, to leave the impression that there are easy ways to "write women" into planning history. The ways in which women (and other marginalized groups) are involved, or not, in any professional endeavor must reflect an acknowledgment of, on the one hand, agency and personal autonomy, and, on the other, oppression and victimization. Having room for both in one's analysis should, I think, be an important part of this kind of historical work.

Still, it is the empowerment of planners—those who have been left out of planning, those who continue to feel marginalized within planning, and those who might question their place at "the" center of planning—that is the *raison d'être* of the argument presented in this chapter. They will draw new boundaries in planning scholarship, pedagogy, and practice—boundaries that will hopefully be more permeable and more inclusive than the ones that preceded them. Whether this entails agitating from outside formal planning circles or fighting from within is an ongoing struggle for women and feminists who seek to meet the boundary-redrawing challenge. It remains a personal choice for each of us as to how we reconcile these often competing demands on our time and energy. In true post-modern, boundaries-be-damned spirit, perhaps neither should be privileged but, instead, a balance sought—a balance that might well lead to the drawing of boundaries so blurred and so permeable they might just disappear altogether.

NOTES

Research grants from the Social Sciences and Humanities Research Council of Canada and the Advisory Research Committee of Queen's University enabled me to conduct part of the background work leading to the completion of this chapter. Paul Sajan, Richard McCabe, Sherilyn MacGregor, Jason Pfotenhauer, and George Claydon assisted in collecting and assembling relevant material. Financial assistance for my attending the annual 1996 conference of the Association of Collegiate Schools of Planning was obtained from the Office of Research Services, Queen's University. I thank Leonie Sandercock, Christine Overall, Karen Dubinsky, Evelyn Peters, Brenda Lee, Richard McCabe, and four anonymous assessors of a research grant application for helpful suggestions along the way. Jo-Anne Williamson and Jacqueline Bell helped, as always, with the logistics of putting the chapter together.

1. Zinsser quotes other feminist historians who, talking about students taking history courses in universities, remarked on the fact that "not a single paying customer demanded her money back on the basis that she had paid for a history course and had been sold a male fantasy instead" (1993, 30).

2. Of course, the role of women in planning is only one story that has gone largely untold. As others have discussed, one can also ask about the role of other groups in the profession (people with "other" races, sexualities, abilities, languages, etc.), in addition to the nonprofessional side(s) of planning, and the value it has added (or not) to cities and regions, and so on. The point here is that there are many stories about planning and the passage of time; I have chosen to focus my attention on women-related and feminist aspects of this theme.

3. For example, do early woman "planners" look at issues of sanitation and health because those are issues that have been left for them through their roles as housekeepers? And, if so, were these roles oppressive? What would their interests have been if they had had the freedom and autonomy to select their places in city life? Though women's history allows us to describe the planning activities of women, feminist history enables us to analyze these activities from a more prescriptive point of view (see, for instance, Freestone 1995 for some ideas regarding women's "choices" of planning interests in Australia).

4. Bennett (1989) goes on to argue that patriarchy ought to be a central concept in feminist history. She follows Adrienne Rich here and quotes Rich's definition of patriarchy: "A familial-social, ideological, political system in which men—by force, direct pressure, or through ritual, tradition, law, and language, customs, etiquette, education, and the

division of labor, determine what part women shall or shall not play, and in which the female is everywhere subsumed under the male" (260).

5. Some of these distinctions become more important, not in the nature of historical work in and of itself, but in how this work is used. For example, Rose (1993) speaks of Valverde's claim that gender history can be feminist if it is used in a critical fashion in terms of how it defines gender.

6. The question of who, or what, is "women" in this context will remain largely unanswered in this chapter (see, for example, Riley 1988). Apart from some discussions of urban/rural, English/French and middle/working-class distinctions among Canadian women involved in professional/planning efforts, there is little information pertaining to race, sexuality, ability, etc., in addition to more theoretical questions of how the women involved in planning perceived themselves—as women? as planners? as human beings?

7. This is an important difference. Were their successes due to their planning philosophies, techniques and approaches, and their tenacity in advocating same, or to their being strong, assertive women who refused to take a back seat to men in general, and male planners in particular? Again, were they great planners or great women? Or both?

8. For example, in the Royal Town Planning Institute in Britain, women represented 5.4 percent of full members in 1971; this figure increased slowly to the most recent figures I have of 16.5 percent in 1991 (Greed 1992) and 18.1 percent in 1993 (Greed 1994). Prior to 1970, data on female membership were not recorded; however, it is recognized that only "a handful" were part of the Institute (Greed 1992). Women in the United States appear to have fared a little better; women were less than 5 percent of the membership of the American Institute of Planners in the 1950s and were "estimated to be between 10.5 and 15.0 percent of the [U.S.] planning population" in the 1970s (Leavitt 1981, 223–224).

9. In the United States, women were granted 7.5 percent of planning degrees in 1968 and 31 percent in 1978 (Leavitt 1980). In Britain, women's enrollment in planning programs recently was gauged at between 30 and 40 percent (Greed 1994).

10. Indeed, such concerns continue to interest women (OECD 1995) and often are discussed in explicitly feminist terms.

11. His discussion, for example, is intended to elucidate "the" principles, practices and participants in Canadian planning, as well as a "comprehensive rendering of the origins of the approaches we use in planning today" (Hodge 1998, 15)—these illustrate linguistic turns that signal, to those of us who do not see ourselves in the pages of his book, our own lack of relevance in the development of Canadian communities. See Wolfe (1994) for a history that struggles, to my mind, with the distinction between "the" history and "a" history of Canadian planning.

12. Professional work here refers to medicine, education, law, and nursing. These data, unlike the previous Canada-wide figures, are based on Manitoba statistics.

13. This second category of professional work includes education and nursing; the data are from a study of women's work in Montreal, Quebec.

14. This figure is somewhat misleading in that it includes student members, and this group always has a higher percentage of females than do the nonstudent categories of full/ provisional members (see, for example, Greed 1992 for a British perspective).

15. Together, these figures are comparable to the British and U.S. trends discussed earlier.

16. One has to take care in interpreting participation rates in professional work, how-

ever, in that these figures demonstrate one of the problems inherent in feminist history as discussed earlier. Specifically, these data emphasize particular women from particular classes (for example, Catholic, French Canadian women fared worse than their Protestant counterparts in entering some professions and, in turn, "French Canadian teaching and service orders such as the Grey Nuns, the Sisters of Saint Joseph, the Sisters of Providence and the Sisters of Charity effectively monopolized education, nursing and social work and made the entry of lay women into these professions extremely difficult" (Lavigne and Stoddart 1977, 138). Furthermore, and in this chapter, for example, the women to whom I am referring are undoubtedly primarily white, middle-class women.

REFERENCES

Abbott, Carl, and Sy Adler. 1989. "Historical Analysis as a Planning Tool." *Journal of the American Planning Association* 55, 4: 467–473.

Anonymous. 1925. "Women' [sic] Part in Town Planning." *Journal of the Town Planning Institute of Canada*: 21–22.

Atwood, Margaret Eleanor. 1993. *The Robber Bride*. Toronto, Ont.: McClelland and Stewart Inc.

Beard, Mary Ritter. 1915 [1972 reprint]. *Woman's Work in Municipalities*. New York: Arno Press.

Beauregard, Robert. 1998. "Subversive Histories: Texts from South Africa." In *Making the Invisible Visible: A Multicultural Planning History,* edited by Leonie Sandercock. Berkeley, Calif.: University of California Press.

Bennett, Judith. 1989. "Feminism and History." *Gender and History* 1, 3: 251–272.

Birch, E. Ladner. 1994a. "An Urban View: Catherine Bauer's Five Questions." In *The American Planner. Biographies and Recollections.* 2d ed., edited by Donald Krueckeberg. New Brunswick, N.J.: Center for Urban Policy Research.

———. 1994b. "From Civic Worker to City Planner: Women and Planning, 1890–1980." In *The American Planner. Biographies and Recollections.* 2d ed., edited by Donald Krueckeberg. New Brunswick, N.J.: Center for Urban Policy Research.

Blackie, M. Miss. 1909. "Management of Houses for Working People." In *Report of the International Congress of Women,* by The National Council of Women in Canada. Toronto, Ont.: Geo. Parker and Sons.

Bock, Gisela. 1989. "Women's History and Gender History: Aspects of an International Debate." *Gender and History* 1, 1: 10.

———. 1991. "Challenging Dichotomies: Perspectives on Women's History." In *Writing Women's History: International Perspectives,* edited by Karen Offen, Ruth Roach Pierson, and Jane Rendall. London: Macmillan.

Burgess, Patricia. 1993. "City Planning and the Planning of Cities: The Recent Historiography." *Journal of Planning Literature* 7, 4: 314–327.

Butler, Diana. 1975. "Women in Planning: Career Development." *Plan Canada* 15, 2: 62–67.

Cadbury, G., Mrs. 1909. "Housing." In *Report of the International Congress of Women,* by The National Council of Women in Canada. Toronto, Ont.: Geo. Parker and Sons.

Carr, Edward Hallett. 1964. *What Is History?* Harmondsworth, Eng.: Penguin Books Ltd.

Freestone, R. 1995. "Women in the Australian Town Planning Movement 1900–1950." *Planning Perspectives* 10: 259–277.

Good, D. Lin. 1975. "Women in Planning: A Citizen's View." *Plan Canada* 15, 2: 68–71.

———. 1994. Personal communication. Kingston, Ontario, April 18.

Grant, Judith. 1993. *Fundamental Feminism: Contesting the Core Concepts of Feminist Theory.* New York: Routledge.

Greed, Clara. 1992. "Women in Planning." *The Planner* 78, 13: 11–13.

———. 1994. *Women and Planning. Creating Gendered Realities.* New York: Routledge.

Higgs, M. 1909. "The Housing of Working Women." In *Report of the International Congress of Women*, by The National Council of Women in Canada. Toronto, Ont.: Geo. Parker and Sons.

Hodge, Gerald. 1998. *Planning Canadian Communities.* 3d ed. Scarborough, Ont.: Nelson Canada.

Kealey, Linda. 1979. *A Not Unreasonable Claim: Women and Reform in Canada, 1880s–1920s.* Toronto, Ont.: Women's Press.

Kelly, Joan. 1984. *Women, History, and Theory.* Chicago: University of Chicago Press.

Kinnear, Mary. 1995. *In Subordination: Professional Women 1870–1970.* Kingston, Quebec: McGill-Queen's University Press.

Kleinberg, S. Jay, ed. 1988. *Retrieving Women's History: Changing Perceptions of the Role of Women in Politics and Society.* New York: Berg Publishers.

Krueckeberg, Donald, ed. 1994. *The American Planner. Biographies and Recollections.* 2d ed. New Brunswick, N.J.: Center for Urban Policy Research.

Lavigne, Marie, and J. Stoddart. 1977. "Women's Work in Montreal at the Beginning of the Century." In *Women in Canada.* Rev. ed., edited by Marylee Stephenson. Don Mills, Ont.: General Publishing Co.

Leavitt, Jacqueline. 1980. "Women in Planning: There's More to Affirmative Action than Gaining Access." In *New Space for Women*, edited by Gerda Wekerle, Rebecca Peterson, and C. D. Morley. Boulder: Westview Press.

———. 1981. "The History, Status and Concerns of Women Planners." In *Women and the American City*, edited by C. Stimpson, E. Dixler, M. Nelson, and K. Yatrakis. Chicago: University of Chicago Press.

Lemco van Ginkel, Blanche 1991. "Slowly and Surely (and Somewhat Painfully): More or Less the History of Women in Architecture in Canada." *Society for the Study of Architecture in Canada Bulletin* 17, 1:5–11.

Mehak, Mary Catherine. 1983. "A Comparative Analysis of the Career Development of Men and Women Planners in Canada." Unpublished manuscript.

Newman, Louise. 1991. "Critical Theory and the History of Women: What's at Stake in Deconstructing Women's History." *Journal of Women's History* 2, 3: 58–68.

Oberlander, Page, and Eva Newbrun. 1995. "Catherine Bauer: Ahead of Her Time." *The Planner*: 10–12.

Ontario Professional Planners Institute (OPPI) 1994. Personal communication. November 22.

Organisation for Economic Co-operation and Development (OECD). 1995. *Women in the City. Housing, Services and the Urban Environment.* Paris: OECD.

Perot, M., ed. 1992. *Writing Women's History.* Oxford: Basil Blackwell.

Pierson, Ruth Roach. 1991. "Experience, Difference, Dominance and Voice in the Writing of Canadian Women's History." In *Writing Women's History: International Perspectives*, edited by Karen Offen, Ruth Roach Pierson, and Jane Rendall. London: Macmillan.

Rendall, Jane. 1991. " 'Uneven Developments': Women's History, Feminist History and Gender History in Great Britain." In *Writing Women's History: International Perspectives*, edited by Karen Offen, Ruth Roach Pierson, and Jane Rendall. London: Macmillan.

Riley, Denise. 1988. *'Am I That Name?' Feminism and the Category of 'Women' in History*. London: Macmillan.

Rose, Susan. 1993. "Gender History/Women's History: Is Feminist Scholarship Losing Its Critical Edge?" *Journal of Women's History* 5: 89–101.

Roth, Michael. 1988. "Cultural Criticism and Political Theory." *Political Theory* 16: 636–644.

Sandercock, Leonie. 1994. "Making the Invisible Visible: New Approaches to City Planning History." Paper prepared for the annual conference of the Association of Collegiate Schools of Planning, Tempe, Arizona, November.

———. 1995. Personal communication, January.

———. ed. 1998. *Making the Invisible Visible: A Multicultural Planning History*. Berkeley, CA: University of California Press.

Scott, Joan Wallach. 1988. *Gender and the Politics of History*. New York: Columbia University Press.

Sherwood, David. 1994. "Canadian Institute of Planners." *Plan Canada* (July): 20–21.

Smith-Rosenberg, Caroll. 1985. *Disorderly Conduct. Visions of Gender in Victorian America*. New York: Alfred A. Knopf.

Stephenson, Marylee. 1977. *Women in Canada*. Don Mills, Ont.: General Publishing.

Strong-Boag, Veronica Jane, and Anita Clair Fellman. 1986. *Rethinking Canada: The Promise of Women's History*. Toronto, Ont.: Copp Clark Pitman.

Tong, Rose Marie. 1998. *Feminist Thought*. 2d ed. Boulder, Colo.: Westview Press.

Wills, Jacqueline Gale. 1989. *Efficiency, Feminism and Cooperative Democracy. Origins of the Toronto Social Planning Council, 1918–1957*. Ph.D. dissertation. University of Toronto, Toronto, Ontario.

Wirka, S. 1994. "Introduction to: Housing by Mary Kingsbury Simkhovitch." In *The American Planner. Biographies and recollections*, 2d ed., edited by Donald Krueckeberg. New Brunswick, N.J.: Center for Urban Policy Research.

Wolfe, Janet. 1994. "Our Common Past: An Interpretation of Canadian Planning History." *Plan Canada:* 12–34.

Wolfe, Janet, and Grace Strachan. 1988. "Practical Idealism: Women in Urban Reform, Julia Drummond and the Montreal Parks and Playgrounds Association." In *Life Spaces. Gender, Household, Employment*, edited by Caroline Andrew and Beth Moore Milroy. Vancouver, B.C.: UBC Press.

Zinsser, Judith. 1993. *History and Feminism: A Glass Half Full*. New York: Twayne.

Chapter 8

Resisting Boundaries?
Using Safety Audits for Women

Caroline Andrew

The title of this part of the book, "Challenging Planned Boundaries," reminds us that boundaries are constructed, reconstructed, and/or transformed in a variety of ways in urban areas, and that gender is a central element of all of these processes. Planning is only one of the ways in which boundaries can be regulated, but it is a particularly important one in that, as a public-policy process, it is open to public debate and scrutiny and to mechanisms of public accountability. Boundaries are also regulated by the market and by civil society, but political processes, such as planning, are particularly important to study to see how women, as political actors, do and/or do not succeed in influencing the ways in which urban boundaries are publicly regulated.

This chapter examines these questions through a very specific focus: the use made by women of safety audits as a planning tool in urban areas. By taking safety audits as a case study, one can look at whether planning processes can promote the reconfiguring of boundaries that constrain women's use of urban spaces, or whether these processes act more to reinforce, construct, or emphasize these boundaries in a constraining manner.

This requires, first of all, thinking about planning as an open-ended process rather than as the imposition of a set of fixed norms. Indeed, the traditional view of local planning as the drawing up and attempt to implement a fixed vision has been described by Elizabeth Wilson as a masculine vision. In *The Sphinx in the City: Urban Life, the Control of Disorder and Women*, Wilson argues that men have tried to impose order and boundaries on urban space and that women have been one of the elements of disorder seen by men as something that needs to be brought under control. The disorder of the city involves women, either "as temptress, as whore, as fallen women, as lesbian" or "as virtuous womanhood in danger" (1991, 6).

It is men who want boundaries, limits, order; women's experience has been differently shaped.

> Perhaps the 'disorder' of urban life does not so much disturb women. If this be so, it may be because they have not internalized as rapidly as men a need for over-ratio-nalistic control and authoritarian order. The socialization of women renders them less dependent on duality and opposition; instead of setting nature against the city, they find nature in the city. . . .
> We shall also explore how women have lived out their lives on sufferance in the metropolis. For although women, along with minorities, children, the poor, are still not full citizens in the sense that they have never been granted full and free access to the streets, industrial life still drew them into public life, and they have survived and flourished in the interstices of the city, negotiating the contradictions of the city in their own particular way. (Wilson 1991, 8)

Thus, Elizabeth Wilson's argument is that women's experience in the city is not one of creating boundaries, drawing limits, or establishing categories; it is one of movement in the margins, between and through categories, connecting rather than distinguishing and relishing contradictions rather than rejecting them. Yet these boundaries exist, and therefore the question to be asked is to what extent planning processes can be used by women to reconfigure boundaries or actively to resist them. More specifically, can safety audits be used to challenge conventional ideas about boundaries and about women's place in the city?

When we think of the kinds of boundaries that constrain the lives of women in cities, we can think of boundaries that are time defined, space defined, and defined by the segmentation of social relations (Semblat 1993). Women's use of urban space is heavily marked by considerations of time. A large number of women limit their activities in cities at night (WACAV Women's Safety Audit Guide 1996a; Whitzman 1995). Women are seen, and see themselves, as illegitimate users of urban space at night, or at least as people whose right to be there is questionable. Little insists on the impact expectations have on behavior: "These expectations are adapted widely by society—for example, women are advised not to go out alone after dark—those who do are frequently seen as 'asking for trouble.' . . . It is acceptable for women to be out shopping during the daytime but not in the city center at night (especially alone)" (1995, 62). This of course limits the ability of women to participate in the full range of urban life. Carolyn Strange's 1995 book on the "girl problem" in Toronto from 1880 to 1930 illustrates this point—it was the leisure-time activities of the single girls that particularly posed problems to Toronto society. Women out in urban space past regular working hours represented a particularly disturbing transgression of social limits, at least according to those groups and associations worried about the social fabric of Toronto. We have certainly evolved in our thinking since 1880, or even 1930, but time-defined boundaries on women's use of urban space still remain.

In addition to boundaries of time, there are also boundaries of space. Booth and Gilroy place this question in the context of urban planning practices: "The work that has followed has concentrated mainly on the difficulties created for women by the mismatch between their dual role of homemaker and waged worker, and the form of the built environment particularly exemplified by the physical separation of different functions brought about by the land-zoning policies of planners (1996, 72). Dichotomies between public and private are written into the urban form through zoning; residential areas are only residential, with often even the nearest store outside the immediate neighborhood. By the same token, public areas exclude housing. The rigidities of zoning reinforce what Booth and Gilroy call "the false dichotomy of public and private space" and, in doing so, serve "to constrain women in their role both as career and as waged worker" (1996, 73). Women are certainly expected to be in residential zones; they will be less expected in areas defined as industrial zones.

However, our understanding of boundaries imposed by space must include not only material boundaries such as those created by zoning but also boundaries created out of discursive constructions of the sense of urban space. Jacqueline Coutras, in her *Crise Urbaine et Espaces Sexués* (1996), makes this point elegantly. A gender analysis of urban space needs to look at material reality, but it also needs to take account of the symbolic representation of space. There may be as many women as men using some street to go to work, but both women and men may be acting as though the street, as public space, belongs more to men than to women. Averting eyes, giving way on the sidewalk are more typical of women's behavior.

Resisting these boundaries of space could mean acting to increase mixed uses of urban space and therefore to diminish the association between particular areas and a gendered understanding of "public" and "private." We are still surprised to see women with small children in downtown office areas during the week, because we have difficulty imagining what they could be doing there. But if these downtown office areas also had residential functions and a wide variety of services, we would not find the presence of women with small children surprising.

The third dimension of boundaries that women might want to resist in urban spaces is that of social relations. Modern cities impose a segmented order where functional relationships dominate. It is unusual for women, and indeed even more unusual for men, to bring their children to the office; even now, this is barely tolerated. The unusual nature of this is illustrated by the fact that there is now an official day in the year when school children are encouraged to go to their parent's place of work. With the exception of this day, one's role as parent is strictly segregated from one's role as worker. Resistance to this can come from a desire to create and/or reaffirm conviviality and a sense of connectedness. As Dolores Hayden argues, properly constructed urban spaces can play this role; "diverse citizens need places to spend time that connect them to the possible meanings of city life as a social bond" (1995, 247). Women may be prime actors in this resistance, as they are particularly disadvantaged by the present segmentation of urban space.

SAFETY AUDITS

Let us begin by describing what we mean by a safety audit. METRAC's (Toronto's Metro Action Committee on Public Violence against Women and Children— the acronym no longer fits the name of the organization but has been kept because it is well known) definition is simple: "The basic idea of a safety audit is to look at a place that bothers you and note problems" (Wekerle and Whitzman 1995, 157). A slightly more elaborate definition was used by the Women's Action Center against Violence (WACAV) in its examination of the use of safety audits across Canada. "The Women's Action Center against Violence understands safety audits as a process which brings individuals together to walk through a physical environment, evaluate how safe it feels to them, identify ways to make the space safer and organize to bring about those changes" (1995, 2).

The description goes on to list the steps involved in safety audits: organizing the audit, orientation of the facilitators, doing the walk about, debriefing, and implementation (WACAV 1996a, 3). Typically, the actual audit will involve a group of users of that space, often with resource people, spending several hours, usually in the evening, examining the space from the point of view of their sense of safety. Out of this activity will come a series of recommendations that the group will then attempt to have implemented. The recommendations may be addressed to a wide variety of public and private bodies (municipal governments, provincial governments, individual landlords, store owners, schools) and may range across physical improvements (better lighting, changes in landscaping) to social changes (greater use of public space, public education about vulnerable groups).

Safety audits were first developed in Canada by METRAC, which was formed in 1982 in Toronto. Through its work with women's groups, the Toronto police, and the Toronto Transit Commission, METRAC developed the safety audit concept in 1985. METRAC published a *Women's Safety Audit Kit* that was widely distributed to women's groups and community groups. In order to bring diversity into the program, the original guide was adapted in a number of ways; for use on campuses, in rural areas, and by francophone groups. In turn, WACAV did a study in 1995 of the use made of safety audits across Canada. Two-hundred and fifty questionnaires were sent out to organizations and people who had been identified as possibly having had involvement with safety audits. One hundred seventeen questionnaires were returned, and of these, 69 indicated that they had participated in safety audits. This would suggest that safety audits have been used fairly extensively in Canada. A further breakdown of the results gives somewhat more information on the use of safety audits: 29 respondents who had been involved in safety audits came from universities and colleges, 26 from community groups, and 14 from municipalities. People who had used safety audits were generally positive about this tool, feeling that it had resulted in improvement to the areas surveyed and that it had increased participants' sense of their ability to create change. At the same time, people were aware of the limitation of safety audits, particularly the difficulties of implementing recommended changes.

Using this very brief description, we can structure our argument about the ways that safety audits can be seen as having important potential as a tool for women mobilizing to resist the mental and physical boundaries that mark their use and representation of urban space. This potential can be seen in a variety of ways: in creating a sense of ownership over the spaces used, in strengthening the women's sense of control over their environment, in increasing women's sense of their social and political effectiveness, in empowering women with a sense of positive social action and, finally, in fostering a sense of women having a right to the city and the unfettered use of urban space.

Being part of a group that moves about in a familiar urban space discussing and identifying things about that space that make people uncomfortable can increase women's feelings that this is their space and that they should feel at home using it. This leads to the realization that changes in this environment can be made so that the environment is made more friendly. Once people feel ownership of a space, they feel they can make decisions for this space. And, in turn, this leads the participants to have a greater appreciation of their own capacity to act collectively. At this point, community development is taking place as participants, with an increase in their political efficacy, work to ensure implementation of the recommendations that have come from the actual audit. This leads to an improved sense of social action and the increased likelihood that the community may be capable of acting collectively. For all these reasons, the safety audit process visualizes women's right to the city and to the use of urban space.

The boundaries imposed by time are directly addressed in safety audits. Questions of adequate lighting are always central to recommendations emerging from safety audits; the discussion assumes that women have the right to and should feel comfortable using urban spaces at night. Recommendations argue, on the level of physical improvements, that space should be usable at night.

Questions then become more general—why has urban planning worried about lighting streets rather than sidewalks? Should cities not be planned for people to use at night, not only in cars but as pedestrians? This raises questions not only about physical planning but also about social planning—how can we create cities that are livable if lighting experts worry only about cars and not about the people using the streets?

Safety audits also deal centrally with boundaries that are space defined. The sharp differentiation between residential neighborhoods and commercial zones creates problems for women feeling safe. In *Death and Life of Great American Cities* (1961), Jane Jacobs criticizes the rigid zoning and the development of unifunctional areas that relate to feelings of insecurity. By looking at the patterns of use that have developed and at the way women feel about these patterns of use, questions can be raised as to the impact on women of the rigid demarcation of the city into zones for work, zones for shopping, zones for sleeping. The boundaries imposed by the segmentation of social relations develop from this last point. Not only are our cities separated into unifunctional zones, but our social relations are also increasingly segmented into a multiplicity of interacting social roles: worker, parent, volunteer activist. The spaces of citizenship are absent from our lives and from our cities. Safety audits that are well organized can raise the questions of these boundaries and the ways in which our collective spaces, and our use of these spaces, reinforce the segmentation of social relations and the narrowing and fragmentation of modern urban life.

Safety audits have a particular ability to relate the very concrete to the more abstract. By engaging women in thinking about what they like and use in their immediate environment, and what they do not like and indeed fear, the audits create opportunities for linking the physical environment to the social one and for concretely imagining a more secure and more livable city. Women are experts, as the Elizabeth Wilson quotation indicated, at getting on with their lives in the cities and therefore at figuring out how their "bits" of them work; safety audits therefore build on, and are successful because of, women's knowledge and understanding of the interstices of the city. This knowledge is a base for thinking of ways urban space could be restructured to work better for women. Safety audits can give women not only the sense of their own knowledge and expertise, but also the sense that together it is possible to create better urban spaces.

Safety audits can facilitate a better understanding of the ways boundaries are socially constructed, and can instill a collective will to resist the imposition of boundaries that restrict the lives of women. However, safety audits do not always meet their progressive potential and, indeed, like most planning tools, depend very much on the social forces involved, the ways the tools are used, and the kinds of political participation that occur. Nancy Fraser's classification of needs discourses allows an analysis of different ways safety audits can be constructed and the ways in which this influences the choices of participants and the nature of participation. Fraser describes three kinds of needs discourses: oppositional, reprivatization, and expert (1989, 121). Oppositional discourses occur when "needs are politicized from below" and subordinate groups contest their subordination. Reprivatization discourses happen in reaction to oppositional needs talk; they make explicit the need for interpretations that were previously taken for granted, but, in making them explicit, these needs interpretations are also subtly changed. Expert discourses are "closely connected with institutions of knowledge production and utilization" (173).

These are useful categories for reflecting on the politics of safety audits; they allow us to contrast safety audits dominated by women and/or women's groups (oppositional), those dominated by municipal governments and/or the conventional media (reprivatization), and those dominated by professionals—be they planners, lighting engineers, or architects (expert). The variety of safety audit experiences is clearly being simplified by this limited number of categories, but this does allow us to focus on a number of central questions that distinguish the categories: who should participate, how should they participate, and why should they participate.

Oppositional

Oppositional safety audits are those where there is a clear link between using this tool and advancing the equality claims of women. Women do not now have full access to urban citizenship, but this right can be advanced by the use of safety audits. The right collectively to structure urban space in a way that would create a more equitable access to citizenship is an important goal for women.

The oppositional interpretation of safety audits argues that women have the right to take control over urban space and more particularly that urban space used by them. For the most part, the argument made is that women have this right in their quality as a vulnerable group; women are acting as a visualization of the greater vulnerability of certain groups in the urban context. "Safer for women, safer for all" is the most common formulation of this understanding, with the "all" seen as being inclusive of groups such as the elderly, the handicapped, gays and lesbians, visible minorities, and so on. There is also a clearly collective understanding to this right; communities have the right to have control over their urban space, and women organizing a safety audit are acting as the organized leadership element of the community. Safety audits can put women into a central role if the issue of vulnerability is made clear; in practice, women do take the lead because of their greater willingness to talk about their feelings of insecurity, which can facilitate an inclusive discussion about the ways in which the whole range of the population can better feel ownership of their collective space.

The question of how the participation should take place is answered by the oppositional discourse in terms of political organization. The recommendations will be implemented because the group will be sufficiently strong to press effectively for these recommendations. It will be bottoms-up mobilization. There will be recommendations for physical improvements but also more that relate to social questions and issues of social organization. Physical and social issues will not be separated, and the physical improvements will be understood in relation to their social impact.

The basis of this participation is the lived experience of those people taking part. The safety audit process is predicated on the idea that indigenous knowledge can, and should be, the basis of policy. People know the quality of the urban space that they use, and they understand how things work in this space. The community thus has the knowledge needed to improve its security and bring about community development. Women are the leaders in this process because the pattern of their use of community space, particularly in relation to the question of security, gives them this knowledge base.

In practice, it is extremely difficult to develop this sense that the lived experience of participants can, and should, be the basis of expertise. In our society, expertise is usually seen as something that is held by "experts," and both those receiving the results of the safety audits and those participating in them are likely to be doubtful about the status of indigenous knowledge. This sense that the participants in safety audits are the experts has to be developed and articulated and is certainly not something that can be taken for granted. The argument has to be made and clear links established between the role of the participants and the development of solutions.

Reprivatization

As Fraser (1989) indicates, the reprivatization discourse is aimed primarily at depoliticizing the question of women's access to urban space. Its major message is that there is no real problem and that any minor irritants can be satisfactorily solved by traditional leadership groups. Conventional policies—by the police, by planners, by municipal politicians—are the most appropriate ways to act in relation to questions of security. Where there are problems, they come from the general problems of modern society, and government is only one, and probably not the most important, actor in addressing these questions.

There are different versions of the argument that women's public security is not really a political question. Some of the conventional media argue that security issues stem in part from the decline of the family. Unsafe cities have resulted from the breakdown of the nuclear family, and only a return to conventional families, with stay-at-home mothers disciplining and socializing children, will make cities safe. Other versions support the view that the real solution lies in women avoiding "dangerous" areas and that each individual is personally responsible for her or his urban safety. Still other versions argue that in Canada we have avoided the dramatic urban problems of the American cities and that therefore urban safety does not at this time rank as a major political problem here. The analyses vary in why we have avoided these problems—our more livable center cities, more regional governments with regional tax bases, and different ethnoracial makeup being only three of the arguments—but the basic message is the same: urban public safety is not an issue to which we should be devoting new political resources at this time.

A reprivatization discourse does not, however, eliminate safety audits being done. They can be useful tools for making minor adjustments to physical space, for making residents feel more comfortable with their particular urban space, or, indeed, for making residents feel that their municipal government is receptive to their expressed concerns. All these argue for safety audits being done, but within a framework that does not question the basic gender and power assumptions of urban space. Participants are more likely to be defined as all residents in an urban area with little or no effort made to ensure the participation of vulnerable groups or to insist on the centrality of women's urban experience.

Participation follows the model of pluralist democracy. Particular groups of residents formulate recommendations, and these recommendations are weighed by the political authorities who must allocate scarce resources among a variety of groups, each with its own priorities. In this model, governments are seen as essentially beneficent, doing their best to use their scarce resources to maximize the improvements to the safety of the physical environment. The state is socially neutral; it responds to pressures from outside. The role of the public sector is therefore quite limited, as initiatives come from civil society. The allocation of public resources is marginal to the resolution of the problem of urban safety.

The real resolution will take place through private mechanisms—through women buying whistles and other security devices, through increasing the use of private security companies, through women and other vulnerable groups altering their behavior and making less use of urban space. In this version of safety audits, concrete and often limited improvements to the physical environments are often the priority—crisis telephones, surveillance cameras, improved lighting. The emphasis on technological solutions reinforces the apolitical cast of this vision: public safety is not a political problem, the solutions are to be found (where they are not reached through individual responsibility) through the power of technology. Technology is reassuring, and the principal message of the reprivatized version of safety audits is reassurance.

Expert

Expert discourses are well articulated in the different forms of safety audits. Public safety is seen to be an important, and often a new, issue for the society and one that requires the expertise of professionals to successfully solve. These professionals may be people with technical skills such as lighting experts, police, engineers, and so on. They may also be people with social knowledge of crime prevention through environmental design, crime prevention through social development, and even, of course, through the techniques of safety audits. The people who participate in these safety audits are seen as needing their results organized and interpreted in order for their messages to be taken seriously. Women can be focused upon as participants, and indeed vulnerability can be a useful criterion for participation, but the participants are only the subjects of political action, not political actors in their own right.

The "how" question falls in the same pattern; the participants need to channel their "raw material" to the experts so that the experts can come up with the appropriate solutions. The safety audit as such is simply a beginning; the real process begins with the reworking of the basic results by the experts.

The basis of participation is professional understanding of practice, and indigenous knowledge, or the knowledge of those who live in and use the city, is seen as something to be interpreted by experts. Indigenous knowledge does not, in this version of safety audits, form the basis of policy. It is the policymakers—the police, planners, university researchers—who define the relationship between the residents and policy. Once again, as in the reprivatization discourse, technological solutions have some popularity, but they are not the only kinds of solutions. The planners, for instance, may think of traditional planning solutions for reducing insecurity, whereas the police may depend more on technology. But in all cases, what is clear is that solutions emerge from expert analysis, not from the knowledge and organized activity of those who live in and use the city. Safety audits are seen as specialized tools or techniques for the creation of more secure cities, but they are tools that need to be used, and their results interpreted, by those trained to do so. The message of the expert version of the safety audit is that it is possible for the city to be safer for women, but it is the experts who have the power to make the decisions.

CONCLUSION

Articulating these three versions of the safety audit—oppositional, reprivatization, and expert—illustrates clearly their crucial differences, particularly as they relate to women. In the oppositional version, not only are women the central focus for the safety audit, women are also the primary political actors. Women are empowered by the safety audit process because it is their knowledge, their experience, and their organizing that form the base for successful action. The reprivatization version has a very different impact on women; it attempts not to empower, but to depoliticize the question of urban safety. It aims to reassure people—either that there is not a serious problem, or that its solution falls outside of politics. The expert version also does not consider women to be important political actors; instead the central players are the experts who have learned to use and interpret safety audits. The knowledge and experience of women who use these spaces are discounted; what is important is the analysis of experts.

If we are interested in the progressive potential of safety audits, the question therefore becomes: how can women ensure that safety audits follow an oppositional model and thereby ensure that this tool will facilitate the capacity of women to contest the imposition of boundaries? In part this depends on the balance of political and social forces at levels—national, provincial, global—far beyond those at which safety audits are being done. Looking across time, one can see moments when the objectives of gender equity were stronger and other moments where these objectives were far more muted. These levels of broad social support influence the ways in which safety audits are actually being done and the ways in which they can be presented.

However, there are some more locally based factors that relate to the safety audit process that are important to underline. First, safety audits must lead to concrete results if they are to be tools for resistance. Participants must get the sense that changes can be made, that collective action is possible. The implementation stage of safety audits is therefore crucial—recommendations must be the basis for action. A number of organizational factors are relevant here. There are important questions of resources—both financial and organizational; if there are clearly resources available for implementation, then the potential for organized action is higher. Where groups have been able to maintain their organizational effort, implementation has been more successful, reinforcing the group's potential for mobilization.

Second, safety audits must be women centered. This follows from the first point; focusing on women is a way of achieving better results and a better community development process. The focus on women is both accurate theoretically and effective practically. This must be clearly explained and discussed within the community.

Third, the social aspects of security must be highlighted. Technical or physical solutions will be part of the overall changes to be made, but these must be related to explanations about how "safe" and "unsafe" public spaces are constructed socially. The real solutions are through political organization and action.

Fourth, safety audits must reinforce the validity of indigenous knowledge. People's understanding and knowledge about how their space operates should form the basis of public policy. Women's intricate use of urban space—and here we go back to Elizabeth Wilson (1991), with her sense of women's greater capacity for variety, multiplicity, and even disorder—must be celebrated and built upon so that women will claim their rights to the unboundaried city.

Successful safety audits can lead cities to impose fewer boundaries on women. They can result in more women using a full range of urban space, and doing so throughout the full twenty-four hour cycle. Truly successful safety audits can encourage a wider range of women and other vulnerable groups to use this space, leading to a wider variety of uses of the space. Pushing success still further, safety audits can allow women to realize that, through community mobilization, they are able to participate in the definition and creation of their communities. Safety audits are a tool for women to use in resisting and reformulating boundaries.

REFERENCES

Booth, Christine, and Rose Gilroy. 1996. "Dreaming the Possibility of Change." *Built Environment* 22: 72–82.

Coutras, Jacqueline. 1996. *Crise Urbaine et Espaces Sexués.* Paris: Armand Colin.

Fraser, Nancy. 1989. *Unruly Practices.* Minneapolis: University of Minnesota Press.

Hayden, Dolores. 1995. *The Power of Place: Urban Landscapes as Public History.* Cambridge: MIT Press.

Jacobs, Jane. 1961. *The Death and Life of Great American Cities.* New York: Random House.

Little, Jo. 1995. *Gender, Planning and the Policy Process.* London: Pergamon Press.

METRAC. 1989. *Women's Safety Audit Guide.* Toronto: Metro Action Committee on Public Violence against Women and Children.

Semblat, Marie-Lise. 1993. "Les européennes et le développement local." *Animer: le magazine rural* 113–114: 21–22.

Strange, Carolyn. 1995. *Toronto's Girl Problem: The Perils and Pleasures of the City, 1880–1930.* Toronto: University of Toronto Press.

Wekerle, Gerda R., and Carolyn Whitzman. 1995. *Safe Cities.* New York: Van Nostrand Reinhold.

Whitzman, Carolyn. 1995. "What Do You Want To Do? Pave Parks? Urban Planning and the Prevention of Violence." In *Change of Plans,* edited by Margrit Eichler. Toronto: Garamond.

Wilson, Elizabeth. 1991. *The Sphinx in the City: Urban Life, the Control of Disorder and Women.* Berkeley: University of California Press.

Women's Action Center against Violence (WACAV). 1995. *Safety Audit Tools and Housing: The State of the Art and Implications for CMHC.* Ottawa: Canada Mortgage and Housing Corporation.

———.1996a. *Women's Safety Audit Guide.* Ottawa: WACAV.

———.1996b. *Women's Safety Audit Implementation Guide.* Ottawa: WACAV.

Chapter 9

Sex, Lies, and Urban Life: How Municipal Planning Marginalizes African American Women and Their Families

Marsha Ritzdorf

Marsha Ritzdorf died on March 28, 1998. She left behind two manuscripts, both works-in-progress, that her husband, Paul Brosovsky, identified as consisting of portions that she was working on for this chapter. One of these manuscripts was heavily dependent on a previously published work, "Family Values, Municipal Zoning, and African American Family Life" (Ritzdorf 1997a). Because Marsha had been so supportive of this project and to us personally, as well as to so many other women scholars, we felt committed to having her contribution published in this volume. Thus, we have remained as faithful as possible to her thoughts and words throughout this chapter. Our comments are in italics and are only offered when we felt there was need for clarification or edification.

—The Editors

In 1965, Daniel Patrick Moynihan released his now infamous report, *The Negro Family: The Case for National Action*, which catapulted into the national limelight the view that the African American family was broken and needed to be corrected. The stage for this report had been set long ago, however, by deliberate actions of white American policymakers. Their actions had been based historically on the assumption that the problems of the black family stemmed, in large part, from women being at the head of the family as "matriarchs." Today, though presented in far more subtle language, those same views are at the forefront of the Family Values Debate, the welfare reform movement, and numerous other policies promulgated by various factions of the American political spectrum. Such views are representative of a narrow cultural opinion of what a family was, is, and can be in the future. In addition, though we almost never hear this material discussed in the context of urban planning policy or urban policy history, it is central to the way our cities are planned and zoned.

The purpose of this chapter is to discuss the ways in which politically influential people have constructed a vision of the black family as "deviant" or "dysfunctional," and then to show how that construction has framed a public policy discourse that discriminates against black women and their families. Although there are more obvious public issues that are constructed in response to this discourse (the current welfare reform debate, for example), this chapter will focus on the quieter and more insidious ways in which these assumptions permeate spatial public policy by drawing on examples from municipal land-use planning and zoning.

Zoning and other tools of urban planning are guided by a concept of boundary that encourages inclusion and exclusion at the same time. Strict divisions of physical space, such as racially segregated neighborhoods, are highly visible and codified. In addition, social organization and language reinforce each other as sexualizing physical spaces, and social roles re-create existing boundaries. These boundaries are maintained by state policies and laws, economic and educational opportunities, discrimination, and the desire to be around others who share similar values. Yet some of these factors can also provide opportunities for transcending and reconfiguring these boundaries.

CONTRASTING VISIONS OF THE AFRICAN AMERICAN FAMILY

At the heart of the historical policy debate about appropriate family life is the ethnocentric view that assumes that the only acceptable norm is a nuclear family consisting of a husband, wife (who, in the best possible case, stays at home), and one or more children. This was coined the "family ethic" by social welfare historian Mimi Abramovitz, who suggests that "the family ethic articulates expected work and family behavior and defines women's place in the wider social order" (1996, 37). The linchpin of the family ethic is "the assignment of homemaking and childcare responsibilities to women." Abramovitz further suggests that "fulfilling the terms of the family ethic theoretically entitles a woman to the 'rights of womanhood' including claims to femininity, protection, economic support, and respectability. Non-compliance brings penalties for being out of role. Encoded in all societal institutions, the family ethic also reflects, enforces, and rationalizes the gender-based division of society into public and private spheres and helps to downgrade women in both" (1996, 38).

Even though the explosion of divorce and separation creates more and more white families configured outside this norm, the brunt of historical disparagement of alternative family norms falls upon African American women and their children.

The majority of scholars of the African American family fall into two major schools of thought. The first is referred to in the literature as the pathological or dysfunctional view. I argue that governmental policymakers rely upon this per-spective in defense of their own policies and programs. Most often associated with the work of E. Franklin Frazier and Daniel Patrick Moynihan, this view as-sumes that the black family is unstable, disorganized, and unable to provide its members with the necessary support systems to thrive and assimilate into main-stream American society (see Frazier 1939; Moynihan 1965). A concurrent prem-ise is that an intrinsic pathology of matriarchal households exists within the black community. This assumption blurs the historical racism and sexism of social pol-icy and solidifies the need to explore them both, concurrently and separately, as motivating forces in the application of these ideas in planning policy.

The second, or cultural relativity school, advocates the intrinsic functionality of the black family unit. The primary scholars supporting this view are Billings-ley (1968), Staples (1971), Hill (1971), McAdoo (1997), among others. Although there is debate among these scholars as to what proportion of black family life in the United States is reflexive of its African heritage, there is consensus that black America has developed family patterns that are useful in overcoming the racist conditions of American society. These patterns reveal a much broader con-struct of family that includes real and fictive kin beyond the bonds of mother, father, and children (see Stack 1974).

There is also a growing literature opposing the pathological view of the black family, including a challenge to the construct of matriarchy. Ground-breaking work, primarily by black women scholars, has sought to critique the construct from a feminist as well as racial direction. These scholars have focused on reex-amining the historical record as well as the theoretical terrain in order to chal-lenge the matriarchal theory based on its inaccurate use and misinterpretation of statistical data and historical records (see, for example, Baca Zinn 1990; Dill 1986; also see Higginbotham 1992). *This evolving scholarship, which challenges past findings while purporting new theories of gendered domain, does much to reveal how black women act within the confines of race, culture, and history in order to exploit opportunities for survival and improve their family's life chances. Working from margins, these women, in particular poor single mothers, learn how to move between and through physically and socially constructed boundaries.*

THE POLITICAL CONSTRUCTION OF THE
AFRICAN AMERICAN FAMILY

The literature on black family deviance is firmly rooted in the soil of white Amer-ican politics. In the years immediately following the American Revolution, politi-cians argued that the loose morals of blacks made them poor candidates for citi-zenship. In 1844 John C. Calhoun, then U.S. Secretary of State, argued in defense of slavery that whenever a state changes the relationship of whites and blacks from one of slavery to freedom, blacks then degenerate into a state of vice and poverty accompanied by deafness, blindess, insanity, and idiocy (Niven 1988). The reasons given were lack of morals and the absence of family values. By contrast, he suggested that in the slave states, blacks were greatly improved "in number, comfort, intelligence and morals."

In 1889, Phillip A. Bruce, a prominent historian of the era, began the academic solidification of the mythology that branded black families as disorganized or deviant. The black family did not exist, he wrote, and since the end of slavery, children were born into a state of "moral degeneracy" reflecting a severe deterioration in blacks' moral and social condition. He also began the process of castigating African American women, suggesting that they were unattractive to black men because of their "wantonness" (see Bruce 1889).

Herbert Gutman (1976) identifies Bruce's work as an important link between the popular view of African Americans as degenerate and the theory of Social Darwinism, which dominated in the United States from the Progressive Era through the end of World War I. This train of thought helped justify the most vicious patterns of segregation. Blacks were portrayed as being so degenerate that the race was not likely to survive. The solution, as proposed by the majority of white America, was to quarantine black people so that the white race could remain pure (Gutman 1976, 536–538).

In the 1930s, E. Franklin Frazier, a sociologist of the Chicago School, set forth the theory that slavery and migration had destroyed any natural order to black family life, leaving a vacuum they had not been able to fill (Frazier 1939). The truth, however, may have been different. Gutman's work shows that between 1855 and 1880, 70 to 90 percent of black households contained two parents, and about 70 percent were nuclear families (Gutman 1975, 191). Furthermore, he suggested that family ties were extremely strong despite the fact that slave owners could separate families at will, and that what white analysts called debilitating matriarchal structures were actually close approximations of a "healthy sexual equality" (Gutman 1975, 198).

It is true, however, that the black family developed in a different form than that held up as the white, middle-class ideal. The viability of a nuclear household supported by one male breadwinner was problematic as job opportunities diminished for black men and women in the aftermath of the depressions of the 1870s and 1890s: "The exclusion of African-Americans from skilled trades and factory work led to poverty and unemployment that made it necessary for many families to pool their resources and for others to split up, as members went in different directions in search of work or security. . . . [As a result] married black women were five times more likely to work for wages than were married white women" (Amott and Matthaei 1991, 166). By the turn of the twentieth century, urban poverty, under employment, and unemployment had led to the creation of a higher proportion of both female-headed and other alternative household forms for African Americans.

Studies of many late nineteenth-century and early twentieth-century cities also revealed strong kinship ties among African American families (see Taylor 1993). By the 1950s and 1960s, researchers were demonstrating that alternative family forms in black communities were flexible, effective ways of coping with long-term poverty and growing unemployment among black men (see Stack 1974). In other words, the history of the black family reveals a wellspring of historical strengths (see Giddings 1984).

Still, it was during this period that Moynihan (1965) wrote the report that was later released by the U.S. Department of Labor as *The Negro Family: The Case for National Action.* In the document he described the black family as a "tangle of pathology." Specifically, he referred to the natural (or moral) rightness of the patriarchal family. Thus, female-headed households were deemed to be pathological with no reference to any characteristic other than the sex of the head of the family. Moynihan's chilling portrait of the black matriarchy has been an enduring one for both the general public and policymakers, despite nearly 30 years of research refuting the view that female-headed households in particular, or black families in general, are intrinsically deviant (see Baca Zinn 1990).

THE IMPACT OF MYTHS ON BLACK WOMEN AND THEIR FAMILIES

In *The Black Image in the White Mind* (1987), historian George Fredrickson explains why these myths have had such a hold on the public imagination and, by extension, public policy. Because it was assumed that blacks' inferiority would keep them from surviving for many more generations, the major social concern became how to "control" them from blending into the larger, white population during the period of their decline and disappearance (Fredrickson 1987). Segregationist policies such as exclusionary zoning and restrictive residential covenants were a logical outgrowth of such thought (see Ritzdorf 1997a). *In this way, state policies created a highly visible border between blacks and whites while also isolating black families from resources available to whites.*

No matter how "middle class" black families became, in both economic and social terms, they were closed out of the opportunities available to other (white) Americans. For example, in the post–World War I housing boom, blacks were denied opportunities to purchase their own homes. In the era following World War I, "the most striking feature of Black life was not slum conditions, but the barriers that middle-class Blacks encountered in trying to escape the ghetto" (Jackson 1985, 203). These barriers included federal home ownership programs that were rooted in bigotry, the redlining of many black neighborhoods, and the inability of blacks to find financing for old homes since preference was given to new homes in suburban areas that were not open to black homeowners (Ritzdorf 1997a, 80). Many of these patterns of discrimination continued openly until the 1970s (Jackson 1985).

Although black families had been excluded from certain residential neighbor-hoods for generations by virtue of tools such as racial zoning, it was the massive building of American suburbs after World War II that showed the determination of housing developers, builders, and bankers to use governmental policies and monies to create a society clearly segregated by both economic class and race. For example, in 1960, not one of the 82,000 residents of Levittown on Long Is-land, New York, was black (Jackson 1985, 240). With the explosion of affordable suburban housing, it was no longer the privilege of only the very affluent to buffer themselves against "blight" (a euphemism for the poor and blacks). This opportunity for self-segregation expanded across the broad range of the white middle class. A not-often-discussed fear, however, also fueled the suburban exo-dus: a "pervasive fear of racial integration and its two presumed fellow travel-ers—interracial violence and interracial sex" (Jackson 1985, 290).

Although the fear of violence is discussed in the planning literature, white fear of interracial sex is not, except in rare cases. Yet this fear played, and still plays, a significant role in fueling segregation. The persistent untruths about black men's uncontrollable sexuality and the "loose morals" of black women have created a racial stereotype that brands them as unacceptable neighbors to whites. "For most, if not almost all, critics of the Black family, there is always at the back of the mind this myth, this image of Black America as Babylon" (Bennett 1986, 123). Maintaining segregated communities eases this fear. Thus, "traditional family values" remains the bedrock on which communities can legally build bar-riers to an integrated future.

These various methods of exclusion have had a particular impact on black women and their families. Forced into increasingly segregated areas by various private and public planning policies, black women find themselves traveling within a racialized and gendered domain. It is a domain that provides limited access not only to housing but also to other resources such as jobs, schools, and shops. Locating their problems within the built environment, however, is but one step in the process of determining how their marginal status affects their ability to develop survival strategies for themselves and their families. The social con-struction of poorer neighborhoods acts as a boundary as much as the regulated physical space that relegates certain individuals to live within those confines. These neighborhoods are thought to be places of violence, depravity, and lazi-ness, and there is the fear that the residents will bring these perceived character flaws with them should they move into other areas. Thus the attempt by many middle-class communities to use zoning to "keep them out."

THE FAMILY CONCEPT IN PLANNING AND ZONING

Discussions of urban planning policy almost never explicitly center on the con-cept of family, but it is implicitly central to the way our cities are planned and zoned. Both racial prejudice and sexism drive the use of the supposedly neutral ways in which family is defined for the purposes of municipal zoning. The historical use of family definitions in zoning ordinances is to discriminate against those who, by choice or chance, live in family arrangements that do not conform to the traditional white middle-class nuclear, family model (Ritzdorf 1987; Ritzdorf n.d.; Ritzdorf 1997a). Yet in 1992, a census report revealed that 50 percent, or 32.3 million, of all American children (children are defined by the U.S. census as individuals under the age of eighteen) lived in a nontraditional family that contained people other than the biological parents and their offspring. Eight million lived in an extended family containing, for example, a grandparent, an aunt, or an uncle. Thirty percent of all children of single parents lived in an extended family situation. For African American children, only 26 percent lived in a traditional nuclear family (Ritzdorf 1997a, 83).

Zoning is consistently used to prevent the spatial extension of people of color into white, middle-class America. Stereotypes influence zoning regulations that attempt to keep alternative living arrangements out of neighborhoods called "single-family," where the mythical nuclear family resides (see Coontz 1990). Perin (1988) found that Americans were discomforted by the presence in their neighborhood of those of different status, especially female-headed and minority-headed households. Female-headed households, whether white or black, were seen as culturally deviant and "not like us." However, nonnuclear families are more likely to occur among disenfranchised groups, the impoverished, and those from different races and cultures. For women who are both poor and of color, race becomes a "second axis of oppression" with rules that often benefit whites while exploiting or diminishing black women's chances (see Dill 1986). The literature on zoning shows that communities are generally resistant to changes in their local ordinances. However, major changes in household composition, maternal employment, and the number of elderly needing creative household and care arrangements in today's society leave room for debate on the legitimacy of traditional American residential zoning. In 1984, I conducted a nationwide zoning survey, the purpose of which was to gather empirical information about how municipal land-use and zoning policies were responding to the needs of changing households and families. In 1994, I conducted a longitudinal follow-up using the same stratified random sample set. The set was designed to include one SMSA, the central city, and a random sample of suburbs within the urbanized area from each state.

The 1984 survey showed that communities were making little effort to respond to demographic changes in their communities. The 1994 data revealed a slow and minimal movement toward more responsive change, primarily in the areas of child-care definition and the location of child-care homes, and a more liberal attitude toward home occupations. What has not changed however, is the way that most communities continue to narrowly define the family (see Table 9.1). The

Marsha Ritzdorf

remainder of this chapter is focused on how communities, including suburban communities, define family.

Family Definitions

Municipalities have the right (in all but three states—Michigan, New Jersey, and California) to establish zoning ordinances that determine the number of unrelated individuals who may share a household and whether they are to be considered a family (see Ritzdorf 1997a, 83). Almost all American zoning ordinances contain a definition of family. These definitions have become more restrictive, especially since the 1960s when, faced with changing life styles and a strong desire to preserve the existing small, nuclear-family oasis, local governments began to incorporate strict family definitions into their ordinances. The new, post-1960 definitions most typically define a family as an unlimited number of individuals related by blood, adoption, or marriage, but they limit the number (typically four or five) of unrelated individuals who are allowed to live together as a single housekeeping unit. In some communities, no unrelated individuals are allowed to live together.

In a 1983 study of the Seattle-Everett metropolitan area, for example, all the communities had legislated family definitions from 1950 on, and 74 percent had been passed or substantially revised in the 1960–1962 time frame. Nine (29 percent) of the communities allowed no unrelated individuals to live together; eight were small suburban communities, but the ninth was Everett, with a population in excess of 50,000 (Ritzdorf 1983).

The new definitions provided the courts with a chance to clearly establish whether zoning's function was restricted to regulating land use or whether it could be extended to the regulation of household composition. Generally speaking, the cases that have dealt directly with the right of alternative families (such

Table 9.1   U.S. Community Responses to Demographic Changes

	1984	*1994*
Percent of ordinances that define families	.91	.93
Comparison of the ways family is defined		
No unrelated people can live together	.06	.00
No more than:		
2 unrelated persons	.05	.10
3 unrelated persons	.09	.10
4 unrelated persons	.10	.10
5 unrelated persons	.28	.24
6 unrelated persons	.01	.01
More than 6	.01	.01
Defined broadly as a housekeeping unit	.40	.36

Data compiled by Marsha Ritzdorf, 1984, 1994.

as a group of elderly women or a lesbian couple and their children) have often been decided in favor of municipalities, as these individuals fall outside the category of "traditional family." Indeed, the landmark family decision, *Village of Belle Terre v. Boras*, decided by the Supreme Court in 1974, leaves no doubt that alternative family formation is suspect and legitimately controllable by municipal regulation. This decision allows for local zoning authorities to reach inside the household and regulate its composition. It gives single-family zoning, as a legitimate objective, the right to protect and encourage the institution of the traditional family (Ritzdorf 1997b, 48).

In the two decades since *Belle Terre* was decided, the impact of the decision has increased significantly. Restrictive ordinances continue to be judicially supported, as demonstrated by the 1991 case, *Dinan v. Town of Stratford*. In that case, the Connecticut Supreme Court upheld a locality's restrictive family definition, which allowed only a maximum of two individuals unrelated to the family of the occupant to live in a single-family unit. The court praised traditional family districts and vacated the lower court decision, which had invalidated the regulation since it controlled the user and not the use.

Family definitions thus remain relevant because communities continue to adopt and enforce them, as I found in the surveys I conducted. Between 1984 and 1994, the percentage of communities defining family in their ordinances went up slightly, from 91 percent to 93 percent. There was also a slight increase in the percent of communities that established a numerical limit to the number of unrelated persons who could live together as a family group, from 60 percent in 1984 to 64 percent in 1994. Therefore, only about 40 percent of the communities each year defined family broadly as a "single housekeeping unit." Most ordinances set numerical limits of six or fewer unrelated persons living together, though also giving broad discretion for interpreting who is related to whom. For example, two single mothers with two children each and one grandchild wishing to share a five-bedroom home could easily be prevented from doing so if the ordinance allows only three people unrelated to each other to live together.

Planners are being called upon to investigate and enforce their communities' family definitions. In 1984, 55 percent of the respondents said they had been asked to investigate complaints related to the violation of local family definitions. In 1994, that percentage had remained almost steady, at 54 percent, but more importantly, these family definitions had been enforced. In 1984, 42 percent of the communities had enforced their family definition and required nontraditional family groups to change their life style or location. In 1994, 47 percent responded that they had enforced their family definition.

However, some groups are organizing and lobbying for changes in their communities' restrictive zoning ordinances. In a 1980 landmark California case, *Santa Barbara v. Adamson*, the state court invalidated numerical family definitions. At issue was a ten-bedroom, owner-occupied house where the owner rented nine bedrooms to other adults, all of whom shared in the household life. Santa

Barbara had a family definition allowing only five unrelated people to live together regardless of the size of the house or ampleness of off-street parking. The
court rejected the city's argument that there was a rational relationship between
the definition and use of the property, and invalidated the utilization of numerical
definitions in California zoning ordinances, citing the state's constitutional right
to privacy. The California case demonstrates how citizens with pressing needs
for more flexible communities have developed greater sophistication about the
social impact of zoning. They are now bypassing the municipalities and going
directly to the state government for change. The passage in 15 years of 17 state
pre-emption statutes related to child care is an example. Research shows that
these pre-emptions were passed, in most cases, over the opposition of the local
governments themselves (Ritzdorf 1997b).

The use of family definitions has proven effective in segregating traditional
families from nontraditional ones. But it is also an insidious way of separating
white, middle-class families from poorer families of color. There is never any
mention of race, ethnicity, class or gender; so it appears that communities are
only enforcing ordinances which address the definition of family. In reality, however, communities are reaching inside the home and affecting familial relationships. Such intrusions are particularly burdensome to single mothers in African
American communities. These women likely need to share housing with other
adults and children, for any number of economic, social, and security reasons
(Ritzdorf 1997a, 85). For example, sharing a traditional single-family dwelling
unit may allow two single-parent families to own or rent a home that they might
otherwise be unable to afford. Thus, disallowing this housing arrangement may
end their hope of ever fulfilling the "American dream."

CONCLUSION

One of the challenges of the twenty-first century is to extend the boundaries that
shape urban life styles and life choices, primarily because of the changing patterns of people's lives, especially those of poor women. Implicit in the granting
of land-use and zoning powers to U.S. municipalities is a mandate to employ
those powers in a socially responsible way (Ritzdorf 1983). Now that economic
and social changes are impacting more families, zoning must change, too. Both
men's and women's lives would be enhanced by residential neighborhoods that
allowed them the freedom to work at home, to have their children (or parents)
watched at small neighborhood-based child-care centers, to share living spaces
with the companions of their choice, and to use the spaces within their homes as
they choose. All of these would of course be accomplished within parameters
that assure the safety and health of the entire community. Undue noise, inappro-
priate uses of property, disruptive neighbors and other potential problems that
may arise in any neighborhood are easily handled through nuisance laws that

apply equally to all community residents, regardless of age, sex, race, or relationship to other.

Yet regardless of changes in the American family, most zoning laws remain basically unyielding in their nostalgic interpretation of "correct" community land patterns in which work, home, and services are spatially separated. Nostalgia is also at play when communities use family definition laws to try to maintain the traditional, Eurocentric concept of family, a concept that is gendered, raced, and classed. Alternative family patterns still create feelings of unease among community residents, and therefore they are explicitly disallowed in most zoning ordinances. But, "for [many] African-Americans, especially, the nuclear family models tend to offer an inadequate survival or pragmatic nurturing strategy. Instead, for African-Americans, extended families increase the chances for improving one's situation" (Ford and Turner 1990–91, 80). *Thus, maintaining zoning ordinances that privilege the traditional nuclear family puts African American poor families at a great disadvantage. The story of that disadvantage, as played out against a backdrop of cultural hegemony reflected in the family ethic, should also serve as a cautionary tale for white, middle-class women who must now juggle work and family.*

Traditional zoning histories generally give two main reasons for the rise and acceptance of municipal zoning ordinances. The first is the desire to do something about the continually disintegrating quality of urban life. The second is the growing realization that it was to the advantage of the burgeoning capitalist economy in the United States to spatially separate home and work life and to romanticize that separation in order to create a consumer-oriented society. The more isolated one's residential environment from the work place, services, and those with a different socioeconomic status, the "better" the neighborhood (Cibulskis and Ritzdorf 1989).

I propose an additional interpretation of the historical suppositions behind municipal land-use and zoning policies: that the family ethic reinforced the growing industrial expansion and provided a way to translate the increasing economic separation between middle-class and working-class lives into a spatial reality. Furthermore, the social importance of the separation of middle- and lower-class life styles was of keen significance to middle-class women and men who participated and still participate in its enforcement.

The language of municipal zoning ordinances, like any culturally bound discourse, is a language that both persuades and informs us about values and attitudes. It supports a specific type of social tie—the nuclear family unit—in a neighborhood separated from the work place and removed from commercial and social services. The relatively narrow range of choices this creates in most American environments needs to be altered to meet the needs of a changing population while preserving the shared standards of behavior that are culturally important to most Americans. In many communities, land-use planning and zoning have become more environmentally and economically sophisticated, but they have not necessarily become more socially attuned to the realities of contemporary life.

For most Americans, a family is a unit from which they draw their nurturance and sustenance. It is not a particular form, nor is it a simple, symbolic image. The development of planning policies that build upon the strengths of a plurality of family forms will be necessary as we continue to undergo demographic and economic changes that affect our racial/ethnic composition, the structure of the labor market, and changing gender roles. Only by extending its vision to a diversified structure of family life will the United States move towards a more egalitarian future and away from the continuing and escalating racial tensions in our communities. Only then will it have stretched the boundaries that affect women's lives and made the space within more inclusive.

REFERENCES

Abramovitz, Mimi. 1988. *Regulating the Lives of Women: Social Policy from Colonial Times to the Present.* Boston: South End.

———.1996. *Under Attack, Fighting Back: Women and Welfare in the United States.* New York: Monthly Review Press.

Amott, Theresa, and Julie Matthaei. 1991. *Race, Gender and Work.* Boston: South End.

Baca Zinn, Maxine. 1990. "Family, Feminism and Race in America." *Gender and Society* 4, 1: 68–82.

Bennett, Lerone, Jr. 1986. "The Ten Biggest Myths about the Black Family." *Ebony* 42: 123–124.

Billingsley, Andrew. 1968. *Black Families in White America.* Englewood-Cliffs, N.J.: Prentice-Hall.

Bruce, Phillip A. 1889. *The Plantation Negro as Freeman: Observations on His Character, Condition, and Prospects in Virginia.* New York: G. P. Putnam's Sons.

Cibulskis, Ann, and Marsha Ritzdorf. 1989. Zoning for Child Care. Chicago: American Planning Association.

Coontz, Stephanie. 1990. *The Way We Never Were: American Families and the Nostalgia Trap.* New York: Basic Books.

Dill, Bonnie Thornton. 1986. Our Mothers' Grief: Racial and Ethnic Women and the Maintenance of Families. Research Paper #4, Center for Research on Women, Memphis State University.

Dinan v. Town of Stratford Board of Zoning Appeals. 1991. 595 A.2d. 864 (Conn.).

Ford, Donna Yvette, and William L. Turner. 1990–91. "The Extended African American Family: A Pragmatic Strategy that Blunts the Blade of Injustice." *Urban League Review* 14, 2: 25–38.

Frazier, E. Franklin. 1939. *The Negro Family in the United States.* Chicago: University of Chicago Press.

Fredrickson, George. 1987. *The Black Image in the White Mind: The Debate on Afro-American Character and Destiny, 1817–1914.* Middletown, Conn.: Wesleyan University Press.

Giddings, Paula. 1984. *When and Where I Enter: The Impact of Black Women on Race and Sex in America.* New York: William Morrow.

Gutman, Herbert G. 1975. "Persistent Myths about the Afro-American Family." *Journal of Interdisciplinary History* 6: 35–49.

———.1976. *The Black Family in Slavery and Freedom: 1750–1925*. New York: Vintage Books.

Higginbotham, Evelyn Brooks. 1992. "African-American Women's History and the Meta-language of Race." *Signs* 17: 251–274.

Hill, Robert. 1971. *The Strengths of Black Families*. New York: Emerson Hall.

Jackson, Kenneth. 1985. *The Crabgrass Frontier: The Suburbanization of the United States*. New York: Oxford University Press.

McAdoo, Harriette Pipes, ed. 1997. *Black Families*. 3d ed. Thousand Oaks, Calif.: Sage Publications.

Moynihan, Daniel Patrick. 1965. *The Negro Family: The Case for National Action*. Washington, D.C.: U. S. Department of Labor, Office of Policy Planning and Research.

Niven, John. 1988. *John C. Calhoun and the Price of Union: A Biography*. Baton Rouge: Louisiana State University.

Perin, Constance. 1988. *Belonging in America: Reading Between the Lines*. Madison: University of Wisconsin Press.

Ritzdorf, Marsha. 1983. "The Impact of Family Definitions on American Municipal Zoning Ordinances." Ph.D. diss., University of Washington.

———. 1987. "Planning and the Intergenerational Community: Balancing the Needs of the Young and Old in American Communities." *Journal of Urban Affairs* 9, 1: 75–89.

———. 1997a. "Family Values, Municipal Zoning, and African American Family Life." In *Urban Planning and the African American Community: In the Shadows*, edited by June Manning Thomas and Marsha Ritzdorf. Thousand Oaks, Calif.: Sage Publications.

———. 1997b. "Locked Out of Paradise: Contemporary Exclusionary Zoning, the Supreme Court, and African Americans, 1970 to the Present." In *Urban Planning and the African American Community: In the Shadows*, edited by June Manning Thomas and Marsha Ritzdorf. Thousand Oaks: Sage Publications.

———. n.d. "Zoning and the Changing Family: Resistance or Change?" Unpublished manuscript.

Santa Barbara v Adamson. 1980. 610 P.2d. 436 (Calif.).

Stack, Carol. 1974. *All Our Kin: Strategies for Survival in a Black Community*. New York: Harper and Row.

Staples, Robert E., ed. 1971. *The Black Family: Essays and Studies*. Belmont, Calif: Wadsworth.

Taylor, Henry L. 1993. *Race and the City: Work, Community, and Protest in Cincinnati, 1820–1970*. Urbana: University of Illinois Press.

Village of Belle Terre v. Boras. 1974. (416 U.S. 1.39LE2d797, 94S.Ct.1536).

Chapter 10

Manipulating Constraints: Women's Housing and the "Metropolitan Context"

Christine Cook, Marilyn Bruin, and Sue Crull

Where we live and how we are housed are important concerns of research, public policy, and human activity. During the 1990s, because of a reduction in the availability of low-cost housing and the physical and social deterioration of America's cities, urban housing conditions and neighborhood quality emerged as especially critical issues for single mothers and their children (Mulroy 1995). The decline of cities and the strategies to revitalize them have been the subject of much planning literature, but current research does little to illuminate the extent to which improved opportunities in the metropolis result in improved housing and neighborhood quality for single-parent women and children. Heretofore, the dominant theme in urban economic development strategies has been job creation. These employment opportunities, however, are not for existing residents but to bring middle- and upper-income households back to downtown (Turner 1995). Apparently the plan is to "recapture" the city from the poor—those responsible for its decline—many of whom are single mothers and their children.

For a majority of single mothers, however, "cities are not simply the scenery for the playing out of gender; place is central" (Garber and Turner 1995, xviii). The proportion of single mothers living in the metropolis, both central city and suburbs, continues to grow. Understanding the dynamic of the metropolitan housing market is vital to understanding the housing and neighborhood choices and constraints—the challenges and opportunities—single mothers face in securing housing and creating a home for their families. For example, precipitous drops in income following marital dissolution often force women into the rental market and thus to the central city, where rental housing is most available. This available housing, however, is often older and more physically inadequate than

183

that in the suburbs. Rental housing in suburbia, on the other hand, may be less affordable and can raise transportation costs for women without automobiles. Postdivorce income changes leave other women "house poor" in suburbia— reluctant to move and struggling to retain the family home for the sake of residential stability, educational continuity for children, and existing support networks (Cook 1988). Thus, "the nature of housing problems for single-parent families is tied to their location of residence" (Mulroy 1988, 27).

In this chapter, we turn first to a review of literature that includes both the importance of housing and the meaning of home for women and children, thus avoiding the "narrowness of much writing on 'women and housing' which has concentrated on women's disadvantaged access to housing" (Darke 1994, 12). We also include a selected review of literature on housing choice and decision making. Taking into consideration "boundaries" from within and outside the family that restrict women's housing options, we discuss from a woman's perspective the issues being raised by those interested in the "geography of opportunity," since much of that literature does not attend to families headed by women specifically. Our work begins to address questions posed by Spain (1987) about housing problems experienced by single mothers and the role of the metropolitan context in explaining them: How is housing quality affected by local housing markets? Do women, in general, and minority women, in particular, experience more gains in housing quality in some metropolitan areas than others? Do differences in the socioeconomic characteristics and/or the economic vitality of the metropolis affect the housing quality of women?

Since "indices of a housing problem generally include two factors: housing quality and tenure status" (Mulroy 1995, 27), we focus on the housing adequacy and homeownership opportunities of white, black, and Hispanic single-parent women. Our sample of women consisted of those without a spouse present either because they are divorced, never married, or widowed. They are women with at least one child under age 18 living with them. We examine data from 22 cities collected in 1991 and 1992 by HUD in the American Housing Survey to determine the extent to which the metropolitan context in which women find themselves shapes the housing opportunities available to them and their families. The metropolis, both central city and suburbs, is treated as a whole. This view is a decidedly broad sweep, shaped by recent research that suggests that the overall opportunity structure of the metropolis is by far the most important determinant of individual neighborhood conditions (Jargowsky 1997). We define the metropolitan context as the opportunity structure—the overall education and income levels of the city's population—to correspond with the themes of urban revitalization efforts to affect the resource pool within the city. Do cities with high education levels and low levels of poverty provide benefits to single mothers in the form of improved housing and homeownership opportunities? Do racial and ethnic disparities among single mothers persist in high- compared to low-resource cities? In the end, the examination of the literature and the data raise more questions than they answer. We pose those questions back to the reader as research opportunities. As advocates for advancing housing and neighborhood research, we argue for attention to the near environment that is both qualitative and quantitative in nature and that focuses particularly on single-mother families, because more than half of all children will live a portion of their lives in a single-parent family, because these families are often economically vulnerable, and because their housing problems appear lost in efforts to revitalize and "reconstruct" the city (McLanahan and Sandefur 1994).

THE IMPORTANCE OF HOUSING TO WOMEN AND CHILDREN

Housing has far-reaching implications for families and their children—socially, psychologically, and economically. Research on the psychological significance of housing asserts that the home is a "mirror" and "symbol" of self (Cooper 1974; Marcus 1995; Rubinstein and Parmelee 1992). Theorists view the development of the self as a process of separation of the person from the environment (Proshansky and Fabian 1987). To become a healthy adult, children must have experiences that allow for the growth of autonomy, the development of a sense of competence and mastery, and supportive relationships with others. The home—both one's housing and neighborhood—has significance as both a social and physical environment. Miller (1986) found that adults' characterizations of their childhood homes illustrated that home and neighborhood met important psychological needs for nurturance, territoriality, privacy, identity, stimulation, manipulation, sociability. Although the meaning of home as a nurturing and safe haven may be similar for men and women, Darke (1994) suggests that women value their homes in a way that is a mixture of affection and resentment at the demands of the home. For homeless, poor, or abused children, the meaning of home may be similarly "conflicted." A nurturing home environment, privacy, regulating territory, and personalization may be unattainable. Very little research has examined the meaning and the effect of housing and neighborhoods that do not meet psychological needs. "It is important for those making housing policy or delivering housing services to understand the central significance of the home in women's lives" (Darke 1994, 28). Housing that is both physically inadequate and insecure in terms of tenure or safety, neighborhoods that are distressed and high-crime, "cannot constitute a home which enhances a woman's sense of herself or of being socially valued" (28).

"Make yourself at home" hints at the importance of housing as a social phenomenon. Environmental designers and community psychologists have contributed a body of research that illustrates that the "near environment" can be shaped to enhance or detract from social interaction. Chairs, benches, and furnishings inside and outside the home can be arranged to promote social engagement. There is also evidence that housing can stymie or enhance friendship formation and is a component in building social capital in distressed neighborhoods (Lang and Hornburg 1998). Adolescents who live in "mobile homes," for example, do not feel good about inviting friends from outside the "park" to their homes. Site-planning strategies that allow for the definition of semipublic and semiprivate space have been, and continue to be, espoused as methods to improve neighboring and invest in social capital formation (Bothwell, Gindroz, and Lang 1998; Newman, 1972, 1996). Residents of redesigned neighborhoods report improved community involvement.

Often neither social nor community programs recognize the need to support kinship, friendship, and neighborhood networks nor the contribution that housing makes to the formation of these networks. Past research suggests that black single parents, for example, depended on friends and family as sources of social support (Stack 1974). However, some more recent research hints that these informal sources of support may be eroding (Peake 1997). Might the failure to attend to the physical dimensions of social interaction cause some of the denigration of these relationships?

> Housing design and location conventions have been recognized increasingly as being insensitive to and indeed oppressive of women in general and female-headed and single-parent families in particular: in terms of geographical isolation and inaccessibility; in terms of site plans that do not facilitate neighboring, mutual aid, and child supervision. . . . Single-parent families disproportionately are forced to live in inappropriate, unsupportive, or inaccessible settings, because proper housing does not exist. (Smizik and Stone 1988, 231)

The economics of housing is another important dimension that has received perhaps more than its fair share of the literature on women and housing (Gilroy and Woods 1994). Throughout the 1980s and early 1990s, there was a surge of research attending to the housing and neighborhood experiences of women. The feminization of poverty, discrimination, and the rising number of families headed by women were recognized as major factors contributing to a shortage of decent and affordable housing. The lack of affordable housing, however, continues to plague single mothers, yet public assistance for housing costs reaches only a fraction of poor and near-poor women and their children (Cook and Bruin 1994; Newman and Schnare 1988, 1992). It is perhaps the most pervasive and deep seated of housing problems. For many families, the "squeeze between inadequate incomes and high housing costs means that after paying for their housing they are unable to meet their nonshelter needs" (Stone 1993, 23). The crisis in housing affordability has been shown to affect disproportionately single mothers, most especially those who are minority heads of household. Fully 40 percent of Hispanic and 33 percent of black, single-parent mothers have cost burdens in excess of 50 percent of their monthly income, compared to 24 percent of their white counterparts (Cook and Bruin 1994).

Housing that has serious problems with plumbing, heating, electricity, and maintenance is designated by the Department of Housing and Urban Development (HUD) as inadequate, and although the physical condition of housing in the United States continues to improve overall, there are families still trapped in unsafe housing. For them unsafe wiring, plumbing, and heating systems, and the presence of lead paint and vermin, threaten not only physical safety but also emotional security (Stone 1993). When landlords fail to make critical repairs or when homeowners have neither the money, skill, nor time to maintain their housing, women and children alike suffer. Nationally, black, single-parent women's families are five times more likely than their white or Hispanic counterparts to experience housing problems categorized as "severely inadequate" (*American Housing Survey* 1995). Physical inadequacy of housing often goes hand-in-hand with affordability, since one strategy a poor family can use to reduce housing costs is to live in substandard housing, where housing expenditures (rent or mortgage payments and utilities) are sometimes lower. The strategy is not foolproof, however, because increased demand for less expensive housing can create a submarket in which the price of housing actually rises. Building codes and standards, demolition or redevelopment of affordable units, and little increase in the stock of low-cost housing can further limit the availability of affordable housing.

HOUSING DECISION MAKING

A View from the Household

Our choice of housing and neighborhoods is the result of an intricate, dynamic process of gathering information about housing, considering alternatives, making a decision, and reaffirming that decision (Lawton 1983). Prior to selecting housing, families assess their needs relative to resources and constraints (Morris and Winter 1978, 1996). In their theory of housing adjustment, Morris and Winter argue that cultural norms play a large part in shaping a family's definition of its needs. We often define the adequacy of our current housing based on characteristics such as numbers of bedrooms, the availability of a separate kitchen, a private bath, and whether it is owned or rented. No doubt, society's conception of women's roles as homemakers and family nurturers contributes to their housing choice (Spain 1992). Thus both societal norms and women's roles shape housing goals and aspirations. "The household endeavors to make the residential situation and the aspiration picture as congruent as possible" (Priemus 1986, 31). Adjustments to housing exist along a continuum that is anchored by *staying in place* at one end of the continuum and *moving* at the other end. Adjustments range from the active—moving one's family or remodeling an existing structure—to more passive methods that involve changes within the household rather than to the structure (Morris and Winter 1978, 1996; Priemus 1986; Quercia and Rohe 1993).

Regardless of the configuration of one's family, there are constraints that predict the outcome of housing adjustment. The literature that examines housing decision making and housing choice falls broadly into two areas: those that examine housing decision-making processes and resources within families, and those that examine the role of macrolevel effects—conditions external to the household that affect both the supply of and demand for housing. In the former view of housing and neighborhoods, characteristics of women's housing are seen through the lenses of household boundaries. These boundaries may be economic or sociopsychological. Position in the family life cycle and position in the labor market are linked because of their underlying ties to the type and composition of the household. Together they "form the household situation that creates conditions that further or hamper" the adaptation process (Priemus 1986, 35). Those that conceptualize constraints and resources as internal to the family (an inside-to-outside view) also emphasize women's income, finances, and ability to manage their families' resources and employment characteristics (Buehler and Hogan 1986). Other individual and family characteristics such as adaptability, problem-solving skills, self-esteem, locus of control, and perceived discrimination can also influence one's housing decisions (Bruin and Cook 1997; Morris and Winter 1996).

Household reconfiguration, adopting new standards, and social action may result when other, more active means of housing adjustment are restricted. Families that double up, launch adult children, ignore peeling paint, or withhold rent to protest increases are engaging in creative adaptation processes (Priemus 1986). There is generally agreement, however, that "nonadaptation" is the result of the inability to bring housing in line with goals and aspirations. Constraints so severe as to result in apathy and "nonadaptive behaviors" produce enormous amounts of unresolved, continuous stress on families and may ultimately be pathological (Priemus 1986; Morris and Winter 1978, 1996). Chronic stress may result in apathy, anomie, and helplessness. Severe stress of this type may result in chronic mobility—a newly named, though not a new, phenomenon (Bartlett 1997). Though the description of restrained housing choices, nonadaptation, and chronic stress may resonate with single mothers, there is not much research that identifies their housing situations or coping strategies specifically, except as outside the mainstream. Even in the midst of dramatic welfare reforms, there is little attention to how single mothers will meet their housing needs as they are terminated from welfare or move into low paying jobs (Kingsley 1997; Mulroy 1995; Shlay 1995; Wiseman 1996).

A View from the Neighborhood

Even those whose research has tended to focus on housing choice from a household perspective acknowledge that "external factors play an important part in the selection of an adaptation mechanism" (Priemus 1986, 31). Their work acknowledges that some families are in a weak position in the housing market. That position in the housing market, though related to the structure of the society, is usually operationalized by specification of household characteristics such as income, education, age, employment, marital status, race, and numbers of children. Until recently, factors actually external to the family—quality of the schools, availability of jobs—were not usually an integrated part of conceptual or operationalized models. Over the last several years, however, many studies have been conducted examining the impact of both social and economic characteristics of urban neighborhoods on individuals' and families' lives (Galster 1998; Galster and Killen 1995; Galster and Mikelsons 1995; Jargowsky 1997; South and Crowder 1997; Tempkin and Rohe 1998).

"Spatial development patterns affect residential location choices" (Turner 1995, 272). Racially and economically segregated neighborhoods within cities establish boundaries that restrict choice of housing, schools, employment, child care, and services. Thus for single mothers who are black, Hispanic, and/or poor, the options for housing and its location are critical to understanding their life chances (Shlay 1995). As the context for family life, the neighborhood exerts a strong influence on family outcomes. The literature on the "geography of opportunity," often said to be spawned by Wilson's observations of the isolation and perpetuation of urban poverty (Wilson 1987), suggests that neighborhoods can undermine individual motivation and family support (Galster and Killen 1995). Distressed neighborhoods reduce employment and educational prospects, increase exposure to crime, and limit the availability and variety of services and facilities (Galster and Killen 1995; South and Crowder 1997). For youth who are poor and living in distressed neighborhoods, friends, neighbors and kin influence decisions regarding education, fertility, work, and crime—in effect, helping them choose alternatives and options beyond those that they themselves might have considered (Galster and Killen 1995).

Although there is no agreement on precisely how to operationalize social capital, it is conceptualized as community and community building, mutually supportive institutions within neighborhoods, and the familiarity and trust that form the basis of relationships and social participation (Tempkin and Rohe 1998). Some authors emphasize social networks between and among families and friends—the extent and quality of these relationships—involvement in tenant associations, and the existence of community organizations (Saegert and Winkel 1998). Political participation, voting records, and the number of social and community organizations available are often used to characterize the social infrastructure. Still others suggest that both the former, social milieu and the latter, institutional infrastructure combine to give the best measure of social capital (Tempkin and Rohe 1998). The social capital available to residents of urban neighborhoods appears to contribute to housing quality and lower crime rates (Saegert and Winkel 1998) and, to some extent, can compensate for financial capital. However, single mothers have many demands on their time, and their ability to participate in either social networks or community organizations is limited.

The literature on social capital formation as part of the geography of opportunity often fails to consider the time limitations single mothers experience. Saegert and Winkel (1998) found that there was greater social capital and better management in buildings where householders were employed, but the physical conditions of the buildings were worse than those where householders were unemployed. They argued that these "worse conditions" might be attributed to "lack of time at home" (Saegert and Winkel 1998, 46). Peake (1997) suggests that these limitations on kinship and neighborhood activities may extend even to black women, traditionally known for strong, informal support networks. "While there were examples of participation of African-American women in organizations concerned with the safety and level of amenities in their neighborhoods and of small networks of mutually supporting households, overall there were more cases of fragmented and isolated households" (Peake 1997, 358). It appears that profound poverty may mediate social capital formation differently by race and gender in ways that are only hinted at in current investigations.

Escaping the effects of the poor neighborhood is not easy. South and Crowder (1997) report that there has been surprisingly little attention to residential mobility into and out of distressed neighborhoods. In their research, differences were especially pronounced for black households compared to white. Blacks who moved out of poor neighborhoods were substantially more likely to move to another poor tract than they were to move to a nonpoor tract (South and Crowder 1997, 1058). White movers, on the other hand, were more than twice as likely as black movers to escape a poor neighborhood. Concurrently, there is evidence that concentrated poverty is increasing (Jargowsky 1997). In all metropolitan areas in the United States, "the physical areas of urban blight have expanded rapidly and a greater proportion of the population lives within their borders but still the majority of the poor do not live in high-poverty neighborhoods" (Jargowsky 1997, 3). In contrast to the literature that examines the opportunity structure of individual urban neighborhoods, Jargowsky asserts that his findings suggest that metropolitan-wide factors and not the characteristics of the residents and local culture explain high-poverty neighborhoods. A macrostructural explanation accounts for most of the variation in neighborhood poverty, and "changes in the overall opportunity structure, as measured by the mean income of all metropolitan residents, are by far the most important determinants of poverty" (1997, 144).

Much of the dialogue about revitalization of cities seems to revolve around reducing the negative effects of poor neighborhoods on the suburbs and attracting capital, new middle- and upper-income residents, and buyers to the central city. Very little in mainstream research is focused on the consequences of the racialization of women's lives and the feminization of poverty for the social geography of the metropolis (Peake 1997). Central-city poverty is self-perpetuating and has an effect on the wider metropolis (Jargowsky 1997). Continued draining of the nonpoor, who are leaving urban neighborhoods at higher rates than their poor counterparts, creates "economic segregation and worsens fiscal tensions between the poor central city and rich suburbs (Jargowsky 1997, 5). "A region noted for its welfare-dependent, undereducated, crime-prone populace cannot retain or attract a capital base" (Galster and Hornburg 1995, 6). Often the very definition of a poor neighborhood is based on the characteristics of the households (Ricketts and Sawhill 1988; South and Crowder 1997) rather than upon objective spatial variations that occur in the metropolitan opportunity structure (Galster and Killen 1995, 7). Characterization of the distressed neighborhood as one in which poor people predominate does very little to untangle the complexity of housing inadequacy and affordability, the availability of neighborhood services and resources, or the overlay of racial and ethnic discrimination facing the poor household.

Although there is clearer definition of the metropolitan context as the geography of opportunity than in the past, the "dynamics of women and poverty, of the economy and work, and of women's work in all of its facets (must be) recognized" (Young and Miranne 1995, 202). There is still much in the literature that reinforces the notion that the victims in the high-poverty neighborhood, often a single mother and her children, are to blame for their "distress." Although some see single mothers as a social problem or evidence of pathology in neighborhoods, others dismiss them with a single stroke: "For those in two-parent families, the primary causes of poverty can be traced to the vicissitudes of the labor market, and for those in female-headed families to the lack of financial support from absent fathers" (Jargowsky 1997, 4). Young and Miranne explain this view as common: "The argument seems to be that women's chances for moving out of poverty are tied to their chances of being attached to a man. The lack of jobs produces poverty for men, but for women the source of poverty is the lack of a husband" (1995, 203).

METROPOLITAN CONTEXT

We now turn to an examination of the housing conditions—housing adequacy and tenure status—of single mothers in 22 cities across the United States.[1] We examined the housing and neighborhood choices women have made, evaluating the cities in which they live along two important, metropolitan-wide dimensions: educational resources—the proportion of residents with a four-year college degree or more—and the city's economic resources—the proportion of residents who are above the poverty level.[2] The proportions of housing that was inadequate and of homeownership are reported to determine the extent to which the metropolitan context affects housing outcomes for them.[3]

Cities were classified as high or low in education and economic resources.[4]

Among the 22 cities, eight were classified as both high in proportion of college graduates and high in economic resources: Anaheim, Denver, Seattle, Atlanta, San Diego, Newark, Hartford, and Kansas City. Over one-third of the population in Anaheim, Denver, and Seattle had college degrees. Eight cities were categorized as low in both education and economic resources: New Orleans, San Antonio, Pittsburgh, Miami, San Bernardino, St. Louis, Cincinnati, and Columbus; the city with the lowest proportion of college graduates—just one-in-five—was San Bernardino. In New Orleans and San Antonio, for example, almost 20 percent of the population was below the poverty line. The proportion of single mothers with children under 18 years ranged from 9.1 percent in cities categorized as low resource to 7.4 percent in high-resource cities. Specific city characteristics are illustrated in Table 10.1, and characteristics of single-mother households in each city are illustrated in Table 10.2.

HOUSING CONDITIONS OF SINGLE MOTHERS IN HIGH- AND LOW-RESOURCE CITIES

In cities classified as high in resources, the housing inadequacy for the total population was lower than that in low-resource cities, 4.1 percent compared to 6.7 percent (see Table 10.3). For single mothers, housing was better in high-resource cities than in low-resource cities (9.4 percent compared to 12.9 percent were classified as inadequate). Regardless of the cities' categorization, however, single mothers were twice as likely to be housed in units with plumbing, heating, electric, or other problems as the population overall. The metropolitan context had the opposite effect on homeownership rates. In cities categorized as low resource, homeownership rates were slightly higher than those in the high-resource cities, 64.7 percent compared to 62.6 percent. Similarly, for single mothers there was no gain regardless of the resources in their cities. In both the low- and high-resource cities, 37 percent of single mothers were homeowners, a percentage considerably lower than that of the general population.

Housing Conditions of Single Mothers in High- and Low- Resource Cities by Race

Housing inadequacy for white, black, and Hispanic single mothers in cities with high and low education and economic resources is illustrated in Table 10.4. Regardless of the status of the city as high or low resource, there was little variation in the proportion of white women heading families in housing classified as inadequate. For black and Hispanic women, however, the gains in housing adequacy in high-resource cities were marked. About one in five units in which black, single mothers lived was classified as inadequate if the city was categorized as low resource compared to 15 percent in high-resource cities. In the high-resource

Table 10.1 City Characteristics Based on Total Households in Each City, Classified by Metropolitan Context

City	Context	% College*	% Above Poverty	% Black	% Hispanic	% Inadequate Units	% Total Ownership	% Female Head of Household	% Suburban
Cincinnati	L-ed L-econ	23.4	88.5	12.2	0.9	4.4	63.1	31.4	71.2
Columbus	L-ed L-econ	27.0	89.4	10.3	1.1	4.2	62.0	31.3	52.7
Miami	L-ed L-econ	25.2	86.2	14.8	27.9	6.3	61.8	31.4	78.9
New Orleans	L-ed L-econ	23.5	78.3	30.0	3.7	15.6	59.2	34.1	56.6
Pittsburgh	L-ed L-econ	21.7	85.4	6.8	0.6	4.8	70.9	32.9	81.2
St. Louis	L-ed L-econ	25.8	87.7	15.0	1.3	3.5	69.6	32.0	80.1
San Antonio	L-ed L-econ	21.5	80.9	6.2	40.0	20.4	60.2	32.7	30.6
San Bernardino	L-ed L-econ	20.3	87.7	6.2	18.1	4.0	65.2	26.9	78.8
Baltimore	L-ed H-econ	27.3	89.7	22.2	1.2	4.5	65.6	31.3	69.8
Portland	L-ed H-econ	26.2	90.3	2.1	2.2	3.8	61.3	28.9	71.8
Rochester	L-ed H-econ	27.7	90.4	8.0	2.7	5.1	68.9	31.4	72.7
Chicago	H-ed L-econ	29.1	88.9	17.6	8.3	4.9	61.4	30.6	60.1
Houston	H-ed L-econ	28.9	87.5	18.4	14.9	12.0	55.9	26.9	48.9
New York	H-ed L-econ	29.4	86.7	18.5	13.7	10.5	45.5	33.2	35.1
Anaheim	H-ed H-econ	35.0	93.5	1.6	14.6	4.1	60.2	25.1	80.3
Atlanta	H-ed H-econ	31.9	89.9	23.7	1.5	4.9	64.4	29.3	84.3
Denver	H-ed H-econ	34.8	90.2	4.4	9.4	2.6	62.6	28.1	71.0
Hartford	H-ed H-econ	30.1	92.4	7.8	5.4	3.7	65.8	31.7	86.3
Kansas City	H-ed H-econ	28.1	92.6	11.2	2.8	4.3	66.8	28.9	68.9
Newark	H-ed H-econ	30.4	92.2	10.9	8.8	4.9	64.1	28.6	88.0
San Diego	H-ed H-econ	31.5	92.0	5.5	12.7	3.0	54.6	27.8	53.2
Seattle	H-ed H-econ	33.5	93.6	4.1	2.7	3.4	63.0	27.0	64.5

L-ed   Low education resources
H-ed   High education resources
L-econ   Low economic resources
H-econ   High economic resources
*Proportion to total households with at least a college degree.
Source: *American Housing Survey*, 1996, Bureau of the Census.

Table 10.2   Characteristics of Single-Mother Households Based on Total Single-Mother Households in Each City, Classified by Metropolitan Context

City	Context	% College	% Above Poverty	% Black	% Hispanic	% Inadequate Units	% Owner
Cincinnati	L-ed L-econ	8.3	64.6	35.4	2.1	10.4	36.2
Columbus	L-ed L-econ	11.6	62.8	33.3	0.0	11.6	33.3
Miami	L-ed L-econ	13.2	69.8	43.4	28.3	10.4	39.6
New Orleans	L-ed L-econ	11.3	49.1	64.8	3.7	28.3	30.2
Pittsburgh	L-ed L-econ	9.6	52.7	27.4	0.0	9.5	44.6
St. Louis	L-ed L-econ	9.9	58.0	45.1	1.2	6.2	37.0
San Antonio	L-ed L-econ	8.0	54.9	11.8	60.8	29.4	41.2
San Bernardino	L-ed L-econ	10.3	62.8	17.7	26.6	8.9	30.4
Baltimore	L-ed H-econ	11.0	67.5	57.3	0.0	13.3	30.1
Portland	L-ed H-econ	11.9	69.0	7.1	2.4	4.9	40.5
Rochester	L-ed H-econ	10.7	60.7	31.0	10.3	10.7	32.1
Chicago	H-ed L-econ	11.1	62.5	54.2	10.2	12.0	30.6
Houston	H-ed L-econ	10.5	63.8	43.8	17.1	15.4	27.6
New York	H-ed L-econ	11.4	60.7	39.6	34.8	21.4	18.7
Anaheim	H-ed H-econ	25.0	85.4	4.2	25.0	6.3	43.8
Atlanta	H-ed H-econ	12.6	62.8	67.0	0.0	10.6	38.3
Denver	H-ed H-econ	14.5	68.5	13.0	20.4	5.5	41.8
Hartford	H-ed H-econ	13.3	63.3	26.7	23.3	6.7	30.0
Kansas City	H-ed H-econ	13.5	75.5	30.2	5.7	11.3	46.2
Newark	H-ed H-econ	12.1	66.7	35.9	22.5	12.1	33.1
San Diego	H-ed H-econ	15.2	71.2	17.9	25.4	9.0	23.9
Seattle	H-ed H-econ	19.6	78.6	10.7	5.4	8.9	46.4

L-ed   Low education resources
H-ed   High education resources
L-econ   Low economic resources
H-econ   High economic resources
Source: American Housing Survey, 1996, Bureau of the Census.

city, the gains for Hispanic women heading households were greater than those for blacks. Inadequate housing was reduced from 20 percent to 10 percent for Hispanic single mothers, which, however, was still twice that of white single women.

The pattern of homeownership rates was consistent with that described earlier except for white single mothers. In both low- and high- resource cities, about 46 percent of white women were homeowners. Only 27 percent of black and 32.9 percent of Hispanic women were homeowners in low-resource cities. Those figures declined in high-resource cities to 22.4 percent and 21.4 percent, respectively. Homeownership rates for black and Hispanic single mothers were higher in cities with lower education and economic resources. In short, for black and

Table 10.3   Inadequacy of Unit and Ownership, Classified by Metropolitan Context and Household Structure

	Number in 1000s			Inadequate Units		Homeownership	
Metropolitan Context	*Total N*	*Single Mothers N*	*%*	*Total %*	*Single Mothers %*	*Total %*	*Single Mothers %*
Low ed, Low econ	5,914	534	9.1	6.7	12.9	64.7	37.0
Low ed, High econ	1,839	153	8.5	4.4	10.5	64.9	33.3
High ed, Low econ	8,085	723	9.2	8.9	17.7	52.3	23.7
High ed, High econ	7,650	543	7.4	4.1	9.4	62.6	37.2
Total	23,488	1,953	8.5	6.4	13.5	59.8	31.8

Source: American Housing Survey, 1996, Bureau of the Census.

Table 10.4   Inadequacy of Unit and Ownership of Single Mothers, Classified by Metropolitan Context and Minority Status

	Number in 1000s			Inadequate Units			Homeownership		
Metropolitan Context	*White N*	*Black N*	*Hispanic N*	*White %*	*Black %*	*Hispanic %*	*White %*	*Black %*	*Hispanic %*
Low ed, Low econ	260	189	85	5.8	19.6	20.0	45.8	27.0	32.9
Low ed, High econ	90	59	4	5.6	16.9	25.0	43.3	20.0	25.0
High ed, Low econ	221	321	181	5.9	22.1	24.3	44.8	16.5	10.5
High ed, High econ	294	165	84	5.4	15.2	10.7	50.0	22.4	21.4
Total	865	734	354	5.7	19.5	20.1	46.7	20.8	18.6

Source: American Housing Survey, 1996, Bureau of the Census.

Hispanic women, as the education and economic contexts improved, their home-ownership opportunities shrank. It seems likely that there is more available low-cost, affordable housing in low-resource cities. Conversely, in high-resource cities we expect that median house prices are high and rising. The patterns for poor women are similar: the proportion of inadequate units declined in cities with high resources compared to low-resource cities for white, black and Hispanic single mothers (Table 10.5).

Metropolitan Racial Context and Housing Conditions of Single Mothers

We examined the question of housing adequacy and homeownership rates among black and Hispanic women in cities with high and low proportions of minorities in the overall population (Table 10.6). The proportion of black households living in the 22 cities ranged from a high of 30 percent in New Orleans to a low of 1.6 percent in Anaheim. San Antonio had the highest proportion of Hispanic residents, 40 percent. In the cities with larger proportions of blacks, black women

**Table 10.5	Inadequacy of Unit and Ownership of Poor Single Mothers, Classified by Metropolitan Context and Minority Status**

Metropolitan Context	Number in 1000s			Inadequate Units			Homeownership		
	White N	Black N	Hispanic N	White %	Black %	Hispanic %	White %	Black %	Hispanic %
Low ed, Low econ	73	100	39	9.6	24.0	23.1	23.3	15.0	20.5
Low ed, High econ	24	25	2	8.3	16.0	0.0	20.8	8.0	0.0
High ed, Low econ	38	133	107	10.5	27.3	30.8	31.6	6.8	7.5
High ed, High econ	50	72	39	8.2	19.4	12.8	16.0	11.1	7.7
Total	185	330	187	9.2	23.7	25.1	22.7	10.3	10.2

Source: American Housing Survey, 1996, Bureau of the Census.

**Table 10.6	Inadequacy of Unit and Ownership of Single Mothers, Classified by Metropolitan Racial and Ethnic Contexts**

Metropolitan Context	N in 1000s	Inadequate Units %	Homeownership %
Low Black	102	14.7	22.5
High Black	633	20.2	20.4
Low Hispanic	13	8.3	30.8
High Hispanic	340	20.3	17.9
Average Black	735	19.5	20.8
Average Hispanic	353	20.1	18.6

Source: American Housing Survey, 1996, Bureau of the Census.

heading families were worse off both in terms of the proportion of inadequate housing and in the rate of homeownership. In cities with high proportions of black populations, 20 percent of single mothers lived in inadequate housing compared to 14.7 percent in cities with low proportions of black households. Homeownership rates for single mothers, however, were not impacted very much by the proportion of blacks in the total population of the city. In fact, homeownership rates for them shrank slightly in cities with higher proportions of black households, from 22.5 percent to 20.4 percent.

Hispanic single mothers did not experience gains in housing adequacy when the proportion of Hispanic households increased in the metropolis. In high Hispanic population cities, 20 percent of single mothers lived in inadequate housing compared to 8 percent in low Hispanic cities. Homeownership rates for Hispanic single mothers were 39.8 percent in low Hispanic cities and 17.9 percent in high Hispanic cities.

Discussion

The data presented on housing adequacy can be interpreted as a half-full or half-empty cup. Cities with more resources generally have less housing inadequacy. Everyone appears to benefit when there are more resources available at the metropolitan level. Although the reduction in housing inadequacy in high-resource cities is not as dramatic for black, Hispanic, and poor women, the tendency is in the same direction. Alternatively, and viewed more broadly, the data underscore the triple jeopardy experienced by families that are headed by a single parent who is a woman and also a minority. The rate of housing inadequacy of black and Hispanic women, regardless of educational or economic context, is three to four times that of white, single mothers. Not surprisingly, poor women are the least well housed regardless of the characteristics of the metropolis. The data do not help us to understand how women view the choices before them, the tradeoffs made, nor how explicitly these choices come to be made. Bounded by constraints within the household and with few choices in the housing marketplace, single mothers may choose the deteriorated, undermaintained housing units because they are affordable. This coping strategy theory seems to erode, however, unless we believe that black and hispanic women in low- and high-resource cities use different coping strategies. Discrimination, apparently most experienced by black women, is a more likely explanation. We also take the view that cities with more resources can, and apparently do, devote those resources to improved housing stock. The physical condition of the housing stock appears to be a low priority for local and federal policymakers, but we have tried to show that these conditions do have long lasting and meaningful social and psychological effects beyond mere physical discomfort.

Unfortunately, an improved housing stock appears to be a mixed blessing since it affects affordability negatively. American Housing Survey (AHS) data show that homeownership opportunities are reduced in cities categorized as high resource. Women's chances for homeownership are better in low-resource cities, where housing is likely to be more affordable. Only about one in five black and Hispanic single mothers are homeowners in high-resource cities, where 23 percent of black and 31 percent of Hispanic single mothers are homeowners in low-resource cities (Table 10.6). Blacks and Hispanics, poor or not, have very low rates of homeownership overall, but white single mothers in high- and low- resource cities have homeownership rates that approximate cities' overall ownership rates and that are two times that of their minority counterparts. The likely scenario for white single mothers is that they received "their house" in a divorce settlement and that neither black nor Hispanic single mothers were homeowners prior to becoming single parents. Only the rate of homeownership of poor, white, single mothers is similar to that of their minority counterparts. So, are white women generally "house poor," struggling to finance and maintain their housing? There is no definitive answer, but the literature suggests that women who are homeowners are anxious to remain so and put forth extraordinary efforts to retain their houses (Shlay 1995; Sidel 1990; Smizik and Stone 1988; Rohe and Stegman 1994). There is much to suggest that the owned home symbolizes more than just a tax deduction and financial asset; research confirms single mothers' homeownership aspirations (Cook 1988; Sidel 1990; Rohe and Stegman 1994), and, though homeownership opportunities for poor women are sometimes viewed as unrealistic, there is evidence that tenant ownership provides economic advancement for poor households and results in improved housing conditions (Saegert and Winkel 1998). Homeownership within and outside the central city warrants local and federal policy attention as one mechanism to break the cycle of economic dependency among women. Public policy and metropolitan revitalization strategies need to recognize that "the desire for homeownership is so strong that families who can afford to buy their own home do so rather than rent" (Mulroy 1995, 49). Thus, efforts to bring professionals and middle-income households to the downtown to revitalize cities must be approached cautiously; since it undermines affordable housing opportunities for single mothers, this revitalization strategy may create more new problems than it solves.

Our investigation and that of others imply that racialized cities do not serve minorities (Jargowsky 1997; Peake 1997). In cities where there were large populations of black households, housing inadequacy was worse for black single mothers and homeownership rates were lower. The same patterns held true for Hispanic single mothers in cities with high Hispanic populations. We would like to see more understanding that the poor and underhoused are disproportionately families headed by women and their children as well as disproportionately black and Hispanic. Given the disproportionate level of black and Hispanic, female-headed, and poverty-level households in downtown areas, minority women are likely to need local and federal housing policies and government intervention to provide them with improved living conditions. Housing market discrimination constricts poor black and Hispanic women to a subset of neighborhoods where they are concentrated (Jargowsky 1997).

There are limits to what large data sets can tell us about the metropolis and its neighborhoods. The American Housing Survey data of metropolitan statistical areas do not permit evaluation of specific neighborhoods within the Metropolitan Statistical Area—social capital and the data are limited to a total of 44 cities. Despite these shortcomings, there is no other data source that so completely details housing, and many neighborhood, characteristics nor one that allows for comparisons of these characteristics across cities and over time. From our review of the literature, it appears to us these data are underused. We suspect, too, that in cities where AHS data are available, they are not used to the extent possible. This is perplexing and seems to point once again to limited interest and concern for housing and neighborhood conditions at the same time that there is renewed interest in the social and economic opportunities available to residents of the metropolis. Our future research plans include evaluating the issues explored here across time and in the additional cities for which there are data available. In our future investigations, as with this one, we want to contribute to an understanding of the housing and neighborhood disparities that exist between and among women. By examining these issues, we heighten awareness of the factors that contribute to the quality of life of single mothers and their children.

CONCLUSION

We are challenged by several unanswered questions that emerge from the review of literature and the data examined. First, what do single mothers want from their housing? How do they conceptualize the meaning of housing for themselves, and particularly for their children? Do they dream the American Dream regardless of race or ethnicity? How does the meaning of housing function as a boundary—or does it? Planners, policymakers, and researchers have not carefully considered the social and emotional aspects of housing needs from a woman's perspective. They have rarely considered the bond between home and family. The simplistic approach now employed in which "housing needs" is characterized as a numerical and physical condition may hide the real importance and meaning of housing. The beginning of any new building, renovation process, or revitalization strategy is the calculation of need. Perhaps our research on the opportunity structure of the city and planning strategies to revitalize urban neighborhoods should begin with an understanding and portrayal of housing in the voices of women themselves. Current literature only hints at the housing histories—the needs met and unmet by previous housing—of single mothers and their children. How do women approach converging needs, for child care, for employment, and for housing? "Theoretical accounts of these issues and the links among them emerge infrequently and only recently in the field of urban planning" (Sandercock and Forsyth 1992, 50). Qualitative research, thick with description, would serve to humanize the discussion of policymakers, planners, and advocates in a way that rigorous quantitative data often fail to do. Research of this type may also bring us closer to understanding the complex formulation of housing meaning. It seems likely that we are bound to our housing histories, and that in turn our housing histories bind our future choices.

A second important question, then, is how do women conceptualize housing choice? How do single mothers see and evaluate the array of housing options before them? Do women stay in housing that appears inadequate because they are committed to existing support networks, as some research has suggested? Do women challenge the constraints before them and reframe them in their own way, and if so, in what ways do they challenge the limits to and boundaries of housing choice? Do they resist and reconstruct these barriers to housing? Furthermore, how do owned homes received in divorce settlements or the receipt of housing subsidies constrain housing choices? Some literature suggests that housing assistance prevents single mothers from moving, yet other research suggests that the need for some degree of control over life increases chronic mobility among poor families. In the model depicting housing adjustment, perceived discrimination, locus of control, apathy, anomie, and other sociopsychological phenomena are viewed as "predispositional" constraints but have received little attention in the literature, particularly from a woman's or child's perspective. Families' housing choices and the housing available in the marketplace have been conceptualized as cyclical. The life cycle of families assumes, however, that both a family's organization and its financial status are linked. Once formed, families move from rental housing to starter homes as children are born and reared. "Buying up" is a natural occurrence in the middle years to be followed by new housing alternatives for empty nesters and retirees. In such a model there is no attention to single mothers' family life cycle, except as it deviates from the "norm." As long as single mothers are seen as an aberration, in search of a breadwinner, neither the issue of housing design, location, or affordability can be accurately assessed, nor can appropriate public policy be advanced. It seems that marriage and divorce, serial monogamy, and alternative family forms warrant theoretical understandings of their own. In the future, a whole range of needs and issues will likely emerge because of the predominance of single mothers and their children. Today's policymakers need more research to understand these emerging needs and issues.

A final perplexing question is, if stable housing keeps families together and productive (DeParle 1996), why is it so often overlooked in discussions about the opportunity structure of urban neighborhoods, in economic development strategies, and welfare reform efforts? Single mothers must often single-handedly provide this stable environment. How can planning and public policy help? First and foremost, policymakers need to understand that women are disproportionately affected by unsatisfactory housing and by reduced federal investment in housing (Gilroy 1994). What kind of housing social policy will foster single mothers' efforts to house themselves? Programs that promote housing location choices should be a cornerstone of housing social policy. Research on distressed neighborhoods firmly supports the role of the metropolitan geographic context in enhancing or restricting opportunities of low-income families. Distressed neighborhoods stymie opportunities; although deconcentration of the poor through assisted housing has been a goal of U.S. housing policy, in fact, housing assistance has contributed to their geographic concentration. We must assess the extent to which our urban policies and housing policies are at cross-purposes. There is research that suggests that low-income, minority households can find success outside the central city. At the same time, improvements to urban neighborhoods to which families are committed must be part of the dialogue of social reconstruction of the city and urban revitalization strategies.

Homeownership opportunities also need to be expanded, particularly for minority women heading families. Though homeownership is not a panacea, it is an undeniable cornerstone of the American psyche (Huttman 1991; Rohe and Stegman 1994; Rohe and Stewart 1996; Saegert and Winkel 1998; Shlay 1995, 1993). Housing in the form of homeownership is an investment and a form of savings, providing a basis for wealth acquisition (Sherraden 1991). The multidimensional nature of the housing bundle and its centrality to socioeconomic advancement in U.S. society mean that housing is an important variable to consider in initiatives designed to foster economic independence: "The housing bundle is an underlying dimension or cause of poverty and welfare dependency through limited access to human capital-generating resources, absence of employment, poor public services, lack of security, and the general troubles associated with the spatial concentration of poverty, including social isolation, greater risks of crime victimization and physical danger, absence of economically mobile role models and support for community institutions, and lack of visible opportunities" (Shlay 1993, 459). For the poorest of the poor, for whom ownership may not be desirable or feasible, social ownership is needed.[5] Social ownership in which a portion of the housing stock is permanently removed from the private sector should be featured in the revitalization of urban neighborhoods.

Finally, the data and literature examined in this chapter imply that the housing conditions of single mothers vary across cities, and it seems likely that differences in local public policy and economic development strategies contribute to these differences. Gender-based literature has given limited attention to the effect of policy approaches on "women's residential-location options and their attendant living conditions" (Turner 1995, 287)—perhaps because the persistent lack of available, affordable, and adequate housing is often viewed as a social problem rather than as a community infrastructure problem (Ziebarth, Prochaska-Cue, and Shrewsbury 1997). Research that draws attention to the unique housing and neighborhood needs of single mothers and assesses the impact of development strategies on them is needed as a companion to the current gender-based literature on welfare reform. Poverty is a thinly veiled women's issue. Despite its pervasive role in women's lives, the need for and cost of shelter are often noticeably absent from literature on welfare reform, where the triad appears to be women, jobs, and child care. Reliance on welfare cannot be reduced without attention to the role that housing and neighborhoods play in shaping families' lives, economically, socially, and psychologically.

For those inclined to think that housing and neighborhoods of poor quality are not important because they are indicative of other, more deep-seated causes of poverty, it would be wise to remember that the physical environment is a powerful communicator to both residents and perhaps more importantly to others outside the community. Over the last 25 years, volumes of research have argued that the home and its surrounds have both a direct and symbolic effect (Becker 1977; Cooper 1974; Marcus 1995; Rubinstein and Parmelee 1992; Sebba and Churchman 1983; Weinstein and David 1987). The meaning of home in peoples' lives is significantly associated with the "need for control and for self expression and when home fails to meet these fundamental needs, the stage is set for a vicious cycle of depravation and decline that damages families and neighborhoods" (Bartlett 1997, 130). Because it is understood that housing and neighborhoods ideally offer more than shelter from the elements (Stone 1993), the nature of the housing and neighborhood choices and opportunities available to women and their families persist as topics of dialogue and debate.

The boundaries that shape women's conceptualization of housing meaning and those that constrain women's choices in the housing marketplace are not irrevocable. Though single mothers may be fragmented by different roles within and outside the home, there is evidence that women can and do affect these boundaries by creating alternative housing and household configurations and by promoting alternative development and policy approaches (Leavitt and Saegert 1989; Ritzdorf 1986; Saegert and Winkel 1998; Sandercock and Forsyth 1992; Turner 1995). In this way, women are shaping and establishing newly constructed boundaries of their own design. Despite these efforts by and for women, women are still frequently marginalized, having both limited access to the professions that plan, design, and reconstruct the city and to the political power necessary to reframe the intersecting boundaries affecting them. The impact of policies on women needs the same attention as class and race in the literature on urban political economy (Turner 1995) and in the education and training of men and women in planning (Sandercock and Forsyth 1992). When we are asked to consider how women imagine space and how they actualize it in practice, we are perplexed. We suspect that women's intepretations of their lives are holistic without separation into tidy ensembles of housing, transportation, child care, zoning, and neighborhood revitalization. We challenge all to view housing and home, neighborhood and city, and the urban structure in this same way so that theory, research, and practice can contribute meaningful solutions to the problems that plague single mothers and their children.

NOTES

1. The 22 cities are: Anaheim, Atlanta, Baltimore, Chicago, Cincinnati, Columbus, Denver, Hartford, Houston, Kansas City, Miami, New Orleans, New York, Newark, Pittsburgh, Portland, Rochester, St. Louis, San Antonio, San Bernardino, San Diego, and Seattle.

The data are from the 1990 and 1991 Metropolitan Statistical Area (MSA) files collected for the American Housing Survey (AHS). Each of the 22 cities represents a separate sample. The MSAs are defined as they were for the 1980 census, and data are collected in these cities on a revolving basis so that there are data every four years. The sample consists of 4,000 to 5,500 houses per MSA, which have been weighted to reflect the actual number of households in each. In the analysis of single mothers, the "Asian" and "Other" groups were omitted because their numbers were too small (2.6 percent) for meaningful analyses.

It is important to remember that the sampling procedures follow housing units, not individuals or households. The AHS was developed to assess the progress made toward legalizing the goal of a decent home and a suitable living environment for every American family. HUD uses AHS information to prepare the Annual Report on National Housing Goals, which the president is required to submit to Congress, and for other special reports to Congress and its committees on the effect of legislation on the housing stock.

2. There are several good reasons for using the variable "above poverty" rather than other economic indicators, such as median household income or per-capita income. Poverty is a continuous variable, depicting the household income as a percent of the poverty level as designated by the Bureau of Labor Statistics. Most important, it is adjusted for region and size of household.

3. The *inadequacy* of a dwelling is formulated using a three-scale index composed of the respondent's answers to questions about plumbing, heating, electricity, upkeep, hallways, and the kitchen. Response categories were coded in the American Housing Survey as designating either an adequate, moderately inadequate, or severely inadequate dwelling. The percentages of households with inadequate units were calculated by combining the samples of the cities in each contextual level and then calculating the percentage of severely and moderately inadequate units combined for the total population of the contextual level. The percentages of *homeowners* were calculated by combining the sample of the cities in each contextual level and then calculating the percentage of households who were buying or owned their units for the total population of the contextual level.

4. In developing the context profiles, cities were classified as either high (top 11 cities) or low (bottom 11 cities) in the proportion of households with a college graduate as the reference person and in the proportion of households living above the poverty line. Then the two profiles were combined into four categories: low education and low economics (8 cities), low education and high economics (3 cities), high education and low economics (3 cities), and high education and high economics (8 cities).

5. Social ownership is the term used by Stone (1993) to characterize housing stock that is owned by public agencies, or by nonprofit organizations, or by residents themselves in limited-equity-type arrangements. He argues for expansion of units that are permanently removed from the private, speculative market, and dedicating them to those who experience "shelter poverty." A recent issue of *Housing Policy Debate* is devoted to the topic (Hornburg and Pomeroy 1995). A variety of housing professionals—academicians, policymakers, directors, and advocates of community organizations—from the United States, Canada, and the United Kingdom argue that poor households need more than a house or apartment. Finance, development, and management strategies are necessary to provide supportive housing located in neighborhoods that themselves are resource- and service-rich.

REFERENCES

American Housing Survey for the United States in 1995. 1996. Washington, D.C.: U.S. Bureau of the Census.

Bartlett, Sheridan. 1997. "The Significance of Relocation for Chronically Poor Families in the USA." *Environment and Urbanization* 9, 1: 121–131.

Becker, Franklin D. 1977. *Housing Messages.* Stroudsburg, Pa.: Dowden, Hutchinson and Ross.

Bothwell, Stephanie E., Raymond Gindroz, and Robert E. Lang. 1998. "Restoring Community through Traditional Neighborhood Design: A Case Study of Diggs Town Public Housing." *Housing Policy Debate* 9, 1: 89–114.

Buehler, Cheryl, and Jan M. Hogan. 1986. "Planning Styles in Single-Parent Families." *Home Economics Research Journal* 14, 4: 352–362.

Bruin, Marilyn J., and Christine C. Cook. 1997. "Understanding Constraints and Residential Satisfaction among Low-Income Single-Parent Families." *Environment and Behavior* 29, 4: 532–553.

Cook, Christine C. 1988. "Components of Neighborhood Satisfaction." *Environment and Behavior* 20: 115–149.

Cook, Christine C., and Marilyn J. Bruin. 1994. "Determinants of Housing Quality: A Comparison of White, African-American and Hispanic Single-Parent Women." *Journal of Family and Economic Issues* 15, 4: 329–348.

Cooper, Clare. 1974. "The House as Symbol of Self." In *Designing for Human Behavior*, edited by T. Lang, Charles Burnette, Walter Moleski, and David Vachon. Stroudsberg, Pa.: Dowden, Hutchinson and Ross.

Darke, Jane. 1994. "Women and the Meaning of Home." In *Housing Women*, edited by Rose Gilroy and Roberta Woods. New York: Routledge.

DeParle, Jason. 1996. "Slamming the Door." *New York Times Magazine* (October 20) 52–57, 68, 94–95.

Galster, George C. 1998. "An Econometric Model of the Urban Opportunity Structure: Cumulative Causation among City Markets, Social Problems, and Underserved Areas." *Research Report, Urban and Metropolitan Issues.* Washington, D.C.: Fannie Mae Foundation.

Galster, George C., and Steven Hornburg. 1995. "Editors' Introduction." *Housing Policy Debate* 6, 1: 1–5.

Galster, George C., and Sean P. Killen. 1995. "The Geography of Metropolitan Opportunity: A Reconnaissance and Conceptual Framework." *Housing Policy Debate* 6, 1: 7–44.

Galster, George C., and Maris Mikelsons. 1995. "The Geography of Metropolitan Opportunity: A Case Study of Neighborhood Conditions Confronting Youth in Washington, D.C." *Housing Policy Debate* 6, 1: 73–102.

Garber, Judith A., and Robyne S. Turner. 1995. "Introduction." In *Gender in Urban Research*, edited by Judith A. Garber and Robyne S. Turner. Thousand Oaks, Calif.: Sage Publications.

Gilroy, Rose, and Roberta Woods. 1994. *Housing Women.* New York: Routledge.

Hornburg, Steven P., and Stephen P. Pomeroy. 1995. "Editors' Introduction." *Housing Policy Debate* 6, 3: 539–558.

Huttman, Elizabeth. 1991. "A Research Note on Dreams and Aspirations of Black Families." *Journal of Comparative Family Studies* 22, 2: 147–158.

Jargowsky, Paul A. 1997. *Poverty and Place: Ghettos, Barrios, and the American City.* New York: Russell Sage Foundation.

Kingsley, G. Thomas. 1997. "Federal Housing Assistance and Welfare Reform: Uncharted Territory." *New Federalism: Issues and Options for States.* Series A, No. A-19. Washington, DC: The Urban Institute.

Lang, Robert E., and Steven P. Hornburg. 1998. "What Is Social Capital and Why Is It Important to Public Policy?" *Housing Policy Debate* 9, 1: 1–16.

Lawton, M. Powell. 1983. "The Dimensions of Well-being." *Experimental Aging Research* 9: 65–72.

Leavitt, Jacqueline, and Susan Saegert. 1989. *From Abandonment to Hope: Community-Households in Harlem.* New York: Columbia University Press.

Marcus, Clare C. 1995. *House as Mirror of Self.* Berkeley, Calif.: Conari.

McLanahan, Sara, and Gary Sandefur. 1994. *Growing Up with a Single Parent: What Hurts, What Helps.* Cambridge: Harvard University Press.

Miller, Stuart. 1986. "Designing the Home for Children: A Need-Based Approach." *Children's Environments Quarterly* 3: 55–62.

Morris, Earl W., and Mary Winter. 1978. *Housing, Family, and Society.* New York: John Wiley.

———. 1996. *Housing, Family, and Society.* Ames, Ia.: Authors.

Mulroy, Elizabeth A. 1988. "Who Are Single-Parent Families and Where Do They Live?" In *Women as Single Parents: Confronting Institutional Barriers in the Courts, the Workplace, and the Housing Market,* edited by Elizabeth A. Mulroy. Westport, Conn.: Auburn House.

———. 1995. *The New Uprooted: Single Mothers in Urban Life.* Westport, Conn.: Auburn House.

Newman, Oscar. 1972. *Defensible Space: Crime Prevention through Urban Design.* New York: Macmillan.

———. 1996. *Creating Defensible Space.* Washington, D.C.: U.S. Department of Housing and Urban Development, Office of Policy Development and Research.

Newman, Sandra J., and Ann B. Schnare. 1988. *Subsidizing Shelter: The Relationship Between Welfare and Housing Assistance.* Washington, D.C.: The Urban Institute.

———. 1992. *Beyond Bricks and Mortar: Reexamining the Purpose and Effects of Housing Assistance.* Washington, D.C.: The Urban Institute.

Peake, Linda J. 1997. "Toward a Social Geography of the City: Race and Dimensions of Urban Poverty in Women's Lives." *Journal of Urban Affairs* 19, 3: 335–361.

Priemus, Hugo. 1986. "Housing as a Social Adaptation Process: A Conceptual Scheme." *Environment and Behavior* 18, 1, 31–52.

Proshansky, Harold M., and Abbe K. Fabian. 1987. "The Development of Place Identity in the Child." In *Spaces for Children,* edited by Carol S. Weinstein and Thomas G. David. New York: Plenum.

Quercia, Roberto G., and William M. Rohe. 1993. "Models of Housing Adjustment and Their Implications for Planning and Policy." *Journal of Planning Literature* 8, 1 (August): 20–31.

Ricketts, Erol R., and Isabel V. Sawhill. 1988. "Defining and Measuring the Underclass." *Journal of Policy Analysis and Management* 7: 316–324.

Ritzdorf, Marsha. 1986. "Women and the City." *Urban Resources* 3: 23–27.

Rohe, William M., and Michael A. Stegman. 1994. "The Effects of Homeownership on the Self-Esteem, Perceived Control and Life Satisfaction of Low-Income People." *Journal of the American Planning Association* 60, 2: 173–184.

Rohe, William M., and Leslie S. Stewart. 1996. "Homeownership and Neighborhood Stability." *Housing Policy Debate* 7, 1: 37–82.

Rubinstein, Robert L., and Patricia A. Parmelee. 1992. "Attachment to Place and the Representation of the Life Course by the Elderly." In *Human Behavior and Environmental Advances in Theory and Research*, edited by Irwin Altman and Setha Low. Vol. 12. New York: Plenum.

Saegert, Susan, and Gary Winkel. 1998. "Social Capital and the Revitalization of New York City's Distressed Inner-City Housing." *Housing Policy Debate* 9, 1: 17–60.

Sandercock, Leonie, and Ann Forsyth. 1992. "A Gender Agenda: New Directions for Planning Theory." *Journal of the American Planning Association* 58, 1: 49–59.

Sebba, Rachel, and Arza Churchman. 1983. "Territories and Territoriality in the Home." *Environment and Behavior* 15, 2: 191–210.

Sherraden, Michael. 1991. *Assets and the Poor: A New American Welfare Policy.* Armonk, N.Y.: M. E. Sharpe.

Shlay, Anne B. 1993. "Family Self-sufficiency and Housing." *Housing Policy Debate* 4, 3: 457–495.

———. 1995. "Housing in the Broader Context of the United States." *Housing Policy Debate* 6, 3: 695–720.

Sidel, Ruth. 1990. *On Her Own: Growing Up in the Shadow of the American Dream.* New York: Penguin Books.

———. 1996. *Keeping Women and Children Last: America's War on the Poor.* New York: Penguin Books.

Smizik, Frank I., and Michael E. Stone. 1988. "Single-Parent Families and a Right to Housing." In *Women as Single Parents: Confronting Institutional Barriers in the Courts, the Workplace, and the Housing Market,* edited by Elizabeth A. Mulroy. Westport, Conn.: Auburn House.

South, Scott J., and Kyle D. Crowder. 1997. "Escaping Distressed Neighborhoods: Individual, Community, and Metropolitan Influences." *American Journal of Sociology* 102, 4: 1040–1084.

Spain, Daphne. 1987. "Racial Differences in Housing, Neighborhoods, and Political Participation: A Comment." *Urban Affairs Quarterly* 22, 3: 421–424.

———. 1992. *Gendered Spaces.* Chapel Hill: The University of North Carolina Press.

Stack, Carol. 1974. *All Our Kin: Strategies for Survival in a Black Community.* New York: Harper and Row.

Stone, Michael E. 1993. *Shelter Poverty.* Philadelphia, Pa.: Temple University Press.

Tempkin, Kenneth, and William M. Rohe. 1998. "Social Capital and Neighborhood Stability: An Empirical Investigation." *Housing Policy Debate* 9, 1: 61–88.

Turner, Robyne S. 1995. "Concern for Gender in Central-City Development Policy." In *Gender in Urban Research,* edited by Judith A. Garber and Robyne S. Turner. Thousand Oaks, Calif.: Sage Publications.

Weinstein, Carol Simon, and Thomas G. David, eds. 1987. *Spaces for Children: The Built Environment and Child Development.* New York: Plenum.

Wilson, William Julius. 1987. *The Truly Disadvantaged: The Inner City, the Underclass, and Public Policy.* Chicago: University of Chicago Press.

Wiseman, Michael. 1996. "Welfare Reform in the United States: A Background Paper." *Housing Policy Debate* 7, 4: 595–648.

Young, Alma H., and Kristine B. Miranne. 1995. "Women's Need for Child Care: The Stumbling Block in the Transition from Welfare to Work." In *Gender in Urban Research*, edited by Judith A. Garber and Robyne S. Turner. Thousand Oaks, Calif.: Sage Publications.

Ziebarth, Ann, Karen Prochaska-Cue, and Bonnie Shrewsbury. 1997. "Growth and Locational Impacts for Housing in Small Communities." *Rural Sociology* 62: 111–125.

Epilogue

Cracks, Light, Energy

Beth Moore Milroy

In drawing this book to a close, the main point I would like to make is that the kinds of investigations feminist urbanists pursue, like those in this book, are critical. The field may seem scattered with landmines now, but researchers should look for new paths, not abandon the task. This field contributes a range of women-centered research not covered by others. It is distinguished first by rooting women in space and taking account of the entailed proximity whether it be physical closeness or in how jointly used space is structured. Second, women are studied in cities, metropolises, and the like, which are specific forms of proximity. Thus, at the same time as investigating sex/gender/woman/sexual differences, these researchers situate them in their historically and geographically relevant cities, asking about the body/city interplay. Such research is often about city-building practices such as urban planning and community development, which forces researchers to tangle with the normative ideals of cities and behavior that inform the empirical struggles over how to shape *this* city *here, now*. It is inevitably a conceptually complex framework that a feminist urbanist brings to her research; it is always about bodies/cities, a term borrowed from Elizabeth Grosz (1992).

But there is trouble in the bodies/cities field. Briefly put, the conceptualizations that served the 1980s are no longer adequate; and the practices needed to act politically in this general field are not obvious or well formed. In the next few pages I specify some of the problems originating from the broad social milieu and others from feminist quarters. I then describe some proposals that deserve further attention.

LOOKING AROUND

A general "conservative tide" has washed over Western democracies, its manifestations including "fear of critical thought" and reassertion of so-called traditional values (Braidotti 1997b; Guberman 1996, 262). Gains made regarding pay equity and reproductive choice are again at risk. The language of the political left has frequently been laundered and put into the service of political conservatism, emptying the left of meaning (Feldstein 1997). For instance, think of the word "revolution," which the American political right appropriated for its phrase "Republican Revolution" and the Canadian ultra-right has used for its "Common Sense Revolution" slogan in Ontario since 1995. Or, the term "politically correct": it used to be a nonironic, positive assessment. Recently its meaning has been reversed so that it now carries a negative evaluation denoting "righteous bullying." Meanwhile, "politically *in*correct" takes on *its* reverse as a positive, rule-resisting sign of independent thought (Brennan 1997; Feldstein 1997; Frye 1992, 781). This isn't merely language, of course. Its political effects are to undermine the equity-seeking investigations and practices that feminists and others have been engaged in and their efforts to displace the correspondence of subject identity with the male, white, able-bodied, rational subject found throughout the academy and social practices. This is threatening work, and perhaps the backlash is understandable if no less welcome.

The context is marked, too, by a certain fatalism associated with globalization of economies. One scholar talks about "the language of fate in contemporary life," which takes a form such as being told repeatedly that "we must adjust to this or that tendency, that we must scramble in order not to lose out and redesign ourselves to fit the imperatives of the new world system" (Angus 1997, 5). This command emanates from economic captains upon whom there is little if any democratic control, but elected officials voice the same sentiments and seem to throw up their collective hands. Linda McQuaig (1998) describes in detail how government and industry interests coalesce around the cultivation of fatalism. She calls it "the cult of impotence," by which governments and businesses persuade their publics that they are powerless to act in the face of global competition. There is something hysterically overdetermined about the image of a few hundred thousand Masters of the Universe (to use Tom Wolfe's term in *Bonfire of the Vanities*) whipping 6 billion of us into frenzied competition. But the image is not fictive. People's opportunities are materially and symbolically changed by globalization.

Cities are also deeply altered by globalization. They are becoming more culturally heterogeneous. Gaps are widening between the interests and character of the most globally connected cities and those that are *not* in this circuit of capital and development even within the same country. The conventional hierarchy between a nation-state and its cities is blurring, as the dominant jurisdiction's mechanisms for controlling the subordinate are mediated by the demands of global competition. The implications are that cities are becoming more important than ever as places where people must work out their sexual, racial, cultural, and material lives.

It is unclear how "woman" will fare in these circumstances. The answer depends on the specifics of her situation. It is precisely this question of who is a woman that the next section addresses.

LOOKING IN

The category "woman" has faced serious theoretical and political challenges in recent years. This is the category that "women and environments" researchers seized upon in the 1980s when trying to make women visible in cities, to discover their city-building contributions, and to achieve equality of access to city spaces for women. In those days, exhilaration accompanied the realization that, though the boundaries that women felt constrained them were indeed boundaries, they were not irrevocable. Their histories and effects could be systematically investigated and analyzed, and ways could be found to change them through concerted actions.

The main analytical tool for these explorations by many North American, British, and Australian researchers has been sex/gender. Sex/gender posits a binary relationship between sex as biology and gender as socially constructed. Built into that binary is another between male and female on the sex side of the relationship, and men and women on the gender side. Underlying this double binary is first of all the idea that men and women are entities who in principle can be defined as distinct "types," and second, a presumption of heterosexuality (Butler 1990). The study of gender, and its companion gender relations, led feminists deeply into what Julia Kristeva calls "identificatory theorizing" (Guberman 1996)—that is, attempting to theoretically specify what a socially constructed woman is in a given era and geographical location. This called for identification not only by gender but also by class, ethnicity, sexual orientation, and many other characteristics. And so the era of identity politics was fueled. The chapters above amply demonstrate how that problem is manifested.

But there have been achievements. Past work has demonstrated that women and men do not have the same urban experiences. Gender has become as common a variable as income or age in most studies. There is less tendency to use "household" as a general variable for deducing movement patterns and choice without questioning its make up. Personal safety in the city is beginning to be accepted by policymakers as a valid ongoing concern for women, not one that has to be disputed every time redevelopment occurs. The type of use women make of a city's pedestrian and transit ways for multitask trips and for wheeling children and elderly people has been recognized in transit schedules and fares, physical cuts in sidewalks at corners, and pedestrian-scale, multiuse (re)development. Zoning for daycare and home occupations has been liberalized—that is, these investigations have supported concomitant political pressures to successfully implement sensible changes. Still, the enterprise has not been wildly successful, and signs of concern are there (Bondi 1998; Hayden 1997).

It is now obvious—as it generally wasn't in those heady, early days—that *not* to identify leaves the category "woman" to represent all facets of all women, an overwhelming and totalizing prospect analogous to the androcentric theorizing it was meant to displace. Yet, on the other hand, to identify leads to infinite regress. Politically, the totalizing of the category "woman" gives power to already privileged women; yet fractionating them according to many identities siphons off the steam needed for strong engagement in political struggles.

Since at least the early 1980s other, quite different feminist approaches were evolving from quite different starting points. If the subject is ontologically given for the sex/gender theorists just discussed, he or she is a pregiven, autonomous subject for whom thought is conducted in one's personal consciousness. Sovereign selves, as a collection of albeit socially constructed conscious subjects, come to the process of city planning, politics, or other urban activities. By contrast, in another feminist approach, the poststructuralist subject is not positively "there" as only a conscious identity. Rather, the subject is mediated both by those facets that concern constructivists and also by the unconscious. After Freud, subjectivity is no longer coterminous with consciousness; therefore, a subject is no longer potentially transparent. Because the unconscious and its structures are significant to the construction of the subject, we need to know what they are. It is forcefully argued that "woman" is symbolized in those hidden structures as the absence of man, and primarily as a maternal or sexual function. There is no symbolism of woman *as* woman (Braidotti 1991; Irigaray 1985). In this ontology, it is vital to recognize that the absence of woman symbolically does not mean she is absent materially. This rupture is significant, because the absence of the symbolic prevents an actual woman from questioning her material exploitation from a position of "woman" in and of herself, and from speaking of her desires and visions. Her only option is to speak from her symbolically represented position of maternal or sexual complement, which is to say she speaks as object, not subject.

This approach is usually referred to as the sexual difference approach, because it begins from the view that it is through sexual difference that women are exploited and it is through that same sexual difference that they will find resolution. Braidotti (1997a, 26) calls sexual difference a political strategy that challenges the equation of individuality with masculinity but also keeps up the search for "a sex-specific redefinition of the subject to empower women." Joan Scott's way of describing it is to say that the "goal of the so-called difference feminists is to disrupt the process that objectifies women for the purpose of constituting individual male subjects by making the difference of women the basis for representing an autonomous female subjectivity" (1996, 173).

The distinction between these two broadly defined approaches (sex/gender and sexual difference) is that the first is more like a reconstruction, a building up from what is concretely seen or what must be there because men are there. There is a will to discover, define, historicize "woman." In the second, "woman" is negative, is "not," is the sex that is not one, where the thing to figure out is how it comes to be that she *is* this. It is akin to projecting outward from having imagined a sex, a body, and from having wondered what powers, if she had any powers, they would be and why they would be those ones than some others. In broad terms, the one is constructivist in approach, the other poststructuralist. In the feminist bodies/cities field, many examples of the constructivist approach exist (as throughout this book). But there has been rather little use of explicitly poststructuralist theorizing (for one example dealing with "bodywork" in cities, see Milroy 1994), although the approach is more commonly found in the not-specifically feminist "cities" field (see especially Sibley 1995).

It can be seen that sex/gender and sexual difference rest on incommensurable premises regarding the ontology of subjects. Importantly, the respective premises are associated with different national and cultural philosophical traditions, which is a point that should not be overlooked (Angus 1997, 210–214; Braidotti 1997b; Guberman 1996, 263–268). For example, poststructuralism (not to be confused with postmodernism) emerged in some continental European schools as a reaction to the structuralism of Marx, de Saussure, and others, which never were influences sufficiently powerful in Britain or the United States to call out a comparable reaction. Psychoanalytic feminists focused attention on the unsaid (but nonetheless influential) of the unconscious, and the women's movement reflected the philosophical struggles. By contrast, in the United States, social constructivism was in part a reaction to structural-functionalism's relative determinism. Gender roles were said to be the basis of women's unequal condition. The women's liberation movement gave prominence to the inequality claims, which often became widely expressed antimen sentiments, the likes of which were not heard in Europe. This had repercussions. A further difference of note that perhaps contributes to framework preferences is the earlier recognition of ethnoracial heterogeneity as a fact in North America; to this point, constructivist approaches have seemed more open to multiplicity than have poststructuralist. Noting the varying traditions, Julia Kristeva (See Guberman 1996) wisely suggests that each country's activists and scholars need to work through their own country's misogyny.

The incongruity of the sex/gender and sexual-difference approaches seems to have preoccupied mainly privileged, Euro-American women and has by now been sidelined, though not obscured. By contrast, the dominance of their fundamental conceptualizations of embodiment and politics are continually challenged. For one, Judith Butler argued at length in her genealogical study, *Gender Trouble* (1990), that the tendency for sex/gender theorists to retain the distinction between women and men as central means that sexuality is attached to those already unstable categories. By default, sexuality is conceptualized heterosexually, and other sexual orientations are ignored. One critic calls it a division of labor, whereby feminists concentrate on the notion of gender and the queer theory movement focuses on sexuality. In doing so, queer theory provides "a critique of gender in terms of its heterosexism" (Braidotti 1997a, 38).

In a different vein, criticisms stem from those who connect oppression, at least in some way as much, with their global origins, skin color or ethnicities as well as being women. They argue that sex/gender/sexual/difference frameworks do not encompass their experiences of making their way in the world. While some try to modify those now-conventional frameworks, others strike out with new conceptualizations using foreignness, exile, diaspora, postcolonial, borders, displacement as ways to question self, group, and society *in situ* and globally. A bodies/cities example that incorporates such concepts is Sandercock's *Toward Cosmopolis* (1998).

Splits and impasses carry the energy of feminist research agendas today. Their poignancy is heightened by the conservative political climate and global changes. Questions abound: Can fractionating be resolved? Do postcolonialist-style approaches stand beside or supplement sex/gender? Can the sexual difference approach ever deal adequately with cultural multiplicity? Can we stop totalizing, yet act? Can the opposition between sex/gender (with its ontologically grounded subjects and drive for equality) and sexual difference (with its ontologically problematic subjects and woman-who-is-yet-to-be) be deconstructed? How are shared projects identified and advanced politically in this multiplicity?

MOVING ALONG

I have been using Elizabeth Grosz's bodies/cities term because I think it is helpful, but also because I want strongly to remind urbanists not to disembody citizens. Grosz posits the connection between the terms as an interface or cobuilding. She proposes "a model of relations between bodies and cities which sees them, not as megalithic total entities, distinct identities, but as assemblages or collections of parts, capable of crossing the thresholds between substances to form linkages, machines, provisional and often temporary sub- or micro-groupings. This model is a practical one, based on the practical productivity bodies and cities have in defining and establishing each other. It is not a holistic view, one that stresses the unity and integration of city and body" (Grosz 1992, 248).

It seems to me that Grosz's model could work well in combination with some approaches to multiplicity. A fascinating one is *métissage*, in which multiplicity already *is*; its legitimacy does not depend on being recognized as multiple. It is reminiscent of Susan Wolf's point that multiplicity is not "out there" but part of who we already are (1992). *Métissage* addresses "connections between subjects by recognizing affiliations, cross-pollinations, echoes, and repetitions, thereby unseating difference from a position of absolute privilege" (Felski 1997, 12). The word itself also evokes this in its play on the French *métis*, meaning half-bred, cross-bred, or hybrid, and *tissage,* which is a weaving. Importantly, it works against cultural superiority, or The One, by reminding us all of our mixed heritage.

A strategy for political action that I believe acknowledges Felski's point while dealing with the more general question of fractionation is Iris Marion Young's "seriality." A series, in her words, is "a collective whose members are unified passively by the relation their actions have to material objects and practico-inert histories. . . . To be said to be part of the same series it is not necessary to identify a set of common attributes that every member has, because their membership is defined not by something they are, but rather by the fact that in their diverse existences and actions they are oriented around the same practico-inert structures" (1997, 27).

For Young, a major virtue of this approach is that it "disconnects gender from identity" (1997, 33). As members of a series, women are not attributed with shared experiences or a shared project, although there is the latent potential for a series to form a group with a mutually recognized common project. Woman, then, "names a set of structural constraints and relations to practico-inert objects that condition action and its meaning. . . . The series is not a concept but a more practical-material mode of the social construction of individuals" (36). The use of seriality does not mean whitewashing even profound opposition among people, yet it wants to keep alive the potential to organize around issues that are not raised by those particular points of opposition. For example, it should allow for organizing around environmental quality of a city's watercourse and yet leave intact the potential for these same people to seek cultural recognition in other groupings. It is a way of thinking about grouping. It does not cast difference or opposition as necessarily negative.

A totally different strategy is the complex one of mimesis put forward by Luce Irigaray (1985) and Rosi Braidotti (1991). It is a strategy for dealing with the argued absence of symbolic structures in the unconscious for women by which women could express their desires and visions as themselves. The idea is not that there is an essential female imaginary to be uncovered, but rather an as-yet-blank place in the symbolic structures where women could be represented as themselves. Because symbolic structures cannot be changed on command or consciously, one approach to bringing about their change is to engage a mimetic strategy that is psychoanalytic in form but social in intent. In effect, one attempts as analyst-researcher to investigate the male unconscious (since that is what needs to be understood in order to create symbolic structures for women), with the imagined male in the analysand role.

> One must assume the feminine role deliberately. Which means already to convert a form of subordination into an affirmation, and thus begin to thwart it. . . . To play with mimesis is thus, for a woman, to try to locate the place of her exploitation by discourse, without allowing herself to be simply reduced to it. It means to resubmit herself so as to make 'visible' by an effect of playful repetition, what was supposed to remain invisible: recovering a possible operation of the feminine in language. (Cited in Whitford 1991, 71)

It is a way of working with the paradox of being caught within a male-focused symbolic system to which not only is one opposed but against which one also does not want simply to establish an oppositional system. For Braidotti, mimesis challenges the paradox that otherwise tends to "essentialize difference into a new universal" (1997a, 34).

Finally, what about tackling the sex/gender versus sexual difference dichotomy itself? Drucilla Cornell's *Imaginary Domain* describes a new theory of legal equality that attempts to do this (1997). Her point of departure is that each of us should be respected as part of a project that is available on an equivalent basis to us all. For this to occur, two minimum conditions of individuation need to be assured: "(1) bodily integrity and (2) access to symbolic forms sufficient to achieve linguistic skills that in turn permit the differentiation of oneself from others" (Cornell 1997, 42). The key features are, first, that feminine sexual difference is not privileged but rather that any sexuate being is included; second, that protection of the imaginary domain means that "a claim to parity does not turn on any comparison with actual men" (1997, 43); and third, that it rejects the "single axis" approach typified in the dichotomy. Drucilla Cornell's double intention with this theory of equality is not only to take on the single-axis model of discrimination but also to include a way to recognize the mirror-reflection problem that sexual difference theorists try to address.

These are but hints of new thinking that may contribute to the work ahead for feminist urbanists. Cities have always been places where diverse social groups interact. How can their spaces enhance positive interaction more effectively than they currently do in light of new theories and political realities? Second, what has been learned and what has been the impact of the field on urban development since the 1970s? Oddly enough, there is no accounting of what has been achieved in the bodies/cities field, what has endured through time, what has failed. Such an overview could set out the most pressing questions and counter the otherwise certain dispersal of energies. Third, frequent, confident interchanges with related fields of inquiry are required. Bodies/cities as a field is robust enough to engage more actively with its neighbors.

Cathryn Bailey's (1997) optimistic view is welcome here. Writing about third-wave feminism, she describes it as accepting ambiguity and multiplicity, as keen to take "the religion out of feminism," but most important of all as ready with new energy to counter the neoconservative, antifeminist actions and potential loss of gains from second-wave struggles.

REFERENCES

Angus, Ian. 1997. *A Border Within: National Identity, Cultural Plurality and Wilderness.* Montreal and Kingston: McGill-Queens University Press.

Bailey, Cathryn. 1997. "Making Waves and Drawing Lines: The Politics of Defining the Vicissitudes of Feminism." *Hypatia* 12, 3: 17–28.

Bondi, Liz. 1998. "Gender, Class, and Urban Space: Public and Private Space in Contemporary Urban Lanscapes." *Urban Geography* 19, 2: 160–185.

Braidotti, Rosi. 1991. *Patterns of Dissonance.* Oxford: Polity Press.

———. 1997a. "Comments on Felski's 'The Doxa of Difference': Working through Sexual Difference." *Signs* 23, 1, 23–40.

———. 1997b. "Uneasy Transitions: Women's Studies in the European Union." In *Transitions, Environments, Translations: Feminisms in International Politics,* edited by Joan W. Scott, Cora Kaplan, and Debra Keates. New York: Routledge.

Brennan, Teresa. 1997. "Foreword." In *Political Correctness: A Response from the Critical Left,* edited by Richard Feldstein. Minneapolis: University of Minnesota Press, ix–xix.

Butler, Judith. 1990. *Gender Trouble: Feminism and the Subversion of Identity.* London: Routledge.

Cornell, Drucilla. 1997. "Comment on Felski's 'The Doxa of Difference': Diverging Differences." *Signs* 23, 1: 41–56.

Feldstein, Richard. 1997. *Political Correctness: A Response from the Cultural Left.* Minneapolis: University of Minnesota Press.

Felski, Rita. 1997. "The Doxa of Difference." *Signs* 23, 1: 1–21.

Frye, Marilyn. 1992. "Getting It Right." *Signs* 17, 4: 781–793.

Grosz, Elizabeth. 1992. "Bodies-Cities." In *Sexuality and Space,* edited by Beatriz Colomina. New York: Princeton Architectural Press.

Guberman, R. M., ed. 1996. *Julia Kristeva Interviews.* New York: Columbia University Press.

Hayden, Dolores. 1997: "Review of 'Space, Place and Gender' by Doreen B. Massey and 'Feminism and Geography' by Gillian Rose." *Signs* 23, 4: 456–458.

Irigaray, Luce. 1985. *This Sex Which Is Not One.* Ithaca. N.Y.: Cornell.

McQuaig, Linda. 1998. *The Cult Of Impotence: Selling the Myth of Powerlessness in the Global Economy.* Toronto: Viking.

Milroy, Beth Moore. 1994. "Values, Subjectivity, Sex." In *Values and Planning,* edited by H. Thomas. London: Gower Publishing.

Sandercock, Leonie. 1998. *Toward Cosmopolis: Planning for Multicultural Cities.* New York: John Wiley.

Scott, Joan Wallach. 1996. *Only Paradoxes to Offer: French Feminists and the Rights of Man.* Cambridge: Harvard University Press.

Sibley, David. 1995. *Geographies of Exclusion: Society and Difference in the West.* London: Routledge.

Whitford, Margaret. 1991. *Luce Irigaray: Philosophy in the Feminine.* London: Routledge.

Wolf, Susan. 1992. "Comment." In *Multiculturalism and The Politics of Recognition: An Essay by Charles Taylor,* edited by Amy Gutmann. Princeton: Princeton University Press.

Young, Iris Marion. 1997. *Intersecting Voices: Dilemmas of Gender, Political Philosophy and Policy.* Princeton: Princeton University Press.

Index

Abbott, Carl, 151
Aboriginal peoples, 42–43; and surveillance, 32. *See also* First Nations people; First Nations women
Aboriginal Peoples Survey (APS), 46, 57n7
Aboriginal Women's Council of British Columbia, 53–54
Aboriginal Women's Unity Coalition, 51
Abramovitz, Mimi, 170
Acker, J., 4
Adams, Jackie, 49
Adler, Sy, 151
African American family: history of development of, 171–73; impact of myths about, 173–74; and its intrinsic functionality, 171; and literature of opposition to pathological view, 171; and Social Darwinism, 172; view of as "deviant" or "dysfunctional," 170–73; and zoning laws discrimination, 179
African American feminists, 9
African Americans: and anonymity, 31; and intentional borders from whites, 173–74; and planning exclusivity, 13; and residential mobility, 190; and sexual myths, 174; and surveillance, 32; and urban poverty, 67
African American women: and community building, 90–91; and exclusion from World's Columbian Exposition, 109–10; and forced racialized and gendered domain, 174; and housing conditions, 192–99; and housing costs, 186; and housing discrimination, 131; and housing options, 189; and inadequate housing, 187; and literacy training, 10, 91–102; and local support networks, 56, 70–82; marginalization of via municipal planning, 169–80; as matriarchs, 169, 175; and redemptive spaces, 9, 105–6, 115; and spatial boundedness, 73; and Worcester, Massachusetts, 69–81
Afro-American Life Insurance Company, 108
Aid to Families with Dependent Children (AFDC), 65, 94, 125, 132–33n1
alternative visions of the city, 8, 14
American Housing Survey, 184, 197, 198, 202–3n1
American Planning Association (US), 149
Andres, Delores, 55
Andrew, Caroline, 5, 7, 12
Anduhyaun shelter, 50
anonymity: definition of, 19, 21; and identity, 22; limits of as a normative ideal, 31–34; not equally accessible to all, 31–33; as pluralism, 33–34; and tolerance, 28–30; and the urban condition, 8, 19–36
Appleton, Lynn, 29
Asians and surveillance, 32
Atwood, Margaret Eleanor, 150

Bailey, Cathryn, 216
Barnett, Henrietta, 145
Bauer, Catherine, 145
Beauregard, Robert, 151
Bethel Institutional Church, 108
Bhattacharyya, Jnanabrata, 90
Billingsley, Andrew, 171
Birch, Eugenie Ladner, 146, 148
black. See African American
Black Image in the White Mind, The, 173
Bluntz, Allison, 41
Bock, Gisela, 143–44
"bodies/cities," 209, 213, 214
Booth, Christine, 158–59
boundaries, 2, 7–8, 14; and boundedness,
   67; and breaking of, 101–2; definition
   of, 1, 7, 8; and the household, 188; and
   housing, 202; low literacy and, 93–97;
   and networks, 81–82, 131; as order, and
   men, 157; of social relations, 159–60,
   162; as space, 102, 158–59, 161–62;
   and time, 158, 161; and urban planning,
   151–52, 157, 170; and women as recon-
   figurers of, 158
Braidotti, Rosi, 212, 215
Britt, Harry, 24
Brooke Amendments of 1969 and 1971,
   125
Brooks, Catherine, 50
Brosovksy, Paul, 169
Brown, Hallie Q., 110, 112
Bruce, Phillip A., 172
Bruin, Marilyn, 13, 183–207
Burgess, Patricia, 139
Burroughs, Nannie Helen, 106, 110–16
Butler, Judith, 213

Calhoun, John C., 171–72
Canadian Institute of Planners, 149
Canadian planning history. See planning,
   Canadian history of
Canadian Royal Commission on Aborigi-
   nal Peoples, 43, 45, 47–48, 53, 56
capitalist-patriarch, institutional aspects
   of, 4
Carr, Edward Hallett, 144
Castells, Manuel, 25

Castro Street (San Francisco), 24
Charity Organization Movement, 108
Charlotte Court (Lexington, Kentucky),
   120–30
chronic mobility, 188, 200
cities: and anonymity, 19–36; and "bodies/
   cities" approach, 209, 213, 214; complexity of, 26–28; and interplay with
   feminine body, 209; opportunity structure of, 184; as predominately female,
   29; and tolerance, 28–30
City Beautiful Movement, 109
Clarkson, Julie, 74
Clinton, William, 122
Cole, Tanya, 77–78
collective empowerment, 8
College Settlements Association, 105, 115
Colored Women's League, 109, 110
community building, 90–91
community planning, 12
Community Planning Association of Can-
   ada (CPAC), 149, 150
connected knowing, 4
conservative political climate, 209–10, 214
constructivist approach, 213
Cook, Christine, 13, 183–207
Cook, Helen, 109
Cope, Meghan, 121
Cornell, Drucilla, 216
Coutras, Jacqueline, 159
Crise Urbaine et Espaces Sexués, 159
Crowder, Kyle D., 190
Crull, Sue, 13, 183–207

Darke, Jane, 185
Darrow, Clarence, 108
Davis, Madeline D., 32
Davis, Patricia, 76–77
Death and Life of Great American Cities,
   The, 10, 161
D'Emilio, John, 24, 31–32
de Saussure, Ferdinand, 213
devolution: and housing policy reform,
   126, 131; and welfare reform, 120, 130,
   131
difference, social construction of, 66
Dinan v. Town of Stratford, 177

dismantling: and housing policy, 126–27, 129, 131; and welfare reform, 120, 131
disorder and women, 157
diversity/plurality, honoring of, 8
domestic virtue as avenue of acceptance into white society, 114
Douglass, Frederick, 110
Dubec, Bernice, 54
DuBois, W.E.B., 108, 113

Edwards, Laura, 77
Ellison, Kula, 50
"embounded" women, and welfare reform and public housing policy, 119–33
employment and literacy, 94
English, Vicki, 54
Esquimox-Hamelin, Jackie, 50
ethnicity, 2, 6
European cities and American influences, 6
expert needs discourses, 162–63, 165–66

Faderman, Lillian, 22
family: definitions of, 176–78; ethic, 170; and housing decisions, 188; and invalidation of numerical definitions of, 177–78; nuclear, as only acceptable norm, 170; and urban planning policy, 174–78. *See also* African American family; single mothers
family literacy programs, 10, 91–102
Family Values Debate, 169
Fasheh, Munir, 90
fatalism, 210
Federal Housing Administration (FHA), 127
Fellman, Anita Clair, 149
Felski, Rita, 214–15
feminist: approaches to category woman, 211–14; geography, 5, 41–42, 56; history, 141–44; research methods, 3–4, 211–14
feminist urbanists: future directions for, 214–16; importance of, 209
feminization of poverty, 68–69
Fincher, Ruth, 4
First Nations people: and Aboriginal institutions in Winnipeg, 48; and colonial

policies, 43–44; and loss of status, 43–44
First Nations women: and affordable housing and community environments, 51–52; and colonial policy relative to political decision making, 44, 45; definition of, 57n1, 57n2; and loss of status through marrying out, 44, 46; and need for particularized First Nations women programs, 49–51; and political participation, 52, 55–56; and racism and stereotyping, 49; and reserve geographies and funding, 53–55, 56; and residency on reserve, 44–46; and statistical comparison to all urban women, 46–47; and urban services needs, 41–58
Fontaine, Marilyn, 51
Fraser, Nancy, 162, 164
Frazier, E. Franklin, 171, 172
Frederickson, George, 173
Freud, Sigmund, 212
Friendship Centres, 44, 57n6

Garber, Judith, 5, 8, 19–39
gay men: and anonymity, 20–21, 23, 34; and community-formation strategies, 24
Gazhaadaawgamik Native School, 50
gender: bias, 1; and the city, past studies of, 4–8, 14; and heterosexualism, 213; and history, 142–43, 148; and sex/gender approach, 211–14; as socially constructed, 66; study of, 211; and urban boundaries, 7–8; and urban space as an area of study, 2
Gender Trouble, 213
General Federation of Women's Clubs (GFWC), 110
geography: male bias in, 5; of opportunity, 12, 184, 189–90, 191, 199; and social construction of space and place, 66
geography, feminist, 5, 41–42; new terms for conducting of, 42; and significance of space, 66; and "spatial entrapment" model, 56; and universal womanhood myth, 41
Gilbert, Melissa R., 9–10, 56, 65–87
Gilroy, Rose, 159

Giroux, Henry, 89
globalization, 210
Goldsmith, William, 6
Good, Lin, 150
Gordon, Linda, 141
"Gospel of the Toothbrush," 114
Graham, Barbara, 79–80, 81
Grant, Judith, 144
Greed, Clara, 11, 148
Grosz, Elizabeth, 209, 214
Grube, John, 21
Gutman, Herbert, 172

Hall, Darlene, 50
Harrison, Helen, 139–56
Hayden, Delores, 159
Heath, Shirley Brice, 90
Hendler, Sue, 12, 139–56
her-story, 142, 145
Higgs, Mary, 147
Hill, Robert, 171
Hispanic. *See* Latinos
historiography versus history, 141–44
history: and gender, 142–43; and historiography, 141–44; social, 142
Hodge, Gerald, 148, 150
housing: affordability crisis of, 186, 187; decision making relative to, 13, 187–91, 199; and homeownership, 197–98, 200–201; importance of, to women and children, 185–87, 199, 201–2; inadequacy, 192–99, 203n3; and nurturance and safety, 185; physical inadequacy of, 187; and unanswered questions relative to, 199–200; women's, and the metropolitan context, 183–203. *See also* public housing policy
Housing Act of 1949, 125
Housing and Community Development Act of 1987, 125–26
Housing and Urban Development, U.S. Department of (HUD). *See* U.S. Department of Housing and Urban Development (HUD)
housing policy. *See* public housing policy
Hughes, Mark A., 67
Hull House, 108

Human Rights Committee of the United Nations, 45

identity categories, 8
identity group affiliation, 24; and anonymity, 22, 24, 34
Ikwe Widdjiitiwin, 49
Imaginary Domain, 216
Indian Act, 43
Indian Affairs Branch (Department of Indian Affairs), 45
Indians. *See* First Nations people; First Nations women
Institutional Church and Social Settlement, 108
International Congress of Women of 1909, 147
intersection of race, ethnicity, and class, 8–10, 42, 122, 132
Interval House, 50
Irigaray, Luce, 215

Jacks, James W., 109
Jacobs, Jane, 4, 10–11, 161; and anonymity vs identity, 27
Jargowsky, Paul A., 190
Johns, Elizabeth, 74–75

Kahn, Bonnie Menes, 27
Kealy, Linda, 149
Kelly, Joan, 142, 151
Kennedy, Elizabeth, 21, 32
King, Margaret, 52, 55
Kleinberg, S. Jay, 144
Knopp, Lawrence, 24
knowing, connected, 4
knowledge and feminist research, 3
Kristeva, Julia, 211
Krueckeberg, Donald, 150

language and power in society, 97–98
Larner, Wendy, 42
Latinos: and housing costs, 186; and housing discrimination, 131; and housing options, 189; and surveillance, 32; women, and housing conditions, 192–99

lesbians: and anonymity, 20–21, 22, 23, 31, 34; communities of, 25
literacy, 89–103; and choice, 96–97; and community building, 90; critical understanding of and political action, 90; cultural understanding of, 89–90; and dependence, 94–95; and employment, 94; functional understanding of, 89, 102–3n3; and self-worth, 95–96
literacy training, 10, 89, 91–102
Little, Jo, 5
local public housing agencies (LHAs), 125, 126, 130
locational choices, 22–28
Lofland, Lyn, 19, 27
Lovelace, Sandra, 45
lynching, 106, 109

MacGregor, Sherilyn, 11
Maracle, Lisa, 51
marginalization of people, 6, 100
Marx, Karl, 213
Massey, Doreen, 66, 81
Mathews, Shailer, 108
matriarchs, family, African American women as, 169, 175; and housing inadequacy, 195–96
McAdoo, Harriette Pipes, 171
McDowell, Mary, 108
McIvor, Sharon, 53
McQuaig, Lisa, 210
men and boundaries as order, 157–58
métissage, 214
Metro Action Committee on Public Violence against Women and Children (METRAC), 160
metropolis. *See* cities
migration: of blacks from South to North, 107; and long term residency of working poor women, 75–78
Miller, Jill, 80–81
Miller, Stuart, 185
Milroy, Beth Moore, 5, 14, 209–17
mimesis, 215–16
Mink, Gwendolyn, 69
minorities. *See* Aboriginal peoples; African

Americans; First Nations people; First Nations women; Latinos
Miranne, Kristine B., 1–16, 119–36, 190
Morris, Earl W., 187
Moynihan, Daniel Patrick, 169, 171, 172
multiplicity, 214
municipal housekeeping, 105, 106, 108, 111, 116, 146
municipal planning: construction of its policy and the family, 174–78; and exclusion of groups, 13; male dominance of, 11, 12; and the marginalization of African American women, 169–80; necessity for change in, 179–80; as an open-ended process, 157; reconceptualization of, 11. *See also* planning, Canadian history of
municipal zoning regulations, 12–13; and definitions of families, 176; and discrimination of those not in nuclear families, 13, 175, 176–78, 179; and forced separation of black and white, 175; necessity for change in, 178–80; and spatial separation of middle-class and working class, 179; and support of nuclear families, 13, 175, 176–78, 179

National Association of Colored Women (NACW), 105, 106, 109–10, 111–12, 115, 116; and lack of boundaries between religious and secular, 111–12
National Association of Housing and Development Officials (NAHRO), 125
National Association of Wage Earners, 113
National Baptist Convention, 111, 113
National Center for Family Literacy, 91, 92
National League of Republican Colored Women, 113
National Training School for Women and Girls, 106, 112, 113, 114–16
Native Women's Association of Canada, 53
needs discourses, 162–66
Negro Family, The: The Case for National Action, 169, 173
Neighborhood: effects of poor, 190–91; and housing decisions, 188–91

networks, women's social, 70–82, 131; and
    housing, 186, 189, 199
New Era Club, 109
Nineteenth Street Baptist Church, 108, 112
nuclear family. *See* family, nuclear

Ontario Good Roads Association, 150
oppositional needs discourses, 162,
    163–64
order and men, 157
Organisation for Economic Co-operation
    and Development (OECD), 49, 51, 52

parents, single, identity as, 78–81
patriarchal ideology of economics, 121–22
Peake, Linda, 5, 42, 190
Pearce, Diana, 68
Perin, Constance, 175
Personal Responsibility and Work Oppor-
    tunity Reconciliation Act (PRWORA)
    of 1996, 65, 119, 122–23
Peters, Evelyn, 7–8, 41–62
place and poverty, 81
planning, Canadian history of, 12, 139–54;
    and beautification by women, 146; and
    inclusion of theoretical and women's/
    gender issues, 140–41; professionaliza-
    tion, and women's involvement, 146,
    149–50, 151, 153–54n16; social as-
    pects of, and women, 146; women's
    place in, 144–48. *See also* municipal
    planning
Planning Canadian Communities, 148
pluralism as anonymity, 33–34
politics: and new feminist poverty agenda,
    82; and organizing after anonymity, 25
postempiracal approach, 3, 14n1
poststructuralist theorizing, 212, 213
poverty, 65; and feminization of, 68–69,
    81, 82, 190; new agenda relative to, 82;
    and urban underclass, 67–68, 81, 84
power, theory of, 3–4
privacy rights, 31
private patriarchy, 29
privatization: and housing policy reform,
    126–27, 129, 131; and welfare reform,
    119–20, 131

production and reproduction, 5
public housing policy: and failure to recog-
    nize spatial variation, 128; and housing
    shortages, 129; and intersection with
    welfare reform, 128–31; and propensity
    of poorer to move, 130; restructuring of,
    124–28; and stigma associated with it,
    126, 128; and vouchers, 129–30; and
    welfare reform, 119–33; and women's
    poverty, 128–29
publicity, 19
public patriarchy, 29–30
public versus private: and anonymity ver-
    sus identity, 27–28; and zoning and
    gender, 159

Quality Housing and Work Responsibility
    Act of 1998 (QHWRA), 128–29

race and racism, 2, 6; and housing condi-
    tions of single mothers, 192–99; and lit-
    eracy, 97–99; recognizing of and acting
    to change, 99–101; as socially con-
    structed, 66, 82n1, 122; and survival
    strategies and identities, 72–75; and
    urban underclass, 67–68
Ransom, Reverdy, 108
Rayside, David, 22
redemptive spaces, 9, 105–6, 115
Regina Friendship Centre, 53
Reinvention Blueprint, 126
Rendall, Jane, 143
reprivatization needs discourses, 162, 164–
    65, 166
Richardson, Pat, 5
right to be let alone, 30–31
Ritzdorf, Marsha, 13, 124, 169–81
Rose, Gillian, 41
Roth, Michael, 144
Round Table on Urban Issues (1993), 53
Ruffin, Josephine St. Pierre, 109, 110, 112
ruling apparatus, 3–4, 14–15n2

Saegert, Susan, 190
safety audits, 12, 157, 160–67; and needs
    discourses, 162–66; as a tool for
    women, 161–62, 163–64, 166, 167;

Salvation Army, 105, 108, 115
Sandercock, Leonnie, 139, 141, 214
Sanders, Rickie, 41
Santa Barbara v. Adamson, 177–78
Saskatoon Urban Treaty Indians, 55
Scott, Anne Firor, 106
Scott, Joan, 141, 142–43, 212
Section 8 housing, 75, 124–25, 129–30
self-sufficiency, 124, 126, 128, 130
Sennett, Richard, 34
"seriality," 215
sex/gender approach, 211–14, 216
sexism, 8, 122
sexual difference approach, 212–13, 216
sexual identity, 2
Shiloh Church, 108
Simkhovitch, Mary Kingsbury, 145
single mothers: and blame for poverty, 191; and housing, 183–84, 191–202; and work, 78–81, 123–24
Small, Sherry, 55
Smith, Dorothy, 12, 91
social capital, 189–90
social construction, dynamic of, 10, 14
Social Darwinism and mythology regarding blacks, 172
Social Gospel theology, 105, 106, 108–9, 116
social history, 142
social networks. *See* networks, women's social
social policy restructuring: devolution, 120; dismantling, 121; privatization, 120–21
social relations and boundaries, 159–60
solidarity and literacy programs, 97
South, Scott J., 190
space: as a container, 67, 81; boundaries of, 158–59, 161–62; boundedness and African American women, 73; and identity formation, 24; and place-based networks, 81; use of by women, 1, 2–3, 202, 209
Spain, Daphne, 5, 9, 105–17, 184
Sphinx in the City: Urban Life, the Control of Disorder and Women, 157

Standard English, 98
Staples, Robert E., 171
Stephenson, Marylee, 149
Strange, Carolyn, 158
Strong-Boag, Veronica Jane, 149
Subban, Jennifer, 10, 89–104
Suffrage Movement and black women, 112
Supplemental Security Income (SSI), 110
symbolic system and women, 213, 215–16

"Talented Tenth," 113
technological solutions, 165, 166
Temporary Assistance to Needy Families (TANF), 94, 110, 123, 125, 130
Terrell, Mary Church, 110, 112
Thunder Bay Native Interagency Council, 54
time and boundaries, 158, 161
tolerance, 28–30
Tong, Rosemary, 144
Toward Cosmopolis, 214
Town Planning Institute of Canada, 148
Toyota Families for Learning Program, 91–102
Turner, Robyne, 5

understanding and change, 4, 5
United Native Nations, 55
University of Chicago Settlement, 108
University of New Orleans, 92
urban environment as male made, 11
urban feminist studies, 1, 3, 19, 211–16
urban planning. *See* municipal planning
Urban Revitalization Demonstration Act (HOPE VI), 129
urban underclass, 67–68
U.S. Department of Housing and Urban Development (HUD), 119, 124–27; and American Housing Survey, 184; and inadequate or unsafe housing, 187; and public housing reform, 126–27

Valentine, Gill, 21
Veteran's Administration (VA), 127
Village of Belle Terre v. Boras, 177
voluntary associations and city improvement, 107

Wagner-Steagall Act of 1937, 125
Walker, Maggie Lena, 115
Washington, Booker T., 113, 114
Wasteste, Jolene, 53
welfare reform, 65; and devolution, 120; and differing state rules, 130; and dismantling, 120; and failure to recognize spatial variation, 124; and focus on individual as problem, 122, 132; and intersection with public housing policy, 128–31; and privatization, 120–21; and public housing policy, 119–33; and self-sufficiency, 124, 126, 128, 130; women's mobilization against, 68–69, 82, 83n6
welfare state: and capitalist patriarchal ideology, 121–22; gendered nature of, 121
West, Candace, 1–2
white women: and personal networks, 78–81; and residential mobility, 190; single mothers, and housing conditions, 192–96; survival strategies of, 72–75, 77
Williams, Frannie Barrier, 112
Wilson, Elisabeth, 157–58, 162, 166
Wilson, Pam, 78
Wilson, William Julius, 189
Winant, Howard, 97
Winkel, Gary, 190
Winter, Mary, 187
Wolf, Susan, 214
Wolff, Janet, 32
Woman's Convention (WC) Auxiliary to the National Baptist Convention, 105, 106, 110–12, 113, 115, 116; and blurring of boundaries between religious and secular, 111–12
women: and anonymity, 20; and approachability on streets, 32; as a category, 211–14, 215; and community building, 90–91; and critical mass in an area, 25; and discouragement from knowing too much, 91; and disorder, 157–58; as economically disadvantaged, 122, 123–24;

as head of family, 175; identities of, 2; and identity replacing anonymity, 25–26; and literacy programs, 91–102; and personal networks, 70–82, 131, 186, 189, 199; and political activism, 25–26; and public housing, 127–28; and role as homemaker and childcare provider, 170; and role in changing urban environment, 13; and role in planning history, 144–48; survival strategies and spatial boundedness, 70–72; and symbolic systems, 213, 215–16; and use of city at night, 158; and voluntary associations, 107
working poor, survival strategies of, 65–84. *See also* African American women; single mothers; white women; working poor women
Women's Action Center against Violence (WACAV), 160
women's housing and the "metropolitan context," 183–207
Women's Safety Audit Kit, 160
Worcester, Massachusetts, poverty study regarding, 69–81
working poor women: and housing options, 189; and identities as single parents, 78–81; and migration, 75–78; and racial identity, 72–75; survival strategies of, 9–10, 65–84. *See also* African American women; First Nations women; women
World's Columbian Exposition (Chicago), 109–10

Young, Alma H., 1–16, 89–104, 124, 190
Young, Iris Marion, 20, 22, 28, 33–34, 143, 215
Young Women's Christian Association (YWCA), 105, 107, 115

Zimmerman, Don, 1–2
Zinn, Baca, 68
zoning. *See* municipal zoning regulations

About the Editors and Contributors

Caroline Andrew is currently Dean of the Faculty of Social Sciences at the University of Ottawa. As a political scientist, her areas of research are women and politics, municipal government, and urban politics.

Marilyn Bruin is Assistant Professor and Extension Specialist at the University of Minnesota. Her research focuses on low-income, single-parent women, their residential satisfaction and family management behaviors, and the effects of participation in public policy programs.

Christine C. Cook is Associate Professor in Human Development and Family Studies at Iowa State University. Her research centers on issues of women and housing, children's environment, and the housing needs of special populations, including the elderly.

Sue Crull is Assistant Professor in Human Development and Family Studies at Iowa State University. Her areas of interest include housing issues of low-income women, residential mobility, and rural/urban development.

Judith A. Garber is Associate Professor of Political Science at the University of Alberta, where she teaches courses on U.S. politics and policy, urban politics, and law. She writes on normative and constitutional matters in American and Canadian cities. Her publications include: *Gender and Urban Research*, edited with Robyne Turner (1995); articles in *Urban Resources,* the *Journal of Urban Affairs,* and *Urban Affairs Review*; and chapters in various edited volumes. She is currently writing a book about the urban public sphere.

Melissa R. Gilbert is Assistant Professor in the Department of Geography and Urban Studies at Temple University. Her research and teaching interests include gender, racism, and urban and economic restructuring. Currently, she is focusing on local labor markets, urban poverty, social networks, and the survival strategies of working poor women.

Helen Harrison is a doctoral candidate in the Department of History at Queen's University. Her thesis explores issues of health and gender in Canadian public health education literature, 1920–1960.

Sue A. Hendler is Associate Professor of Planning at Queen's University in Canada. Her research and professional interests are planning theory, social and health planning, environmental issues, and planning ethics. Currently she is involved in a long-range study on women and Canadian planning history. She is the author of *Planning Ethics: A Reader in Planning Theory, Practice, and Education.*

Beth Moore Milroy is Director of the School of Urban and Regional Planning at Ryerson Polytechnic University in Toronto. Her teaching and research fall mainly in the areas of feminist planning theory, participatory planning practices, community work, and the street as civic realm.

Kristine B. Miranne is Associate Director of the Skillman Center for Children at Wayne State University. Her research focuses on a gendered perspective of the changing welfare state; children's poverty; and violence against, by, and between children and youth. Her most recent publications have examined gender relations, community, and women's survival strategies in the wake of recent U.S. welfare reform initiatives.

Evelyn Peters is Associate Professor in Geography at Queen's University. She teaches in the areas of social and urban geography and has long-standing research interests in Aboriginal self-government and urbanization.

Marsha Ritzdorf died in March 1998. She was Associate Professor in the Department of Urban Affairs and Planning at the Virginia Polytechnic Institute and State University. Her fields of expertise were gender, race, and class aspects of planning; land use and zoning; and housing. Her last book was *Urban Planning and the African-American Community* (1997), edited with June Manning Thomas. In November 1997, she was awarded the Association of Collegiate Schools of Planning's Margarita McCoy Award, which recognized her contributions toward the advancement of women in planning at institutions of higher learning.

Daphne Spain is Professor of Urban and Environmental Planning in the School of Architecture, University of Virginia. Her publications include *Back to the City: Issues in Neighborhood Renovations* (edited with Shirley Laska, 1980), *Gendered Spaces* (1992), and articles on housing and neighborhoods in the *Jour-*

nal of the American Planning Association, the *Journal of Planning Literature*, and the *Journal of Urban Affairs*. Her most recent book, with Suzanne Bianchi, is *Balancing Act: Motherhood, Marriage, and Employment among American Women* (1996). She is currently conducting research on the "redemptive" urban places built by women through voluntary associations at the turn of the century.

Jennifer E. Subban is Project Director of the Toyota Families for Learning Program in New Orleans and serves as a consultant on literacy to grassroots organizations. She received her Ph.D. in Urban Studies in 1998 from the University of New Orleans. Her research areas include literacy and community development, race and poverty, and women and community building.

Alma H. Young is Interim Dean of the College of Urban, Labor, and Metropolitan Affairs as well as the Coleman A. Young Professor of Urban Affairs at Wayne State University. She is Chair of the Governing Board of the Urban Affairs Association. Her areas of research include gendered perspectives on the changing welfare state, children in poverty, and the political economy of redevelopment.

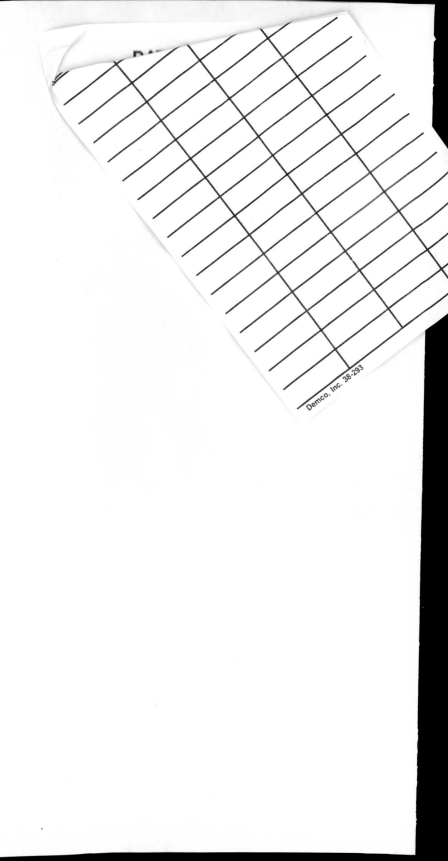

Demco, Inc. 38-293